Globalisation, Convergence and European Telecommunications Regulation

Globalisation, Convergence and European Telecommunications Regulation

Peter Humphreys
School of Social Sciences, University of Manchester, UK

Seamus Simpson
Department of Information and Communications, Manchester Metropolitan University, UK

Edward Elgar
Cheltenham, UK • Northampton, MA, USA

Published by
Edward Elgar Publishing Limited
Glensanda House
Montpellier Parade
Cheltenham
Glos GL50 1UA
UK

Edward Elgar Publishing, Inc.
136 West Street
Suite 202
Northampton
Massachusetts 01060
USA

A catalogue record for this book
is available from the British Library

Library of Congress Cataloguing in Publication Data
Humphreys, Peter.
     Globalisation, convergence and European telecommunications regulation /
Peter Humphreys, Seamus Simpson.
          p.cm.
     Includes bibliographical references and index.
     ISBN 1-85278-931-X
       1. Telecommunication policy–Europe. 2. Broadcasting policy–Europe 3.
     Trade regulation–Europe. I. Simpson, Seamus. II. Title.

HE8085.H86 2006
384.54'094–dc22   2005046152

ISBN 1 85278 931 X

Printed and bound in Great Britain by MPG Books Ltd, Bodmin, Cornwall

Contents

Tables and figures

Tables

Figures

Abbreviations

ABT	Agreement on Basic Telecommunications
ACTE	Advisory Committee for Telecommunications
ADSL	Asynchronous Digital Subscriber Line
AEPSI	Association of Spanish Internet Service providers
AGCOM	Autorità per le Garanzie nella Communicazioni
AOST	Association des Opérateurs de Services de Télécommunications
ART	Autorité de Régulation des Télécommunications
B2B	Business-to-Business
BMWi	Economics Ministry
CAS	Conditional Access Systems
CCS	Common Conformity Specifications
CEPT	European Conference of Postal and Telecommunications Administrations
CMT	Comisión del Mercado de las Telecomunicaciones
COCOM	Communication Committee
CPE	Customer Premises Equipment
CPS	Carrier Preselection
CSA	Conseil Supérieur de l'Audiovisuel
CTR	Common Technical Regulations
DG	Directorate General
DGT	Direction Générale des Télécommunications
DiGITIP	Telecoms branch of the French Industry Ministry
DSL	Digital Subscriber Line
DTAG	Deutsche Telekom AG
DTI	Department of Trade and Industry
DVB	Digital Video Broadcasting
ECE	United Nations Economic Commission for Europe
ECJ	European Court of Justice
ECRF	Electronic Communications Regulatory Framework
ECTA	European Competitive Telecommunications Association
EDI	Electronic Data Interchange
EIC	European Insurance Committee
EPTNO	European Public Telecommunications Network Operators Association

ERG	European Regulators Group
ESPRIT	European Strategic Programme for Research in Information Technology
ETNO	European Telecommunications Network Operators association
ETSI	European Telecommunications Standards Institute
EU	European Union
EuroISPA	European Internet Service Provider Association
FRIACO	Flat–Rate Internet Call origination
FT	France Télécom
GAP	Group d'Analyse et de Prevision
GATS	General Agreements on Trade in Services
GATT	General Agreement on Tariffs and Trade
GODs	General Obligations and Disciplines
HDTV	High Definition Television
HLCG	High Level Communication Group
ICANN	Internet Corporation for Assigned Names and Numbers
ICT	Information and Communication Technologies
IMF	International Monetary Fund
INTUG	International Telecommunications Users Group
IRG	Independent Regulators Group
ISDN	Integrated Services Digital Network
ISO	International Organisation for Standardisation
ISPs	Internet Service Providers
ITC	Independent Television Commission
ITTCC	International Telegraph and Telephone Consultative Committee
ITU	International Telecommunications Union
LLU	Local Loop Unbundling
MEDIA	Measures to Encourage the Development of the Audiovisual Industries in Europe
MFN	Most Favoured Nation
MITI	Ministry of International Trade and Industry (Japan)
MMC	Monopolies and Mergers Commission
MSG	Media Services Gesellschaft
NETS	Normes Europeenes de Télécommunications
NGO	Non-Governmental Organisation
NRA	National Regulatory Authority
NTB	Non-Tariff Barriers
NTIA	National Telecommunications Industry Association
ODETTE	Organisation for Data Exchange by Tele-transmission in Europe
OECD	Organisation for Economic Cooperation and Development
Ofcom	Office of Communications

Oftel	Office of Telecommunications
ONP	Open Network Provision
OSI	Open Systems Interconnect
PIBs	Principles of Implementation and Best practice
PSB	Public Service Broadcasting
PTO	Public Telecommunications Operator
PTT	Postal, Telephone and Telegraph administration
RBOC	Regional Bell Operating Company
Reg TP	Regulierungsbehörde für Telekommunikation und Post
RSC	Radio Spectrum Committee
RSPG	Radio Spectrum Policy Group
SEM	Single European Market
SGEI	Services of General Economic Interest
SMP	Significant Market Power
SNA	Systems Network Architecture
SOGT	Senior Officials Group on telecommunications
ST-FRIACO	Single Tandem Flat Rate Internet Access Call Origination
TA	Telecommunications Administration
TCP/IP	Transmission Control Protocol/Internet Protocol
TEDIS	Trade Electronic Data Interchange System
TO	Telecommunications Operator
TWF	Television Without Frontiers
UMTS	Universal Mobile Telecommunications Service
UNCID	Uniform Rules of Conduct for Interchange of Trade Data by Teletransmission
UNCITRAL	United Nations Conference on International Trade Law
UNCTAD	United Nations conference on Trade and Development
VANS	Value Added Network Services
VATM	The German interest group of new entrants
VAT	Value Added Tax
VoIP	Voice over Internet Protocol
WCO	World Customs Organisation
WIPO	World Intellectual Property Organisation
WTO	World Trade Organization

Acknowledgements

The authors would like to acknowledge the support of the UK Economic and Social Research Council, which funded two independent projects on which a substantial part of the research for this volume is based. Between 2000-2003, Peter Humphreys researched the telecommunications sector as part of a collaborative project entitled 'The European Union as a Medium for Policy Transfer: Case Studies in Utility Regulation' (Grant number L2162001). Colleagues on this project, which also looked at the air transport and electricity sectors, were Simon Bulmer (University of Manchester), David Dolowitz (University of Liverpool), Stephen Padgett (University of Strathclyde), and Simon Roy (Research Assistant). He would like to extend thanks to those officials in institutions of the European Union, notably the Commission, and in a number of EU Member States who agreed to be interviewed in the course of the project. Between 2003-2004, Seamus Simpson was Principal Investigator on the 'European Regulation of Internet Commerce Project' (Grant number RES-000-22-0356). He would like to acknowledge the input of George Christou, who worked as Research Associate on the project. He would also like to extend thanks to those officials at the European Union, the World Intellectual Property Organisation, the World Trade Organization, and government ministries in Finland, Italy, Germany and the UK who agreed to be interviewed in the course of the project. Both authors would like to thank the editors of the journal *Convergence: The Journal of Research into New Media Technologies* for permission to draw on material first published in a special issue on Telecommunications Regulation in Europe (summer 2002, Volume 8, Number 2). The authors would also like to express their gratitude to Professors Edgar Grande, currently at the University of Munich, and Volker Schneider, at the University of Konstanz, for their kind permission to translate from their original German and use Figure 2.1 'Political configurations in telecommunications policy', on page 29. They first presented this diagram in a Max-Planck-Institut für Gesellschaftsforschung (Cologne) Discussion Paper (no. 3, 1991) and subsequently published it in *Politische Vierteljahresschrift*, 32 (3) (1991b), 452-78, p. 472.

1. Introduction: the analytical framework

European telecommunications liberalisation has attracted considerable attention from political scientists (e.g. Schmidt 1998a; Bartle 1999; Eliassen and Sjøvaag 1999; Natalicchi 2001; Jordana 2002) Nonetheless, this book aims to make an original contribution to knowledge and understanding about European telecommunications liberalisation in a number of key respects.

Much discussion of the impact of the European Union (EU) in telecommunications has tended to stress the 'supranational' dimension, in particular the exploitation by the Commission of its institutional resources to draft policy and exercise direct authority (Article 86 directives, and competition rulings) in the field of competition (Sandholtz 1993, 1998; Schneider and Werle 1990, Schneider et al. 1994, Schmidt 1998a, 1998b; Levi-Faur 1999). Recently, this perspective has been powerfully challenged by Thatcher (2001a; 2004b), who relativises the Commission's (and EU's) role. We adopt a middle position, arguing that the Commission was a very important actor. It boldly exploited its direct competition powers, but also achieved much through 'softer' influence – what Héritier (1999) has called 'subterfuge' – moving forward with skill and care, launching consultations and reviews, building support, exploiting the external challenge, and providing a forum for benchmarking and policy learning.

Second, this book examines telecommunications liberalisation from a fresh theoretical perspective; the emergence and character of a 'regulatory state' in the European telecommunications sector. While some useful cross-sectoral and cross-national comparitive work on the European regulatory state has been done (see e.g. Thatcher 2001b, 2002a, 2002b; Jordana and Levi-Faur 2004), detailed and up-to-date work on the emergence of the regulatory state in the telecommunications sector remains distinctly limited (though see Bartle et al. 2002; and Coen et al 2002, both studies comparing the UK and Germany). The concept of a 'regulatory state' has various versions (see Moran 2002, 2003). It is the model that emerged in the USA since the 1930s, but the concept of a distinctly 'European' regulatory state is associated with the work of Giandomenico Majone (1994, 1996, 1997). The core idea is that old forms of intervention associated with the Keynesian welfare state and regulation through public ownership are being replaced by liberalisation and privatisation, but also by new forms of intervention in the shape of statutory economic and social regulation, implemented by independent regulatory bodies. A key aim of this book is to illuminate the emergence and operation of this 'regulatory state' in the European *electronic communications* sector.

This redefinition of 'telecommunications sector' as an 'electronic communications sector' points to third key aim of the book, namely to tell the story of the regulatory impact of digital 'convergence' in the electronic communications sector at large, albeit largely from a telecommunications policy perspective. Traditional telecommunications systems have been revolutionised by a wave of technological change. There has been considerable work done on how the 'convergence' of telecommunications with IT led to the latter fundamentally redefining the former. However, this book aims to break relatively new ground in examining how European policy making is coping with the current 'convergence' of telecommunications, broadcasting and the Internet.

The book's fourth claim to originality is its illumination of the complex interrelationship between technological change and globalisation, 'Europeanisation', national institutional structures, and the transfer of ideas (policy learning), in the reform of European telecommunications regulation. We argue that the transformation of European telecommunications regulation has been driven by market imperatives, unleashed by technological change and 'globalisation', but that the EU has still been significant in 'framing' the rules, sometimes in 'coercively' forcing the pace of adaptation, but more generally in providing softer pressure by serving as an arena for 'ideational convergence' through policy learning. Despite these pressures for convergence, though, a national institutional 'filter' effect points to a significant degree of 'domestication' of the impact of globalisation and Europeanisation.

EXPLAINING REGULATORY CHANGE

This book explores the paradigmatic change in the regulation of the communication sectors – principally telecommunications but also paying some attention to broadcasting in the digital era – that has occurred since the 1980s. This transformation exemplifies the move from the interventionist 'positive state' to the pro-competitive 'regulatory state' (Seidman and Gilmour 1986; Majone 1997). US style independent regulatory agencies – rare in Europe until the late twentieth century – have proliferated, as corporatism, protectionism and public monopoly of the utilities have given way to free market competition (Thatcher 2002a).

The principal dependent variable that interests us – the nature and direction of regulatory change – is explained in terms of three sets of variables, which for heuristic purposes it is useful to categorise as follows:

The *independent* variables driving policy change in a convergent direction, towards liberalisation and the 'regulatory state', are held to be techno-economic change, globalisation, international regulatory competition ('competitive de-regulation' or 'competitive emulation'), interests and group politics and ideas (including ideology). National institutions are approached as an *intervening* variable. They do not determine actor preferences, since these are shaped by our independent variables, but national institutions do constrain actor strategies. Given the diversity of national institutional 'profiles' among the EU-15, this variable is conducive to an element of divergent outcomes ('domestication').

The institutions of the EU, and their capacity for 'Europeanisation' and 'policy transfer', are held to be another *intervening* variable. Here it is held that the EU 'mediates' the impact of the other two sets of variables, seeking to achieve a harmonised European regulatory response to the challenges of techno-economic change, globalisation, and the pressure of regulatory competition. The EU institutions' capacity to do the latter depends on the institutional resources that they command for overcoming national institutional pressures towards divergence.

It is important, however, to understand that telecommunications reform has been characterised by a complex interrelationship between these variables. Thus, for example, globalisation itself can be seen as a dependent variable, explained inter alia by technological change, international regulatory competition, and new ideas. Similarly, while we prefer to emphasise the intervening nature of the institutional variables, at national and EU level, because we believe that they do not fundamentally drive change, they certainly have at important times exerted an independent effect of their own. Finally, there is a complex relationship between structure and agency. Globalisation is often seen only as an exogenous structural constraint on state action. However, state action itself has to be seen as an important cause – among others – of globalisation (particularly state action by the USA). Moreover, structural constraints – whether techno-economic or institutional – are simply that: constraints. 'Politics' still matters in determining the nature and direction of policy outcomes; for instance, the advent of the UK Conservative administration in 1979 had a major impact on UK telecommunications policy, a change of government was important for moving French reform along. That group politics matters is evident when comparison is made between different configurations at the national level (see Chapter 2). With all this in mind, we turn now to a consideration of different theoretical and conceptual perspectives on the causes of regulatory change.

TECHNO-ECONOMIC CHANGE

One obvious explanatory perspective stresses the primacy of techno-economic change in explaining policy convergence in the field of communications regulation. In telecommunications, the simple fact of digitalisation combined with new network technologies such as cable, satellite and mobile telephony – providing scope for a whole new range of networks and services – removed the justification for monopoly. Similarly, in broadcasting, the arrival of alternative means of transmission to the hertzian air-waves, in the shape of cable and satellite, removed the 'scarcity of frequencies' rationale for a public service broadcasting monopoly. Once state monopoly (with its internal regulative element) is removed, there is a need for a new regulatory regime to ensure competition and the continued fulfilment of public interest goals (e.g. universal service). Thus the simple fact of technological change largely explains convergent trends where otherwise divergent preferences and institutional profiles might have been expected to endure.

Moreover, technological change has stimulated international economic competition – and by extension international regulatory competition (see below) – in a number of ways. On the demand side, the range of services rendered possible by the new technologies increased the bargaining power of telecommunications users. Business users (especially multinational companies) became increasingly insistent in their demands for liberalised markets, and favoured competitive service providers with their business. The status of telecommunications as the nerve centre of a global information society gives it a special significance[1]. A modern telecommunications sector became a factor for economic investment and location decisions. On the supply side, new transmission technologies – principally microwave and satellite – meant that national systems could be bypassed, rendering territorial markets indefensible. Further, telecommunications producer firms now needed to expand in global markets in order to recoup the huge investment costs involved in developing the new digital technologies. Incumbent operators, too, began to see their future survival as dependent upon their becoming global service providers, and were led to embark on global alliance and acquisition strategies. National champion firms' embrace of foreign expansion strategies inclined them to favour international liberalisation, the price of which was conceding liberalisation at home (Humphreys and Simpson 1996, p. 115). Moreover, during the 1990s the growth of the Internet and a growing awareness of the implications of convergence of information technology, media and telecommunications, led to a new policy discourse around concepts such as the 'Global Information Society', the 'Digital Revolution' and the 'New Economy'; policy makers and economic actors engaged in a race to capture the benefits (Waesche 2003, pp. 5–10).

To argue that technology is driving change need not entail adopting a discourse of 'hard' technological determinism. Thus, looking at technology driven policy convergence in the field of data protection policy in Europe and the US, Bennett (1988, p. 427) noted that 'technology frame(d) the context of policy choice' but concluded: 'to say that each country was forced independently and inexorably to a common solution ignores the critical role of international communication and learning among the different national elites'.

Further, an interesting literature points to the limits to technology-driven policy convergence, where national institutional structures and politicisation impede convergence (e.g. Levy 1997, 1999, looking at broadcasting policy). These are themes that we pick up in this volume (see below). These are both perspectives that we explore.

GLOBALISATION

Techno-economic change can be seen as a key component of a broader phenomenon, a 'global structural shift' (Waesche 2003, p. 10). In general terms, 'globalisation' is the term used to express the marked internationalisation of economic relations that has accompanied an expansion in international trade and international capital flows, the rise of the global corporation, and the way that modern communication technologies have shrunk distance. Technological change has driven the globalisation of markets by reducing distance, reducing the costs of communication, information processing and trade, and facilitating capital mobility, thereby allowing firms to escape national regulatory constraints. Globalisation has been particularly strong in the information and communications sectors: IT, telecommunications, and broadcasting. Economic strategies have been driven by the technological revolution and the huge investment required for the development of new technologies (for example, digital switching equipment) which cannot be recouped by serving the national market alone. Moreover, the demands on telecommunications policy from multinational companies seeking cheaper and more choice of communications services has been another factor for liberalisation that could be placed under the heading of 'globalisation'.

Some globalisation theorists perceive a more or less ineluctable tendency towards trans-national governance and cross-national policy convergence upon the US-style neo-liberal model of political economy, based on the so-called 'Washington consensus' (see 'ideas' below). American 'ideas' have travelled globally, in the form of 'American-style' regulatory standards, regulatory culture, and indeed even regulatory institutions (Moran 2003, pp. 16–17). Globalisation, it is held, has drastically limited the state's capacity for interventionist government at the domestic level (Strange 1996, Ohmae 1991, McKenzie and Lee 1991). According to this perspective, globalisation amounts to a set of structural imperatives for national adaptation converging on a liberal market model of political economy. In this scenario, the USA serves both as a model and also as an agent of globalisation. Moreover, a 'bandwagon effect' leads to diffusion of the US model; as more states adapt by liberalising, so the momentum of globalisation itself increases. In this process, 'realists' and Marxists alike draw attention to the element of 'structural' power exercised both by US-based multinational corporations and the US government in the global economy (Strange 1994). Attention must be drawn to how the USA has promoted – indeed demanded – liberalisation both through its trade policy and economic foreign policy (demanding reciprocity for US market opening along with threats of market closure), and also through the World Trade Organization (WTO), and formerly the General Agreement on Tariffs and Trade (GATT).

However, not all observers of the phenomenon see policy convergence – around a neo-liberal global order – as inevitable. Vivien Schmidt (2002), for instance, charts the far-reaching political economic transformations at the national level that have accompanied globalisation, yet remains relatively unimpressed by the degree of policy convergence between advanced industrial countries. Although west European countries' policies may be moving in a simular direction in response to globalisation, towards marketisation, Schmidt differentiates between three persistent varieties of capitalism: market capitalism (US, UK), managed capitalism (Germany), and state capitalism (France); importantly, the national policy discourses vary significantly between them. Similarly, Linda Weiss (1998; 2003), too, has concluded that the response of states to globalisation depends very much upon the distinctive character and attributes of their domestic institutions.[2] We explore this institutionalist perspective below.

GLOBALISATION AND REGULATORY COMPETITION

Globalisation should not simply be understood as an exogenous independent variable. Plainly, since globalisation itself has its causes, it can also be viewed as a dependent variable. Indeed, one important cause of the current wave of intense globalisation are the dramatic advances in communications technologies, which have facilitated revolutionary changes in the world's financial structure permitting instant global flows of investment capital (Strange 1994). State action, too, has created globalisation, often in reponse to the stimuli created by internationally active business interests. Here, 'actors such as national governments were both contributors to structural shifts as well as captured within structures' (Waesche 2003, p. 11). As we will see, telecommunications liberalisation is an excellent example of globalisation by imitative state action; pioneering liberalisation in the Anglo-Saxon world stimulated a global bandwagon effect, highly conducive to globalisation of politico-economic outlooks, agendas and strategies. Schiller (1999, pp. 80–5) notes the vital leadership role played by the US administration in this context which prosecuted a strategy aimed at securing for the USA *the* dominant position in the liberalising global information and communications technologies (ICT) infrastructure. Here, the 'overall effort was to interconnect the interests of U.S. information technology companies with those of transnational business, so as to advance both' (ibid., p. 83). Pursuit of similar, though not identical, strategies also proved successful for states such as

France, Germany, Japan and the UK, as measured by increases in shares of foreign direct investment made from the 1980s to the mid-1990s. In this connection, an important driver of globalisation has been international regulatory competition. Techno-economic change and globalisation, it is held, have stimulated international regulatory competition, leading to a global dynamic of 'liberalising re-regulation'. Thus, Vogel (1996, p. 2)[3] cites McKenzie and Lee (1991, p. 1):

> The recent revolution in computer and information technology has enabled firms to move assets around the world at the touch of a button. It has also caused an explosion of competition not only among businesses, but among national governments seeking to attract new businesses and to keep existing businesses within their borders. This competition has forced governments to reduce tax rates, spending and regulation and to lower trade barriers.

This perspective observes that, to attract or retain investment, states competing in the global economy have had to develop competitive policies on a range of fronts: tax regimes, employment and social legislation, regulatory policy in a host of economic sectors, etc. States have had to evolve into competition states (Cerny 1997) and their process of adaptation has fed back into the globalisation process itself. Paradoxically, this has led, not to the much vaunted decline or 'retreat' of the state, but 'the actual expansion of types of de facto state intervention and regulation in the name of competitiveness and marketisation' (Cerny 1997, p. 251). With regard to regulatory policies, the competition state deregulates to the extent that it lifts protectionist old regulations but it also re-regulates by producing 'new regulatory structures that are often designed to enforce global market-rational economic behaviour on rigid and inflexible private sector actors as well as on state actors and agencies' (Cerny 1997, p. 264). However, again, the precise direction of change is not such a foregone conclusion as might at first appear.

As seen, globalisation theorists disagree as to whether globalisation pressures on national actors lead them to converge around a neo-liberal model or whether there remains scope for national policy variation. Proponents of the former viewpoint argue that globalisation seriously reduces nation state autonomy. The capacities of national governments to regulate (and tax) is seriously diminished by the ability of internationally mobile firms to choose between locations on the basis of their relative regulatory attractiveness – referred to in the political economy literature as regulatory arbitrage. This state of affairs, it is argued, encourages a (*de*)regulatory competition – a 'race to the bottom' – between competition states that seek to establish regulatory conditions attractive to investment within their regulatory jurisdictions. However, not all political scientists have been convinced by the literature on the so-called 'Delaware effect', after the US state that attracted firms through offering lax incorporation standards.

David Vogel (1995) pointed to a California effect, whereby that US state was able to impose higher environmental standards on car manufacturers. Vogel's work on consumer and environmental protection found that the EU, too, actually raised standards for some of its Member States as a result of the 'California effect' influence of its greener Member States, notably Germany. Similarly, Steven Vogel's (1996) comparative analysis (principally) of the telecommunications and financial services sectors in the UK and Japan, rejected the notion of a globalisation-driven 'deregulation revolution', suggesting instead that governments 'achieved different levels of liberalisation, adopted different types of re-regulation, and developed distinctive new styles of regulation'[4].

Interestingly, Cerny – who coined the term 'competition state' – allows for competing forms of competition state, based inter alia on states' different strategic capacities and different endowments in terms of competitive advantages and disadvantages. He acknowledges that the original model of competition state was identified by writers like John Zysman (1983) and Chalmers Johnson (1982) as the technocratic, dirigiste, 'strategic state' (e.g. France, Japan). Cerny notes, though, that the 'orthodox model' of competition state nowadays is the flexible, open neoliberal state (e.g. USA, UK). Principal reasons for the diminishing effectiveness of this (once so successful) dirigisme are technological change and globalisation. '[A]s more firms and sectors become linked into new patterns of production, financing and market access, often moving operations offshore, their willingness to follow the [dirigiste] script declines.' Thus, 'in France the forces of neoliberalism have penetrated a range of significant bastions from the main political parties to the major sectors of the bureaucracy itself' (Cerny (1997, p. 265).

Certainly, the pressures of 'regulatory competition' are particularly strong in the communications sector, with the USA setting the standard. As Marsden (2000, p. 20) has noted:

> the regulations of the nation-state that plays host to the most important market – which has the hegemony – set precedents which enable policy-makers in that market to entrench their advantage. In the video, computing hardware and software and telecommunications industries that leading market is undoubtedly the US; European regulators operate in a framework which is coloured if not dominated by US experiences of regulation

Much of the political science debate about regulatory competition might appear value-laden, concerned with 'competitive deregulation' and pressures for a 'race to the bottom'. From an economist's perspective, however, regulatory competition is seen simply as a market-driven process that is capable of achieving more efficient regulation. It is important, therefore, to note that the concept of regulatory competition is consistent with an 'evolutionary' perspective on the transformation of sectoral governance; it emphasises that the most 'efficient' governance regimes can emerge through a kind of 'natural selection process' which favours the emergence of the 'institutional form [ie regulatory regime] best suited to prevailing environmental conditions' (Lindberg et al. 1991, p. 4).

INTERESTS AND GROUP POLITICS

Yet another explanatory perspective is focused on interests and group politics. It is received wisdom in policy analysis that interests matter and powerful interests matter most. Accordingly, policy outcomes are commonly attributed to winning coalitions in the governmental process. Much scholarship stresses the great lobbying power, and further the 'structural power', of business. In regulation theory, interests are often given pride of place. Stigler's (1971) famous 'regulatory capture' argument is echoed by Lindblom's (1977) equally well known observation about the ability of 'privileged' business interests to exercise sway over issues of grand concern to them. Stigler's regulators, like Lindblom's politicians, naturally seek to maximise their political benefits from their activity; just as Lindblom's politicians defer to business interests, regulators are 'captured' by organised economic interests, their formal regulatees, at the expense of less organised consumers (see also Peltzman 1976).[5] Certainly, before the move from the 'positive' to the 'regulatory state', relations between government (the regulator in the positive state) and national champion firms were typically very close (Cawson et al. 1990; Hayward 1986). Vested regulatee interests exercise a degree of veto power over policy change; indeed, political science is replete with cases of entrenched policy communities keeping issues off the policy agenda. According to this perspective, policy change will occur only when powerful new interests seek entry into the sector, when old political coalitions dissolve and new ones form, or when established interests change their calculations of the costs and benefits of reform.

This latter approach might be referred to as the 'utilitarian' perspective, since it suggests that sectoral 'governance transformations occur when rationally calculating economic actors see that alternative forms of governance offer more profitable ways of doing business than those already in place' (Lindberg et al. 1991, p.4). This particular interest-centred approach takes into account that liberalisation is driven by globalisation and technological change (certainly in the case of telecommunications). Here the literature on capital mobility, and also 'forum shopping' and lobbying by multinational companies, is of obvious relevance. In the telecommunications sector, for example, the interest of multinational telecommunications users in benefiting from cheaper communications – and even their desire to construct their own international communication systems – was an important factor explaining the international liberalisation of the sector. Also relevant was the interest of powerful multinational companies like IBM – and now Microsoft –

in entering into the communications sector. States have competed to make their countries attractive for investment by such interests. According to the 'powerful interests perspective', the European Single Market was, above all, the outcome of the ambitions of business interests. Persuaded of their case and deferring to their influence, politicans sought ways of making European economies more competitive. Vogel (1995, p. 5) observed that: '[m]uch of the political support for EU rather than national regulatory standards [came] from Europe's export-oriented producers, who want[ed] to reduce the role of protective regulations as obstacles to intra-Union trade. They …successfully challenged nationally-oriented firms who often had relied upon distinctive national regulations to protect domestic markets'.

From the interest-centred perspective, a powerful argument can be made that the embrace of liberalisation and a new regulatory paradigm is to be appreciated mainly as the result of a strategic re-evaluation of economic self-interest in the context of globalisation and technological change by key economic interests in the sector. In this scenario, erstwhile protectionist actors in a position to influence state policy – e.g. incumbent telecommunications operators – actually positively seek to transform themselves from being national monopolies into global players. They cannot do this while remaining under the state's restrictive tutelle for all sorts of reasons (e.g, they are not free to raise private capital, or make strategic alliances as they like so they can expand in overseas markets). Apprehensive that international competitors will steal a march on them, they come to accept that liberalisation is both necessary and an interesting opportunity for them to expand and diversify their operations; they now explore models that both accord with their own past approaches (reflecting path dependency) and respond to their new preferences. The economic interests 'educate' government officials about the 'new realities', thereby contributing to the process of policy change. With regard to the telecommunications sector, this line of analysis looking at how key vested interests 'came around' has been explored (but only in a preliminary way) by Humphreys and Simpson (1996).

IDEAS MATTER

Another perspective privileges the role of ideas [6] – and how the policy agenda is 'framed' – in explaining policy outcomes. Organisations usually have a guiding philosophy; institutions have their own norms; policy communities and networks have core values. There is likely to be a dominant 'policy paradigm', reflective of an orthodoxy prevailing at a given moment in time. The terms 'Thatcherism' and 'Reaganomics' testify to the remarkable power of ideas and ideology. As Cerny (1997, p. 265) has put it, they provided a 'political *rationale*' (our emphasis) as well as a power base for a 'renaissance of free-market ideology generally – not just in the United Kingdom and the

United States but throughout the world'. They provided a new model for achieving international competitiveness, apparently more in tune with a 'post-Fordist' and globalising world economy, a new model that successfully challenged old ones (e.g. dirigisme). Neo-liberal ideas certainly spread rapidly across the Atlantic, and the English Channel, to continental Europe, as testified by the development of the single European market programme during the latter half of the 1980s (Armstrong and Bulmer 1998). The neo-liberal message was reinforced by influential think-tanks and 'epistemic communities' of experts at national and international level (e.g. Organisation for Economic Cooperation and Development – OECD). The international diffusion of neo-liberal politico-economic ideology might be held to be a very important factor for cross-national policy convergence. The global spread of privatisation and an 'Austrian school' emphasis on entrepreneurship are testament to the contagious power of ideas. Equally, the 'new public management' can be seen as evidence of the transformative power of ideas, leading to cross-national policy convergence around a qualitatively new efficiency- and market-oriented managerialism in the public sector (Christensen and Laegreid 2002).

Globalisation itself can be seen as a form of international neo-liberalism advocated by the the United States, by the EU, by transnational corporations, and by global organisations such as the International Monetary Fund (IMF) and the OECD, the latter organisations playing a key role in transmitting and (technocratically) legitimising values and ideas about policy change. Cerny (1997, p. 256) observes perceptively that possibly globalisation's 'most crucial feature is that it constitutes a *discourse* – and, increasingly, a hegemonic discourse...' and '..the spread of the discourse itself alters the a priori ideas and perceptions which people have of the empirical phenomona which they encounter....With the erosion of the old axioms, the concept of globalisation is coming increasingly to shape the terms of the debate'. Cerny (1997, p. 262) notes that '...the challenge for state actors today, as viewed through the contemporary discourse of globalisation, is to confront the perceived limitations of the state' (p. 262), essentially by evolving from the welfare state to the 'competition state'. Thus, Cerny stresses discourse and perceptions of the failure of traditional state intervention and the need for new 'competitive' forms of intervention in the era of globalisation. The idea (discourse) of globalisation itself thus has a structuration effect, whereby 'globalisation' becomes a kind of self-fulfilling prophecy.

According to this 'ideational' approach, therefore, the main explanatory variable is an epochal ideological shift towards neo-liberalism. It is associated with the ideological shift that arrived with the coming to office of President Reagan in the USA and Prime Minister Thatcher in the UK. Internationally, policy change occurs as a result of a diffusion or 'bandwagon' effect, bolstered by the demonstration effect of the first mover Anglo-Saxon models. At the same time, domestic political factors such as parties' ideological reorientation processes, and the outcome of national elections, remain clearly important. Thus, for example, neo-liberalism came to Britain (1979) earlier than it was embraced in France (1986 onwards). The key turning point in telecommunications policy in the UK was the arrival in power of Thatcherites with a radical privatisation and liberalisation agenda. The key turning point in French telecommunications policy was the great sea-change in French attitudes to economic management that saw the 1986–88 Gaullist-led government embark on Western Europe's second most extensive privatisation programme (second only to Thatcher's in the UK). Moreover, as we shall see, European Commission officials embraced the new ideational orthodoxies about globalisation and liberalisation and served as important EU-institutional agents of 'policy learning' and 'policy transfer' of these ideas. In reorienting the policy agenda and promoting new thinking, these officials – or the Commission collectively (Radaelli 2000a) – acted as classic 'policy entrepreneurs' (Kingdon 1984).

THE NATIONAL INSTITUTIONAL 'REFRACTION' EFFECT

Party ideologies and political incumbency are not, of course, the only way 'politics matters'. National institutions may 'refract' the pressures of global structural shift (Waesche 2003). The institutional features of different countries present different structural constraints and opportunities for political agency (Zysman 1983; Hall 1986; Hall and Taylor 1996; North 1990; Immergut 1998). Historically rooted national institutional and cultural differences and 'policy styles' may explain the continuance of a degree of national idiosyncrasy in regulation. In particular, historical institutionalists stress 'path dependence'. Accordingly, distinct national paths to telecommunications liberalisation can be expected to give rise to continuing national differences in regulatory policies. The core institutionalist hypotheses are that national institutional profiles are persistent and resistant to change, that they vary between countries, that when institutional change does occur, the reforms follow characteristic national paths (path dependence), and that different national institutions provide different constraints on actor strategies and lead to contrasting policy patterns and decisions.

A number of cross-national studies have pointed towards the persistence of deeply embedded national models of capitalism, with very different institutional features and regulatory policy styles (Schmidt 2002; Hall and Soskice 2001; Rhodes and van Apeldoorn 1997; Albert 1993). Schmidt (2002), for instance, shows how Britain, France and Germany have adapted in very distinctive ways to the pressures of globalisation and Europeanisation. Their policies, practices and discourses have remained highly distinctive. As mentioned already, Steven Vogel's (1996) comparative analysis of regulatory reform in advanced industrial societies pointed to the 'many roads to reregulation'. This is not simply a matter of different national state traditions, regulatory cultures and policy styles. It depends also on the 'opportunity structures' of political systems. In political systems with multiple veto points, EU policy models will be moderated by concessions to the interests and policy preferences of domestic veto players. This may be reflected in both 'uploading' of Member State preferences (resulting in directives that allow discretionary scope in the EU framework for national models) and also in 'downloading' (resulting in the 'domesticated' implementation of EU-agreed policies according to domestic norms).

Policy differences – in terms of processes, styles and outputs – between national institutional systems can of course be expected to diminish as a result of technological change, globalisation, Europeanisation, and the mix of regulatory competition and policy learning (the transfer of 'ideas') that they engender. Thus, most recently Thatcher (2004a) has played down the relevance of the 'national varieties of capitalism' perspective for the telecommunications sector, arguing that in this case internationalisation pressures were so strong and mutually reinforcing that they overwhelmed national institutional inertia and led to far-reaching change and a striking degree of cross-national policy convergence. The degree to which policies have indeed converged in telecommunications, and the nature of the EU's impact, is an empirical question, that will be explored in this book, particularly in Chapter 4 on the implementation of the EU's 1998 regulatory package but also in Chapter 5 on the EU's new 2002 regulatory package.

THE ROLE OF THE EUROPEAN UNION

Some analysts have seen the impact of globalisation and technological change as being so overwhelming that the impact of national or European policy is of a distinctly subordinate order of concern. Thus, for Josef Esser (1997), and his colleagues at the University of Frankfurt, the apparent 'Europeanisation' of telecommunications policy and regulation has occurred less because of the Europeanising policies of national policy makers or the European Commission than as the result of the strategies of key private economic interests reacting to the challenges presented by 'triadisation' (see Ohmae 1991), technological change, and the 'crisis of Fordism'. Their case studies of the UK, France and Germany draw attention to how central the transnationalisation of corporate strategies has been for the evolution of national telecommunications in Europe. They are critical of the view – explicit or implicit in many studies – that the role of the European Commission should take pride of place in explaining the direction and pace of telecommunications policy making at the European level. They see the European Commission less as a policy entrepreneur than as a broker for the marketising pressures arising from global competition and the internationalising strategies of large telecommunication enterprises.

We agree that the transnationalisation of corporate strategies has been crucial, but we also argue that the EU's – and in particular the Commission's – role has been far from subordinate. 'Europeanisation' has a very real, independent quality. Telecommunications reform in Europe may have been *driven* by the competitive market dynamics of the global economy, but for Member States it has been *framed* by EU rules. To this extent, European telecommunications policy has been significantly, if not fundamentally, determined in Brussels. The Commission has acted as a policy entrepreneur, responding to the demands of new service providers and user interests, dramatising the extent of the external challenge and coordinating a collective Member State response, generally through persuasion, but backed up by the occasional resort to coercion or the threat thereof. Moreover, the European Union has performed a crucial *alibi* function. Even if national governments have had to adapt primarily to structural pressures resulting from globalisation and technological change, Brussels has served as a convenient excuse vis-à-vis resistant domestic interests ('Brussels requires this reform!'). To this extent, the EU has strengthened the hand of domestic reformers. Moreover, the EU has been an important forum for *policy learning*, about the new technological and market 'realities' of the globalising telecommunications sector. In all these ways, the EU has helped reformers overcome institutional blockages and veto points at the domestic level. Finally, as Chapter 7 shows, the EU has been an important agent – and partner of the United States of America – in contributing to globalisation, which as mentioned earlier can be analysed as a dependent variable as well as employed as an independent variable.

EU POLICY TRANSFER AND POLICY LEARNING

In considering the role of EU institutions in regulatory reform, we make particular reference to two concepts: 'policy transfer' and 'Europeanisation'. With regard to the former, the core idea is that policy experience in one jurisdiction may inform or shape policy making in another jurisdiction (Dolowitz and Marsh 1996 and 2000). Thus, Dolowitz (1997) has explained how UK employment policy in the 1980s drew on the US experience, and Dolowitz et al. (2000) have explored the transfer of social policy. Hills (1986) and Moran (1991) have pointed to the important US influence on regulatory reforms, notably in the UK and Japan, in respectively the fields of telecommunications and financial services. Policy transfer can occur through policy emulation – involving some obvious 'imitating action' – or through policy learning, the latter involving 'a redefinition of one's interests on the basis of newly-acquired knowledge' (Jordana et al. 2002, p. 3). Lesson drawing can be *facilitated* by policy networks and in particular by epistemic communities, which can be defined as 'networks of professionals with recognised expertise and competence in a particular domain and an authoritative claim to policy-relevant knowledge' (Haas 1992, p. 3).

In his work on policy convergence, Bennett (1991a) identifies four transfer processes that help explain why and how elites adopt common policies. First, policy convergence may occur through emulation, which very clearly involves drawing on overseas experience and learning from it (also see Bennett 1991b). Second, Bennett argues that policy convergence may occur because of elite networking and the growth of policy communities. Here convergence arises because of 'the existence of shared ideas amongst a relatively coherent and enduring network of elites engaging in regular interaction at the transnational level'. Another possibility is convergence through penetration, where states are forced to conform to actions taken elsewhere by external actors, such as the USA or multinational companies. Finally, particularly interesting for our purposes, is convergence through harmonisation – where an international regime tackles a common problem among interdependent states. This is plainly relevant for the EU policy process and for policy transfer by the EU institutions. The literature is generally agreed that policy can transfer at any point along a continuum from 'obligated' (i.e. coercive) transfer to 'voluntary' transfer, with a considerable amount occurring somewhere in between these poles. Voluntary transfer clearly involves policy learning whereas coercive transfer occurs where a government is forced, for instance by a supranational institution, to adopt a policy (Dolowitz and Marsh 1996, pp. 344–5).

EUROPEANISATION

The more policy transfer occurs through the agency of EU institutions and the arena for ideational convergence provided by the EU, the more 'Europeanised' we might reasonably expect Member States' telecommunications policies to become. Telecommunications liberalisation has been seen as an excellent example of 'Europeanisation', some analysts seeing the transformation of regulatory governance of the sector in terms of a triumph of the EU's 'supranational' potential (see e.g. Sandholtz 1993 and 1998). Europeanisation itself is a concept that has received increasing attention in recent years and it is important to define it carefully. Risse et al. (2001, p. 1) define it as 'the emergence and development at the European level of distinct structures of governance'. Nonetheless, they are mainly concerned with *the impact* of Europeanisation 'on the domestic structures of the Member States'. Bulmer and Burch (2001, p. 76) actually define Europeanisation restrictively as *the impact* of European integration on national polities, politics and policies. Similarly, Ladrech (1994, p. 69) describes it, in distinction from European integration, as: '…an incremental process of reorienting the direction and shape of politics to the degree that EU political and economic dynamics become part of the organisational logic of national politics and policy-making' (Ladrech 1994, p. 69). However, Radaelli (2000b, p.3) has defined it more broadly thus: 'Processes of (a) construction (b) diffusion and (c) institutionalization of formal and informal rules, procedures, policy paradigms, styles, "ways of doing things" and shared beliefs and norms which are first defined and consolidated in the making of EU decisions and then incorporated in the logic of domestic discourse, identities, political structures and public policies'. Our usage herein takes 'Europeanisation' to refer to both the development of a regulatory framework at the European level and its impact on domestic structures and policies. Regarding the latter, we are principally concerned with exploring the extent of convergence of national regulatory policies for telecommunications as a result of EU membership.

However, we must make two important qualifications at this point. First, it is important to emphasise that we do not ascribe causation or regulatory policy change to 'Europeanisation'; which we view as an intervening variable in this regard. Levi-Faur (2002, p.2) has made the telling point that 'the major features of liberalisation would have been diffused to practically all member states even if the European Commission and other agents of supranationalism had not existed'. After all, as Chapter 7 shows, by 2002 more than 80 states had signed up to the WTO's Agreement on Basic Telecommunications. The aforementioned independent variables – technological change, globalisation, international regulatory competition, and ideas/ideology – can be seen as the key causal elements driving regulatory policy change. Indeed, Europeanisation might be seen as a 'regional manifestation of globalisation' (Anderson 2003, p. 41). Nonetheless, there can be little questioning that 'Europeanisation' has also been an important *intervening* variable. Thus, Majone (1996) has explained how Europe has been an important agent for change from the positive [ie. interventionist] to the regulatory state. Although its main impact has been to reinforce other forces for regulatory change, it could still be expected to exert some independent effect of its own, conserving some elements of a distinctly 'European' approach to liberalisation. With its own huge 'internal' market, Europe clearly has the potential for *either* amplifying *or* moderating 'US style' globalisation (Schmidt 1999; Green Cowles et al. 2001, p. 4).

Second, while much of the literature on Europeanisation is concerned with the convergence of public policies, a number of scholars have drawn attention to the fact that it usually has a differential impact. This is because the degree to which there there is an 'institutional fit' between the EU model and the domestic one varies between Member States (see, for example, Börzel 2002; Börzel and Risse 2000; Knill 2001; Knill and Lenschow 1998; Green Cowles et al. 2001). We treat 'Europeanisation' as an interactive process to take account of the way Member States typically try to shape EU legislation to accord with their own state traditions, institutional profiles, policy styles and policy preferences, thereby minimising any 'misfit' and subsequent adaptation pressures. 'Europeanisation' clearly poses a distinct challenge for Member States, particularly those with strongly defined state traditions, national institutions and policy styles. Accordingly, Börzel (2002), and others, point to the 'uploading' by Member States of their preferred policy models. Equally, EU policy may be 'downloaded' – transposed and implemented at the national level – in ways that reflect national orientations; for this phenomenon, Helen Wallace employs the term 'domestication' (Wallace 2000, pp. 369–70),[7] noting that 'Europeans have ...leverage on the process of Europeanisation; it is a shaped process, not a passively encountered process.'

We shall approach Europeanisation as a complex process. For heuristic purposes it is indeed very useful to distinguish between two broad stages: 'uploading' and 'downloading'. The first stage sees the formulation and negotiation of a series of EU directives that established the ground rules (basic principles, degrees of market opening, etc.). During this formulation and negotiation stage, the Member States have the opportunity to 'upload' their own preferred models of liberalisation. The second, transposition and implementation, stage sees Member States compelled to 'download' the agreed EU model. The transposition and implementation of EU directives into national law allows scope for interpretation and domestication of EU rules by national legislators and regulators.

THE STRUCTURE OF THE BOOK

Chapter 2 briefly looks at the status quo ante and explains how a set of *independent* variables produced a paradigmatic policy change: liberalisation. It explains how the pressures of globalisation, technological change, the diffusion of neo-liberal ideas from the USA and the UK, and international regulatory competition, re-orientated actor preferences so that over time a new consensus emerged in Europe about the need for far-reaching liberalisation. The chapter also points to the importance of a set of national political *intervening* variables. EU Member States' reform capacities varied according to their national political make-up: state traditions, policy styles, governmental orientations, configurations of interests, patterns of group politics, and institutional veto points exploitable by opponents of reform. The chapter shows how, over time, strong pressures of 'competitive emulation' on national telecommunications operators and of 'international regulatory competition' on regulatory policy makers smoothed the path towards the new consensus. A core argument of the chapter is that the state 'retreated' only from the function of owner/operator; otherwise, it remained interventionist, as a 'competition state', actively remodelling telecommunications structures to ensure national economic competitiveness in global markets.

Chapter 3 documents the emergence and growth of telecommunications policy at EU level, culminating in the creation of what came to be known as the '1998 package' of directives, the implementation of which committed EU Member States to an unprecedentedly comprehensive liberalisation of their telecommunications sectors. The chapter stresses the role played by powerful global politico-economic structural forces in influencing policy makers' decisions nationally and within the EU, thereby promoting the development of a European regulatory approach to telecommunications. It provides evidence of the importance of institutional factors, most outstandingly the role played by the European Commission, in shaping policy. Here, whilst the Europeanisation of telecommunications policy was occasionally 'coercive', to give the process a push or to cajole laggards, policy change occurred primarily through consensual decision making.

Chapter 4 returns the focus to the Member State level and examines their transposition and implementation of the EU's policies for introducing competition into Europe's telecommunications markets. Thus, the chapter explores the degree of 'Europeanisation' of national telecommunications policy, that is to say the influence of the EU on domestic policies and regulatory practices. Accordingly, the chapter is principally concerned with the scope for 'domestication' of EU policies by the Member States' adopting European policies in ways that reflect their national preferences, institutions, state traditions and policy styles. The other principal theme of Chapter 4 is the emergence of the 'regulatory state' in telecommunications governance. Rather than retreat, as the rhetoric about 'deregulation' and the reality of privatisation might suggest, the state assumed a host of new *regulatory* functions: enforcing economic competition whilst maintaining national public service (what the French call 'service public'). The chapter argues that the new 'regulatory state' remained as interventionist as the 'old' service provider state.

Chapter 5 explores further the implementation of the EU's liberalising regulatory framework for telecommunications. It examines the development of a new 2002 regulatory package which aimed to streamline regulation, lightening the regulatory burden, and at the same time to cater to the convergence of telecommunications, broadcasting and new systems of electronic communications such as the Internet. The chapter shows how the new 'Electronic Communication Regulatory Framework' (ECRF) was conceived as a strategic factor for Europe's future economic in the emerging 'global information society'. In particular, effective regulatory implementation of telecommunications liberalisation was deemed to be crucial to Europe's up-take of the Internet and competitiveness in the new knowledge-based economy. The chapter pursues the 'regulatory state' theme, arguing that the new framework has the potential to intensify the burden on the regulators. It also examines the tension between the greater regulatory harmonisation sought by the Commission and industry interests, and the continuing resistance of the Member States and national regulators to EU regulatory centralisation. The chapter shows how the flexibility of the new regulatory framework may actually increase 'domestication'; much will depend on how the new regulatory arrangements perform and in particular on the Commission's exercise of its new channels of influence.

Chapter 6 complements Chapter 5 by exploring the restriction of the EU's Electronic Communications Regulatory Framework to infrastructural matters. Here, aside from an account of the detailed politics of the EU's debate on convergence of the late 1990s, we focus on why matters of communications content were excluded from the Framework and some of the complications which arise from this. In terms of broadcasting content, the long established 'gravitational pull' of the national policy context is stressed, which has ensured that the EU's efforts to develop initiatives in broadcasting policy have been often controversial and limited in scope (largely confined to opening up a single market), the convergence debate serving as yet another example. The chapter also focuses on content issues related to the Internet where, in contrast to broadcasting, Member States excluded so-called Information Society services (most notably those associated with Internet commerce) from the new Framework due to the global 'gravitational pull' of this relatively new part of the communications sector, with its attendant uncertainties. The chapter also shows, by focusing on the regulation of 'digital gateways', that despite the EU regulatory framework's confinement to communications infrastructure regulation, carriage (infrastructural) issues do have a bearing on content issues.

Chapter 7 takes a global focus by attempting to locate the position and influence of the EU in the rapidly evolving international governance of the communications sector. It explores the rise to prominence in communications policy of the World Trade Organization (WTO), as well as a simultaneous waning in the influence of the International Telecommunications Union, as trade liberalisation and foreign direct investment regulation have become the new imperatives of global telecommunications. The chapter argues that the EU has served as an effective agent of policy transfer of the agenda of liberalisation in telecommunications, not just to its Member States, but also other WTO members with its clarion calls for liberalisation though it has also served as a shield against international liberalisation of trade in the audiovisual sector. From the character of the WTO's Agreement on Basic Telecommunications (ABT), it is evident also that the EU has been able to upload its policy preferences to the global level. The chapter concludes with an exploration of the role which the EU has played to date in the evolution of the, as yet embryonic, system of global governance for electronic commerce.

The volume's final chapter reflects on the overall significance of the key changes to the European telecommunications policy landscape which it has charted and looks forward, albeit tentatively, to possible future developments. Here, consideration is given, in particular, to the relationship between the EU and national levels in an increasingly complex regulatory scenario, the prospects for further convergence in communications regulation in Europe and, finally, the place of public service provision in a European communications environment increasingly likely to be dominated by overwhelmingly economic goals, targeted either through sector specific or more general regulatory measures.

NOTES

1. The 1994 Bangemann report (European Commission 1994a), which stressed the centrality of telecommunications reform to the Information Society, paved the way for full liberalisation in the EU.
2. See also the collection edited by Hall and Soskice (2001).
3. Though Vogel does not accept that this regulatory competition leads necessarily to a convergence of national regulatory policies towards 'deregulation', a deregulatory 'race to the bottom'.
4. Looking at the specific area of social policy, held to have been rendered particularly vulnerable to retrenchment, Ramesh Mishra (1999) has shown that globalisation has not produced a 'race to the bottom' for the welfare state of advanced industrial countries. Mishra finds that social standards have declined far more in the Anglo-Saxon world than in continental Europe and Japan leading to the conclusion that globalisation is as much an ideological and political construct as an economic phenomenon. Swank (2002) too has argued that capital mobility has not, as commonly argued, led states to engage in a welfare retrenchment 'race to the bottom'; the character of domestic institutions matters in explaining the direction of policy change in developed welfare states.
5. Stigler and Peltzman, on regulatory capture, are commonly referred to as the 'Chicago school'.
6. Bartle (2002b) discusses the role of ideas with regard to telecommunications reform.
7. Wallace employs the term to describe the different ways in which *both* Europeanisation and globalisation are handled at the domestic level.

2. Globalisation and the competition state

Until the 1980s, the general European consensus was that telecommunication was a natural monopoly. The state's role was that of monopoly owner/operator of telecommunications networks and services. However, under the pressure of globalisation, technological change and the diffusion of neo-liberal ideas from the USA and the UK, awareness of the need for liberalisation increased throughout the 1980s. In the 1990s a new consensus emerged around the need for full liberalisation and a harmonised pro-competitive regulatory regime, implemented by the EU Member States but coordinated and supervised by the European Commission. The state now retreated from the function of owner/operator, relinquishing the supply of services to commercial players and privatising the former incumbents. Throughout, however, the state remained interventionist, as a 'competition state', actively remodelling telecommunications structures to ensure national economic competitiveness in global markets.

This chapter charts the transformation in national actor preferences, paying attention to significant cross-national differences in timing. It explores how policy reorientation was constrained by the different national institutional features of the Member States: state traditions, policy styles and institutional veto points exploitable by opponents of reform. In this light, it explains the variations in policy priorities and reform capacities that EU Member States exhibited with regard to telecommunications reform. It also explains how, over time, strong pressures of 'competitive emulation' on national telecommunications operators and 'international regulatory competition' on regulatory policy makers smoothed the path towards the new consensus. The subsequent chapter examines the particular contribution of the EU institutions, especially the Commission, to facilitating this new consensus. These chapters are, therefore, highly complementary.

THE STATUS QUO ANTE: TELECOMMUNICATIONS BEFORE LIBERALISATION

Until the 1980s, the telecommunications sector was characterised by distinct features which made its structure and operation, despite a degree of national diversity, appear inherently stable and narrowly circumscribed. It was widely accepted that fixed telecommunications was a natural monopoly, whether the preserve of a strictly supervised private company (AT&T) as in 'regulatory state' USA or entrusted to public sector monopoly providers, the Postal, Telephone and Telegraph (PTT) administrations[1], as in 'interventionist state' western Europe. The utilities sectors were seen as natural monopolies because competition was not the optimal market structure. Rather, the costs of services to the customer were minimised where supply was concentrated in the hands of a monopoly (or oligopoly) provider able to benefit from economies of scale. These benefits would have been lost under competition; any duplication would have been wasteful. The monopoly was legitimised by a universal service obligation. Indeed, universal service provision was the dominant ideological paradigm of the era. Tariffs were established on political and social rather than on purely economic grounds; in particular, international and long distance (business) calls subsidised local (private) calls. Monopoly also served highly nationalistic industrial policies. The European PTTs sustained an olipogolistic industry of national – or at least domestically-based – equipment manufacturers, protected from outside competition by means of nationalistic policies of R&D, procurement, network attachment certification and standardisation. This protectionism was often legitimised by reference to national security requirements. Consequently, there existed little international trade in telecommunications equipment and services. Europe's market was commonly described as being 'balkanised'. The sector was conspicuous for its lack of market forces. Pitt's (1989, p. 6) description of the US telecommunications sector as a 'club with restricted membership' applied even more in the 'interventionist' states of western Europe with their state-owned monopoly telecommunications service providers.

This sectoral characteristic of a high degree of state intervention transcended diverse state traditions and national policy styles. Despite having contrasting traditions of industrial policy, European countries had essentially similarly structured telecommunications sectors; this is exemplified very clearly by the cases of the UK, France and Germany (Webber and Holmes 1985 p. 16). In each case the demand side of the market was dominated by a publicly-owned telecommunications administration with a monopoly of the rights to provide telecommunications services and to operate the network.[2] In France and Germany, this administration, respectively the Direction Générale des Télécommunications (DGT) and the Bundespost, had been part of the PTT Ministry; in the UK case, the Post Office had become an independent public corporation in 1969. The supply side of the market was similarly dominated by an exclusive group of large firms, some of them foreign giants like the domestic subsidiaries of the US firm ITT, others unambiguously 'national champions': CIT-Alcatel in France, Siemens in Germany, and GEC and Plessey in Britain. The national authorities blatantly favoured domestically-based firms in their purchasing policy. As a result trade in telecommunications equipment was restricted. Right across western Europe, the PTT administrations combined the functions of policy maker, regulator and operator (Steinfeld 1994, p. 7). Policies were guided by two primary concerns: (1) public service provision, which in telecommunications amounted to the provision of a universal service at an affordable price (in broadcasting, of course, it involved rather more than this) and meant the cross-subsidisation of residential user tariffs by long-distance and business calls; and (2) the promotion of national industrial interests, which involved subsidising technical innovation, and the promotion of 'national champion' producers and operators (Humphreys and Simpson 1996, p. 105–6). However, by the 1990s, a new consensus was emerging in favour of a package of reforms: (1) liberalisation, involving the abolition of the state monopoly and the removal of barriers to market entry; (2) the establishment of independent regulatory agencies, to promote competition; (3) 'corporatisation', the organisational reform of the telecommunications branches of public administrations into public corporations; and (4) increasingly, the privatisation of former state telecommunications operators.

The major stimuli to this paradigm change were technological change, the global impact of US telecommunications reform, international competition, including regulatory competition, and the spread of neo-liberal ideas emanating from the Anglo-Saxon 'first movers', namely the USA and the UK. As the next chapter will show, 'Europeanisation' played an important role; but more as an 'amplifier' of these deeper, structural 'global' forces (Humphreys 2002; also see Schneider 2002). Unlike the 'hard', compelling imperatives of technological change and globalisation, the EU's reforms resulted from a 'softer', largely negotiated process. Nonetheless, as will be seen later in this work, the European Commission used all its powers of persuasion, including some coercion, to coordinate a European response to these exogenous structural forces for change, pressing the reform of outmoded structures and practices upon 'laggard' Member States. Also, the EU was a weighty force, aligned with the USA, pressing for global regulatory change, in the pro-competition direction (Simpson and Wilkinson 2002; Young 2002, pp. 50–79). For all its importance, however, the fact remains that given the pressures for change, 'the major features of liberalisation would have been diffused to practically all member states even if the European Commission and other agents of supra-nationalism had not existed' (Levi-Faur 2002, p. 2). Indeed, by 1999, no fewer than 83 countries, of the 188 surveyed by the International Telecommunications Union (ITU), had privatised or part-privatised their incumbent telecommunications operator and more or less the same number had introduced competition (Schneider 2002, p. 28).

TECHNOLOGICAL CHANGE, IT AND TELECOMMUNICATIONS CONVERGENCE, AND GLOBALISATION: 'NATURAL MONOPOLY' BECOMES ANACHRONISTIC

A prime factor for this change was new technology, and the 'merging of space satellite technology, telecommunications and computers' (Tunstall 1986, p. 37). From the 1980s onwards, the idea that telecommunications was a natural monoply lost ground progressively under the impact of a 'communications revolution' (Dyson and Humphreys 1986, 1990). The main technological driver of change was the digital 'convergence' of data-processing and telecommunications. Digital switching and network technologies – combined with 'intelligent' terminal equipment that bridged telecommunications and data processing – opened up the possibility to firms on both sides of the telecommunications/IT fence of offering a range of specialised 'value-added network services' (VANS) in networks that could transmit data at unprecedented speeds and capacities (e.g. through the integrated services digital network, ISDN). The distinction between 'basic' and 'advanced' telecommunications services – and indeed between 'individual' telecommunications and 'mass' communications (broadcasting) – services was also eroded by digitalisation. A third innovation was the development of alternative network technologies like fibre-optic cable and mobile telephony, together with the increased deployment of satellites. Network competition became feasible. By the end of the twentieth century, infrastructural competition was increasingly prevalent, although natural monopoly continued to characterise certain areas, notably the 'local loop' (the 'last mile' of cable from local exchange to the home) and naturally scarce radio spectrum (Coen and Doyle 2000, p. 19). Even here, new digital technologies (ADSL, DSL, digital TV) were diminishing the natural monopoly element, heralding a new age of full competition. It is now widely accepted that telecommunications is no longer a natural monopoly, not even the 'local loop'.

In the 1980s, new telecommunications applications were therefore opening up a new world of international business communication. A diverse range of specific user demands could be met by a host of new services. Seeking lower prices and more choice, business users now demanded the freeing up of markets in the myriad information and communication services that were now possible. Computer manufacturers (e.g. IBM) became interested in producing telecommunications-related equipment and buying into telecommunications companies (such as MCI[3]). Software companies (e.g. Microsoft), cable operators (e.g. NTL), and other utilities (e.g. Energis) became interested in providing telecommunications networks and services. A business 'coalition for change', became vocal at national and international level (Humphreys and

Simpson 1996, p. 106). Governments faced a dilemma. They wanted to protect their national markets, promote their national champion producers and operators, and retain the revenues they gained from their state-owned telecommunication operators. On the other hand, they were pressured by the business coalition for change and they naturally also wanted to gain the anticipated general economic benefits – technological innovation and greater choice of services at lower prices – of having competitive telecommunications infrastructures and markets. Over time, the latter aim came to predominate. In this, globalisation was a crucial factor. It had various components. On the demand side were the globalisation of world trade and the new communication requirements of the global financial structure and transnational and multinational business users. On the supply side, were the new technological possibilities to provide a plethora of high-speed, interactive, content-rich services, opening exciting new opportunities for the conduct of global business. Globalisation pressure was institutionalised when the Uruguay Round of the General Agreement on Tariffs and Trade (GATT – later the World Trade Organization – embraced liberalisation of telecommunications services (Simpson and Wilkinson 2002).

Table 2.1 Phases of technological innovation in communications

1900 – 1930s	1960s – 1970s	1970s – 1980s	1990s – 2000
Voice telephony; radio; experimental TV.	Telex; facsimile; colour TV; cable TV; teletext.	Digital switching; data services (at increasing speeds); 1-G mobile; paging; videotex; fibre-optic cable; satellite TV.	Packet-switching; Broadband (DSL, ADSL); 2- and 3-G Mobile; E-mail; Teleconferencing; Internet; Online services; Internet telephony; digital TV.

GLOBALISATION AND THE REGULATORY COMPETITION 'GENIE' RELEASED BY THE ANGLO-SAXONS

A core feature of globalisation was a dynamic of international regulatory competition. America's communications industry at large – space communications, broadcasting, telecommunications – was 'unleashed' by a number of regulatory and legal decisions taken during the 1980s Reagan era in the USA (Tunstall 1986). Generally described as 'de-regulation', but more properly termed 'liberalising re-regulation', the new policy turn arose from a synthesis of ideological (neo-liberal) and pragmatic (neo-mercantilist) motives (Dyson and Humphreys 1990; Humphreys and Simpson 1996, p. 107).

In telecommunications, a degree of incremental liberalisation had occurred in the USA since the 1950s. However, suddenly in January 1982, one year into the 'new Right' Reagan administration, the Department of Justice made two monumental decisions behind which 'the thinking ...seemed to be that the US had in IBM and AT&T two super-companies which should be unfettered from anti-trust constraints and allowed to engage in uninhibited competition with Japan' (Tunstall 1986, p. 27). One decision released IBM, the world's leading computer company, from a long-running anti-trust case, allowing the company to enter telecommunications markets (in 1985 IBM duly bought into the successful US telecommunications company MCI). The other decision terminated an anti-trust case against AT&T that had been running since 1974 (initiated by MCI). Following the same logic of convergence between the computing and telecommunications sectors, and the new scope for competition that this convergence brought, the Justice Department agreed a solution with AT&T which allowed the company to diversify into data-processing businesses but also provided for the divestiture of its regional telephone companies, a solution that was subsequently agreed by Judge Harold Greene, presiding over the case. This vertical separation, which actually occurred on 1 January 1984, had the desired effect of propelling the old monopoly Bell–AT&T telephone company into world markets (Hills 1986; Tunstall 1986).

Accordingly, AT&T was divested of its 22 local telephony operations. These became 'Baby Bells', seven independently owned regional Bell operating companies (RBOCs), in other words regional telephone systems, which were now required to provide all long-distance carriers with interconnection. AT&T's dominant position in the long-distance market was opened to competition from the likes of MCI and Sprint. At the same time, US markets for equipment and services were partially opened to competition, including from foreign suppliers. The first ripples of the coming tidal wave of globalisation of the telecommunications sector were now felt as US companies began to be propelled into international markets in order to recoup loss of domestic market share, while the US government pressed for reciprocal market access overseas. In 1988 Congress enacted legislation demanding reciprocity from countries with which the USA ran a telecommunications deficit (Humphreys and Simpson 1996, p. 107; Dyson and Humphreys 1990, pp. 5–6; Hills 1992, pp. 125–7; Pitt and Morgan 1992). European markets were a particular target for US companies seeking to expand (Young 2002, p. 52; Ungerer with Costello 1990). The US government championed their interests wherever it could. Thus, the US government appears to have exerted considerable pressure on the Germans (interview in the RegTP, 2001). Lüthje (1997, p. 164) notes that liberalisation of the market for terminal equipment in Germany was accepted by traditional suppliers as a concession to trade political pressure from the USA.

Reform in the UK was the result of an odd mix of ideological and similarly prosaic motives. The neo-liberal Thatcher government elected in 1979 saw telecommunications reform as an opportunity to put into practice radical 'new Right' policies of freeing up markets and privatising 'inefficient' state enterprises. Though widely perceived as radical, the reform had a very pragmatic side. Thus, the Conservatives' 1981 Telecommunications Act deprived British Telecom of its monopoly over telecommunications equipment, but only introduced a limited degree of competition into the long-distance telephone market by licensing a single company Mercury Communications as a duopoly competitor. Moreover, in contrast to the USA's bold divestiture of AT&T, the Conservatives' 1984 privatisation of BT[4] left it as a vertically integrated company. Structural separation, it was feared, would have rendered the company a less attractive privatisation prospect. Value added services were liberalised and, to supervise this new competition, a national regulatory authority (NRA), the Office of Telecommunications (Oftel) was established, independent of the industry. Thus, the PTT model of telecommunications provision was dramatically overthrown. However, not until 1989 was a free market in (resale of) leased lines permitted and not until 1991, following a duopoly review, was full network competition introduced.

Nonetheless, the UK's partial liberalisation in the 1980s fast spread the perception that the UK had the most attractive telecommunications market in Europe. During the 1980s, telecommunications revenues grew impressively. According to Robinson (1992, p. 34) in just one year (1986–87) they increased by 12.4 per cent[5]. At the same time, the UK soon boasted the lowest business call charges in Europe and became an attractive location for foreign multinational companies; a number (e.g. Mitel, NEC, Northern Telecom and Rolm) chose the UK as their chief European location. Western European countries therefore started 'looking closely at the British' (Morgan and Webber 1986, pp. 61–2). Thus, together, the Anglo-Saxons could be said to have unleashed global pressures for 'competitive deregulation', strictly speaking a 'competitive liberalising re-regulation' (Humphreys and Simpson 1996, pp. 107–08). They also provided a compelling policy 'lesson'. Continental Europeans 'learned' from the Anglo-Saxon first movers that telecommunications liberalisation contributed to general economic competitiveness, attracted investment, and stimulated innovation. They demonstrated to entrenched incumbent operators on the Continent that – at least in the context of dynamic telecommunications markets – liberalisation did not pose a threat, rather a commercial opportunity to expand internationally (Humphreys 2002, p. 58). Once the liberalisation genie was released by the Anglo-Saxons, strong pressures of international regulatory competition confronted governments. Continental policy makers watched apprehensively as the Anglo-Saxons, unconstrained by domestic politics obstacles, stole a march in the economically strategic sector. In France, in particular, the competitive threat from Britain concentrated minds (Longuet 1988; Dandelot 1993, both cited in Thatcher 1999). Large multinational business users could clearly engage in regulatory arbitrage. Moreover, the new 'technologies of freedom' (Levi-Faur 1999, p. 200) meant that national systems could be simply 'bypassed' (e.g. by international call-back), rendering territorial markets indefensible. Through the 1980s, into the 1990s, the Europeans faced these mounting pressures of technological change, globalisation and regulatory competition.

THE DIFFERENTIAL WILL AND CAPACITY TO REFORM OF THE EU MEMBER STATES

However, at first, the EU Member States' responses to these pressures varied considerably. In the vanguard of reform along with the UK were only the Scandinavians. Since Finland and Sweden did not join the EU until 1995, during the 1980s the UK was rather a lone voice within the Community advocating   radical   telecommunications   liberalisation.   Moreover, telecommunications reform was not simply shaped by powerful 'exogenous' factors (technological change, globalisation, regulatory competition). 'Endogenous' political factors were very important. As the UK case demonstrated, the political ideology of the government was an important factor; at first, only the UK Conservatives embraced neo-liberalism and their coming into office in 1979 was a crucial contingency for the reform. Group politics was important too. Only in Britain was the balance of group politics overwhelmingly weighted towards the reformers: the demand for new services from commercial users – including the City – outweighed sectoral vested interests (e.g. the UK telecommunications manufacturers) and the unions were divided and weak. By contrast, in France and Germany sectoral vested interests, such as equipment manufacturers and large and powerful public telecommunications bureaucracies, were stronger. In many continental countries, including France and Germany, the resistance of the unions was a much greater obstacle to reform than in the UK. Also, national institutional differences provided different patterns of constraint and opportunity structures. As an early study by Grande and Schneider (1991a, 1991b) explained, the timing and the intensity of reform processes in Europe were conditioned by two principal political variables: the strategic orientations of political actors and the institutional settings in which these strategies had to be formulated and realised. Cross-national differences in national responses to the pressures for change could be explained by how these political factors played in particular countries. Grande and Schneider compared Britain, France, Germany and Italy (see figure 2.1).

Strategic will to reform	State reform capacity	
	High	Low
Strong	Great Britain	Federal Republic of Germany
Weak	France	Italy

Source: Grande and Schneider 1991a, p. 42 , 1991b p. 472.

Figure 2.1 Political configurations in telecommunications policy

In Britain, there existed a strong strategic will to reform and the state capacity to deliver it was also strong in view of Britain's highly centralised political system, its marked concentration of political decision making competence, and the relative weakness of opposition. In Germany, too, there was a strategic will on the part of government to achieve reform, albeit weaker than in the UK due to the greater ideological heterogeneity of government, the lower profile of telecommunications policy on the government's agenda, and the high value given to universal service provision. More significantly, German government was characterised by decentralisation and by a strong fragmentation of decision-making competence. In Germany, social resistance to reform was greater and the country's 'institutional pluralism' (federalism, corporatism, etc.) provided veto actors with the opportunity to impede reform. Moreover, there were high institutional hurdles to reform, notably the need to amend the constitution before privatisation of the incumbent could occur, this amendment requiring a two-thirds majority in both houses of parliament.

In statist and mercantilist France, where a highly interventionist telecommunications modernisation during the 1970s had been markedly successful, there was a much weaker strategic will to reform on the part of policy makers. The French telecommunications industry was relatively strong, having benefited from the state's protection, and the demand for reform was therefore weaker. Grande and Schneider concluded that the late and modest nature of French reform up to this point in time (1991) was attributable to this lack of will to reform in a state which actually had a strong capacity for action. (As will be seen, the strong executive-centred nature of French government meant that, once the political will to reform was present, policy changes could be rapidly enacted and implemented.) Despite an awareness of the need for reform, Italy lacked both a strong strategic political will and the state capacity for reform. The Italian system was characterised by governmental instability, heterogeneous coalitions, and a fragmented party system, which presented minorities with a high degree of veto power and limited the capacity for action on the part of governments. The para-state enterprises that constituted the telecommunications sector were populated by clientelistic networks and special interests, which would be destabilised by reform. The reform coalition was weak, while the unions – despite their ideological fragmentation – amounted to a strong veto force.

A similar approach, again taking into account both actors and institutions as key political variables, was later offered by Willem Hulsink (1999), comparing telecommunications reform in the UK, the Netherlands and France. Hulsink's analytical framework saw individual telecommunications reforms in each country as the product of the interaction of three independent variables: (1) exogenous structural forces (technology, international markets, international deregulation, European integration); (2) the structure of the domestic telecommunications sector and the choices made by dominant actors and coalitions; and (3) and the national institutional variable. Cross-national differences in strategic responses to the commonly experienced first variable are explained by the second and third variables. The second variable produced three quite different pictures of the distribution of political and economic power in the case study countries. In the UK, the dominant coalition consisted of large telecommunication users, most notably the City of London, and an ideologically driven neo-liberal Conservative government, seeking radical marketising solutions. Other stakeholders, such as the political opposition, the unions, and domestic equipment manufacturers, were excluded by the highly majoritarian institutional nature of the UK political system.

By contrast, in the consensual Netherlands, the majority of stakeholders in the telecommunications sector were included in a 'near-inclusive' coalition; technocratic non-political advisory committees and consultancy companies played a key role. France produced yet another contrast. The dominant coalition was 'state-controlled': the government pursued an interventionist strategy of telecommunications modernisation, sponsoring national champions and protecting domestic industry from international competition. The voice of telecommunications users demanding liberalisation was weaker than in the other cases, especially the UK.

In Hulsink's framework, the national institutional variable constrained the policy makers by setting limits on and providing incentives for their strategic behaviour. Broadly, the UK market-inspired strategy, the Dutch negotiated consensual approach and the dirigiste French approach could all be seen as 'path-dependent'. This reflected a complex of national institutional features including the composition of the political system, the role of the state, the pattern of interest mediation, the established approach in industrial and economic policy, and the embeddedness and positioning of the national economy within the international system. In the politically majoritarian and economically liberal UK, with its traditionally hands-off relationship between government and industry, it was much easier for the dominant coalition including an ideologically motivated government to enact comparatively radical telecommunications reform. By contrast, the Dutch were constrained by consensual political institutional structures and their social market economy. The French were inhibited by hierarchical government–industry relationships and a traditionally statist approach to governing the economy. Hulsink concluded that 'both the Dutch and the French were constrained by the institutional disadvantages of their regimes in adapting to market-oriented telecommunications' (Hulsink 1999, p. 296).

The importance of endogenous political factors emerges, too, from Bartle's (1999) comparison of Britain, France and Germany.[6] Bartle pointed to the importance of different national 'policy styles' and different 'models of capitalism'. Thatcherism produced a shift from a traditional consensual policy style to an ideologically driven 'pro-active' policy style that was able to exploit the majoritarian and centralised institutional structures of British government to drive through comparatively early and rapid reform. Also, Britain's 'market orientated capitalism' and the special importance and influence of the City of London[7] greatly facilitated the shift towards neo-liberalism. In Germany, by contrast, reform was constrained by the country's 'consensus-seeking and reactive' policy style, characterised by cooperative federalism (giving the Länder an important voice) and corporatism (giving organised interests, including unions, a say), and by its 'network orientated' model of capitalism, characterised by social partnership, corporate solidarity and commitment to public interest. Reform in France was constrained by its distinctive policy style, characterised by statism and dirigisme, and a model of capitalism that accords a special importance to public service and national control by the state (though this pattern was changing, allowing reform to occur). The importance of domestic ideological, institutional and politico-economic differences in mediating exogenous pressures for change is confirmed by a number of other comparative studies (see, for example, Natalicchi 2001 on France, Germany, Italy and the UK; Thatcher 1999 on Britain and France; Grande 1989 on Britain and Germany) and national case studies (see Humphreys 1990 on France; Humphreys 1992 on Germany).

MODERATE REFORM DURING THE 1980s

Beyond the UK and Scandinavia, reform measures introduced in Europe during the 1980s were essentially designed to capture the benefits of technological change, while retaining the old PTT model. The French and German cases provide a good illustration. In France, the monopoly held by the DGT, the branch of the state administration responsible for telecommunications, over the supply of customer premises equipment (CPE), already liberalised to a degree as early as the 1960s and 1970s, was completely opened up to competition during the 1980s (well in advance of EU rules). However, during this period, the DGT exploited its continued status as the largest supplier of CPE to place orders with French national champion firms, Alcatel and Matra; this practice was continued into the early 1990s by France Télécom until EU rules tightened matters up (Thatcher 1999, p. 254). Similarly, the DGT's monopoly of value added network services was breached by the ambitious 'Minitel' telematics (videotext) programme launched in the early 1980s. While the DGT retained a monopoly of the network, the telematic service providers were overwhelmingly private. Nonetheless, the telematics programme was very much part of a traditional mercantilist industrial strategy geared to challenge US dominance in the field of information and communications, certainly not an exercise in liberalisation (Humphreys 1990). Further, when in 1987 the French enacted a VANS decree permitting the sale of services on leased lines and of telematic services to third parties, it contained a number of restrictions and conditions designed to protect the DGT's monopoly over all voice telephony and most data transmission (Thatcher 1999, pp. 249–50).[8] Throughout the 1980s, France led a coalition of southern European Member States, together with Luxembourg and Belgium, which remained opposed to any meaningful telecommunications liberalisation.

In Germany, as suggested, the reform will was considerable, but a 'consensual' political system was geared to produce only incremental reform. In 1980 the Monopolkommission (Anti-Trust Commission), an autonomous para-public body, produced a report that trenchantly criticised the protectionist procurement policies of the Bundespost and demanded the extensive liberalisation of the terminals market and a limited degree of competition for the telecommunications services offered by the Bundespost (Monopolkommission 1981, pp. 91–110). There emerged in Germany during the 1980s a quite dynamic coalition of interests pressing for telecommunications liberalisation: this coalition included business users of telecommunications services, would-be suppliers of telecommunications equipment from the computer sector (e.g. Nixdorf, IBM), and the German Liberal party, which occupied the influential Economics Ministry. Characteristically, this pressure led to the establishment in 1985 of a corporatist commission, chaired by an expert, Professor Eberhard Witte, given the remit to make recommendations on the 'present and future tasks in telecommunications', essentially the whole balance of state and market in the sector. The majority of the commission's members voted for only moderate reform, with the trade union representative opposing any weakening of the public monopoly. Only a small minority – notably, the representatives of the Liberals and of Germany's industry association – advocated radical reform (Humphreys 1992).

In the light of the Witte report, Germany now set about preparing legislative measures for only moderate reform. In 1989, 'Postreform 1' duly liberalised the markets for terminal equipment and services but excluding voice telephony. Infrastructure remained a Bundespost monopoly, except for mobile telephony. The reform was largely prepared by the Bundespost and shaped in its own interests. The law introduced a reorganisation of the Bundespost into three separate business, Telekom, Postdienst (the postal service) and Postbank (the banking services). Thereby, Deutsche Bundespost Telekom ('Deutsche Telekom') was freed from the loss-making postal operation and granted a welcome degree of corporate autonomy. At the same time, 'Postreform I' in 1989 posed little threat to the incumbent's dominance; as noted, Deutsche Telekom retained its core monopolies of infrastructure and voice telephony, accounting for around 90 per cent of its revenues. Regulation was separated from operation, but it remained the preserve of the Bundespost ministry, raising doubt whether the ministry could be a true referee while remaining so close to the main player (Humphreys 1992).[9]

STRATEGIC RE-ORIENTATION OF CORPORATE STRATEGIES AND THE REFORM BREAK-THROUGH OF THE 1990s: THE PIVOTAL ROLE OF FRANCE AND GERMANY

In the 1990s, however, the national politics obstacles to reform simply gave way. Continental European countries corporatised, then privatised or part-privatised their incumbents. They progressively ended their monopolies, culminating in liberalisation of infrastructure provision and voice telephony. They established new independent regulatory authorities to promote competition in telecommunications markets. By the decade's end, there had occurred a considerable degree of policy convergence around a new paradigm of liberalised markets and pro-competitive regulation. What explains this remarkable reform breakthrough? What lay behind this sudden change of political gear in the drive for reform? Numerous accounts have given pride of place to the 'external' agency of institutions of the EU, notably the Commission, which enacted a series of directives opening up one telecommunications market after another (Schneider and Werle 1990; Sandholtz 1993, 1998; Schmidt 1998a, 1998b). However, Thatcher (2004b, p. 285) has gone so far as to claim that '[in] terms of pressures [on national policy makers], the EU represented at most a further reason for reforms.'

The precise nature and extent of the role of the EU will be explored in the following chapter. In this chapter, we are concerned with the important structural factors of technological change and international competition, including regulatory competition, which were already working away at the national level, inexorably eroding the domestic sources of resistance to change and transforming state telecommunication strategies along 'competition state' lines. The strategic re-orientation of veto actors at the national level – most notably the incumbents themselves – was the prerequisite for regulatory reform at national and EU level. By the early 1990s, this key source of resistance to full liberalisation had eroded in the two Member States which are often seen as constituting the 'core' or 'engine' of the EU, namely France and Germany (Schneider and Vedel 1999). With regard to European telecommunications reform, not only did these two countries provide two of the largest telecommunication markets and have the two strongest telecommunications industries in Europe, they were pivotal because France was widely seen as the leader of the protectionist camp within the EU, while Germany was a laggard in the pro-liberalisation camp. Natalicchi (2001) actually deemed Germany a member of the 'telecommunications-conservative' camp. Bartle (1999, pp. 136–7), too, classed Germany among the 'slow reformers', along with the majority of EU Member States. Once these two countries had swung their weight behind further liberalisation, the centre of gravity among the Member States shifted significantly, constraining others to follow suit, and allowing the Commission to press on with its reform agenda at the European level (see Chapter 3).

Reforms already under way in these two countries during the 1980s could be explained in part by the considerable pressure that their governments had been under both from would-be new entrants and from corporate users of telecommunication. Pressure from computer manufacturers, such as Nixdorf in Germany, previously excluded from the supply of terminal equipment, helps explain why this particular market was so readily liberalised. The impact of 'globalisation' cannot be understated. Globally active business users, notably large multinational companies, like IBM, had been notably vocal in demanding liberalisation of the market for advanced services. Importantly, too, formerly protectionist national champion suppliers in both countries had became preoccupied by the need for global free markets not least to recoup their huge investment in the new digital technologies.[10] Thus, in Germany, liberalisation of the telecommunications equipment market by the end of the 1980s had been helped along significantly by the re-orientation, from 1987 onwards, of the national champion supplier Siemens away from its former protectionist position, in recognition that international liberalisation, European markets included, offered exciting business opportunities (Humphreys 1992, p. 123; Humphreys and Simpson 1996, p. 114). Siemens' reorientation was symbolised by its 1988 takeover of the US company Rolm which now made it the biggest supplier of telephone systems in the world (Lüthje 1997, pp. 166–8). With this new 'global player' identity, the company did not want to cut of its nose to spite its face by adhering to the narrow protectionism, which had traditionally advantaged it within the home market.

Similarly, in France, during the 1990s the national champion telecommunications supplier Alcatel had outgrown its former dependence on the French state and was purposefully reinventing itself as a global player (Sally 1993; Lehmke and Waringo 1997, p. 114). By the mid-1980s, a huge state-led 'catch-up' modernisation of the French telecommunications network had been successfully completed and French suppliers were compelled to turn their attention to international markets (Lehmke and Waringo 1997, p. 132). Through a series of acquisitions at home and abroad Alcatel transformed itself into one of the world's leading telecommunications multinationals. Its 1986 acquisition of the European division of ITT (USA) made it a policy actor with interests beyond the French market and gave it an obvious interest in the opening up of markets in Europe and globally (Humphreys and Simpson 1996, p. 114).

There now occurred a similar strategic re-orientation on the part of Europe's larger incumbent telecommunications operators. Hitherto, their managements had been unenthusiastic about liberalisation. However, a distinct 'bandwagon' effect – in the shape of an imitative, competitiveness-directed, strategic reorientation – was at work. They began to fear losing ground to the international alliance strategies of their Anglo-Saxon competitors, like AT&T and BT. Confronted with the Anglo-Saxon competitive threat and model, senior managements of major continental incumbents came to perceive that their organisations' future lay no longer in being domestic, state-controlled monopolists but in becoming privatised, international players in globalising markets. Thus, from 1989 on, Deutsche Bundespost Telekom rapidly developed an international network of subsidiaries and branches (Lüthje 1997, p. 167). Deutsche Bundespost Telekom and France Télécom placed at the core of their internationalisation strategies the creation of a strategic alliance between them, together with a suitable US partner (Sprint), in order to deliver a 'one-stop' international service. This new 'global player' vocation now led the continental European incumbents to accept the inevitable opening up of their core monopolies of voice telephony and infrastructure. Liberalisation was quite plainly the price that would have to be paid for the privatisation that they now desired for themselves. By the early 1990s, the senior managements of France Télécom and Deutsche Bundestpost Telekom (and also Spain's Telefonica) had accepted the need for 'full liberalisation'. According to a high European Commission official: 'once the monopolies had changed their mind, then the Member States had to follow' (interview in the European Commission, in 2000).

In both France and Germany, there was already strong support for more radical reform from some policy makers. In France, telecommunications reform has to be situated in the context of a much broader decline in traditional French étatisme and dirigisme from the mid–1980s onwards (beginning with the French Socialist government's famous politico-economic

U-turn away from the statist interventionism of the 1981-83 period). Deregulation and privatisation soon became 'the order of the day'. Almost regardless of the political complexion of the government, the business sector generally became much more independent of the state, with business increasingly leading developments and the state now following (Schmidt, V. 1996a, 1996b). Elie Cohen (1995, p. 32) notes that in range of economic sectors, French 'national champion' companies 'began to see state intervention [which had so carefully 'nurtured' them] as a threat to their cash flow, to their own discretionary power and as an impediment to building international alliances.' Telecommunications presented a very good example.

During the latter half of the 1980s, telecommunications suppliers were privatised and developed ambitious international strategies. Just as importantly, the Grands Corps des Ingénieurs des Télécommunications, its prestige greatly enhanced by the successful modernisation of French telecommunication network during the 1970s, became increasingly influential on government as a bureaucratic lobby within the state. The latter sought greater business autonomy for the DGT, the branch of the state administration responsible for telecommunications (Humphreys 1990; Lehmke and Waringo 1997, p. 134). Under pressure from senior telecommunications managers, the Socialists duly corporatised 'France Télécom' in 1991 (i.e. transforming it from a branch of the PTT into a public corporation), thereby giving it relative autonomy of action. However, by the early 1990s, France Télécom's senior management were seeking even greater commercial autonomy. Transformation into a limited company would relieve them of political control, and the customary 'raiding' by the government of their budget to finance other parts of the public sector. It would also allow them to forge international alliances with Deutsche Telekom and US operators.[11]

In opposition, the Right had discussed privatisation. Reform was now given an important stimulus when the Right won the legislative elections of 1993. The new neo-liberal PTT Minister, Gérard Longuet, now set about pushing reform forward towards fully liberalising the market and freeing the incumbent from state control. However, the latter measure in particular was opposed by the unions, the Communists and the Socialists, and the Right's power was constrained by its 'cohabitation' (executive power-sharing) with a Socialist President François Mitterrand. This 'cohabitation' ended with the victory in the 1995 presidential election of the Gaullist Jacques Chirac. The Right, now in full 'majoritarian' control, could exploit France's characteristically strong central executive powers and 'strong state' tradition to push through two major reform laws, one on competition and regulation, the other part transforming France Télécom into a limited company operating under private law. Ironically, it fell to the Socialists – victors of the 1997 legislative elections – to complete the Right's work by presiding over the partial privatisation of the incumbent. Their change of tack could be explained in large part by pressure from France Télécom's senior management (Thatcher

1999, pp. 157–163). Political opposition to liberalisation was defused to some extent by a strong commitment to the provision of a high quality universal service (Bartle 1999, p. 199), a precondition that France 'uploaded' to the EU level (as will be seen in the subsequent two chapters).

The 'consensual' (Lijphart 1984) German political system did not endow government with anything like the same degree of centralised executive power; its 'institutional pluralism' provided veto points to oppositional actors. Nonetheless, here too the resistance to change eroded in the early 1990s, for much the same reasons as in France. During the early 1990s, politicians in all main parties and – crucially – Deutsche Bundespost Telekom managers came to embrace the need for further reform so that Germany's telecommunications industry and services might remain internationally competitive. As in France, a key factor was the awakening ambition of Deutsche Bundespost Telekom management to transform the company from being a state-controlled domestic monopolist into a commercial global player, the price for which was accepting full liberalisation in the domestic market. Privatisation would facilitate the development of international alliances. It would also provide a much needed injection of capital. Since the 1980s the incumbent had acquired a massive debt as a result of ambitious infrastructural investments, notably to construct a national integrated services digital network (ISDN)[12] and also to provide a national cable television network[13] (Lüthje 1997, pp. 160–163). The huge modernisation costs in the East following unification in 1990, too, contributed to acceptance of partial privatisation of the incumbent (Schmidt, S. 1996; Lüthje 1997, pp. 171–2).

Germany's 'Postreform II' took the shape of a 1994 law to partially privatise Deutsche Bundespost Telekom; Deutsche Telekom AG was duly created in 1985 and a 39 per cent share was floated on the stock exchange in 1996. While privatisation certainly opened the way up for further liberalisation, it also constrained liberalisation's *pace*. First, the domestic German policy debate during the period 1992-1994 was almost entirely focused on privatisation of Telekom and not on further liberalisation. Second, as mentioned above, the constitution needed to be amended before privatisation of the incumbent could occur, and this required a two-thirds majority in both houses of parliament, the Bundestag and the Bundesrat. The SPD effectively exchanged support for privatisation for a commitment to protect the privatised Telekom's core voice telephony monopoly until the end of 1997. Waesche (2003, p. 112) observes that the 'incumbent was granted a period of almost two years from summer 1996 [when the telecommunications reform law was enacted] to the end of 1997 during which it could prepare for competition'.[14] This 'period of grace' actually suited the government too. Now a shareholder in Deutsche Telekom AG (DTAG), the government 'was highly interested in a smooth listing. The grace period would guarantee this; there would be no disturbances by the competition'.

Telekom's privatisation achieved, the German government could proceed towards its 'Postreform III', enacted in 1996, opening the way for full competition in network and services from 1998 and implementing what was now known as the EU's '1998 regulatory package' (see next chapter). However, German 'institutional pluralism' continued to complicate the policy process. Although the government's hand was stronger now than in the case of Postreform II because there was no need for a two–thirds approval by both the Bundestag and the Bundesrat, Postreform III was still only achieved after considerable inter-party negotiation and finally recourse to arbitration between the two houses of Parliament. At issue between the CDU/CSU/FDP government and the SPD opposition was the definition of universal service at an affordable price, while the issue for the Länder was their continued influence in the new regulatory structure, the RegTP. The Bundesrat rejected the reform bill in June 1996, the arbitration eventually producing a compromise that both widened the definition of universal service and guaranteed representation for the Länder on an Advisory Council for the RegTP (Bartle 1999, p. 173).

The embrace of full liberalisation by France and Germany gave crucial momentum to EU-wide reform. As early as 1993/94 both France and Germany lent their considerable political weight to EU Council Resolutions envisaging full EU liberalisation of telecommunications services and infrastructures by 1998. However, their pro-liberalisation stance was combined with a 'gradualist' strategy of ensuring that the pace of EU reform (see next chapter) suited the incremental pace of their domestic reforms. In particular, they made sure that it allowed their incumbent operators a reprieve from full liberalisation for a sufficiently long period to allow them to gear up for international competition. Accordingly, France and Germany both held out for (i.e. 'uploaded') a 1998 EU deadline for full liberalisation, while fast track liberalisers, the UK, Netherlands, Sweden and Finland, supported earlier full liberalisation (Bartle 2002a, p. 16)). Both governments were clearly acting as 'competition states'; they wanted the best conditions for the promotion of their part-privatised incumbents as 'national champions' in the globalising markets. This protection of the incumbents had its cost. Waesche (2003, pp. 140–1) points to the high cost of local calls – and Internet access – in Germany as its 'national champion' exploited the temporary reprieve for its core monopoly in order to reduce its debts and to cross-subsidise its development of the new services that would help it undergo the painful transformation from inefficient public monopoly into global player.

Finally, it is important to note that the same pressures that account for France's and Germany's support for full liberalisation were at work on more 'laggard' cases as well. Thus, in the case of Italy, where Natalicchi (2001, p. 170) observes liberalisation was long obstructed by the 'strict links of the telecommunications bureaucracies to the political parties in government', change followed the same pattern, as the strategic orientation of Italy's (several) public telephone operators changed 'from a national focus to an international market focus'. Similarly, a growing reform orientation in the étatiste southern European countries, Spain ('liberal étatiste') and Portugal ('social étatist'), was driven by changing perceptions of what was nationally advantageous under the new technological and international market conditions. EU-liberalisation was perceived as being compatible with continued support for these two countries 'national champions' (Jordana et al. 2003, p. 5). Indeed, there was a 'mercantilist' motivation to their liberalisation. Both countries' governments 'supported the internationalisation of their [national champion] companies who expanded their operations [in their] former colonies, mainly in Latin America' (ibid., p. 27). As in the case of France, Germany, and even Italy, the incumbents accepted domestic liberalisation as the price to be paid for their international ambitions. Indeed, the extent of their reorientation was demonstrated when, having successfully negotiated the principle of five-year derogations from opening up their core markets on 1 January 1998, to allow their companies time to prepare for competition, the Spanish settled in the end for only 11 months of delay and the Portuguese for only two years (ibid., p. 14).

THE ROLE OF THE EU

The picture that has been painted so far might suggest that telecommunications reform in Europe occurred largely independently of any EU agency. Privatisation was certainly not prescribed by the EU, since its treaty base did not give it any competence over ownership. As for market opening and regulatory harmonisation, the French and German reforms plainly occurred in parallel with – rather than primarily as a result of – EU reform. They were driven principally by the competitive strategic re-orientations of the key corporate actors and their sponsor 'competition states'. As suggested, these states determined the incremental pace of EU reform, to which they were pivotally important. Thus Lüthje (1997, p. 165) observes that Germany's 1989 reform of telecommunications services created the 'political weight' that *allowed* the European Commission then to proceed further with the liberalisation of European telecommunications.

However, the role of the EU was still important. Most obviously, the Commission exploited EU competition law to force the pace of reform vis-à-vis 'laggard' Member States, enacting a series of its own Article 86 (ex 90) liberalisation directives that allowed it to by-pass intergovernmental negotiation in the Council of Ministers. In this way, it progressively opened up the market, first for terminal equipment (1989), then for value-added services (1990), followed by satellite (1994), cable (1995), and mobile telephony (1996), culminating in voice telephony (1996), to be fully opened up to competition by 1 January 1998. The Commission also used its direct competition powers to rule on mergers and joint ventures to apply pressure on Member States to liberalise their markets. Thus, the Commission made clear that it would only approve the France Télécom/Deutsche Telekom 'Atlas' joint venture (for international leased lines and services), the 'focal point' for their international strategies, on condition that the French and German governments supported early liberalisation of existing alternative telecommunications infrastructures (Bartle 1999, p. 171; Schmidt 1997, p. 17; Schneider and Vedel 1999).[15] Such leverage was employed on a number of further occasions, on several Member States.

The Commission also exerted softer pressure, contributing to policy learning about the new dynamics driving telecommunications reform. Learning occurred through a number of EU mechanisms (Humphreys 2002). The Commission constantly sought, through its contacts with national policy makers and other interested parties and through its reports, to present strong arguments for reform. It pointed to the external challenge from the USA and Japan. It provided an EU–level industry-wide international forum for discussing policy and exchanging experiences. Most notably, the Commission's 1992 'Telecommunications Services Review' paved the way for an EU consensus about the need, if not the timing, for full liberalisation of voice telephony (interview in the European Commission, 2000). Importantly, the EU also performed a crucial 'alibi' function. 'Europeanisation' gave leverage to national policy makers enabling them to carry through liberalisation measures against recalcitrant domestic opposition by presenting them as faits accomplis from Brussels (Bartle 1999, p. 171; also 2002).

The German government certainly played a two-level game with regard to the EU's 1998 deadline for full liberalisation. At the EU level, it pointed to the domestic political constraints that prevented it from agreeing to an earlier deadline. At the domestic level, its commitments in the shape of the Council Resolutions of 1993/94 to the 1998 deadline pressured domestic actors to accept its reforms (Bartle 1999, pp. 170-; Bulmer et al. 2003, p. 258). Similarly, Thatcher (1999, p. 158) notes that the French reforms were justified inter alia 'by reference to the requirements of EC legislation'. The EU was certainly a very important factor for achieving reform in the 'laggard' Member States of southern Europe and Belgium. The next chapter will now explore the role of EU legislation in detail.

NOTES

1.   The term soon became a misnomer during the 1980s and 1990s as the postal aspect was removed from the telecommunications component, and as the state monopolies were first corporatised and then fully or partly privatised. As a result the terms 'telecommunications authority' (TA) and 'telecommunications operator' (TO) came into wide usage. As this book describes, the regulatory functions of the former PTTs were adopted by National Regulatory Authorities (NRAs).

2. While most European countries shared this unitary and tightly state controlled public telecommunications operator (PTO) structure, there were exceptions. In Italy, rather than one, there were several PTOs, but they were all in the public sector. They were consolidated into Telecom Italia in 1994, which was majority privatised in 1997 (Thatcher 2002c). Portugal and Spain were the main exceptions to the European norm in that neither country had traditionally had a special public telecommunications administration and the government's powers were limited in this field. Spain's Telefónica was a privately-run monopoly, though the state did have a significant interest. In Portugal, telecommunications was a private sector activity until the late 1960s. As in Spain, the government actually only became interventionist in the 1980s (Jordana 2002). This 'intervention' was to re-shape the sector, and can be analysed on 'competition state' lines.

3. This company's name, Microwave Communications Inc. (MCI) itself illustrates the challenge presented to AT&T by technological change. MCI started off as a company using this new technology, which was not a 'natural monopoly', to bypass the AT&T network, serving business users of telecommunications. MCI evolved into a successful rival to AT&T in long-distance telephony. In 1974 MCI opened up the legal assault on AT&T, accusing it of monopolistic behaviour. This culminated in the famous 1982 decision to structurally separate 'Ma Bell' from its regional networks (Tunstall 1986, p. 97).

4. The government sold 50.2 per cent of BT in November 1984. In 1991, it sold of the rest of its share of BT.

5. Robinson also points out that the British economy at large also registered the fastest growth of any OECD country, at a rate of 5.2 per cent.

6. Bartle's study compares liberalisation of telecommunications and electricity. The cross-sectoral part of the study points to the importance of exogenous factors, showing how telecommunications reform occurred earlier and was more intense than electricity reform principally because it underwent much greater technological change and was much more exposed to globalisation.

7. A major user of advanced telecommunications services, the City was a strong proponent of liberalisation.

8. A plan to further open some telecommunications markets and transform the operational side of the DGT into a limited company, albeit state controlled, was developed by PM Chirac's government during 1986–88, but its removal from office impeded developments. This shows that the political will to reform already existed in some quarters. However, the major reforms of this period impacted on broadcasting.

9. One former member of the Witte commission, the Tübingen academic lawyer Wernhard Möschel, observed that the 'Post Minister remain[ed] the *Konzernchef*' (Humphreys 1992, p. 126).

10. Domestic 'captive markets' were now too small to allow the amortisation of escalating R&D costs.

11. In 1993, the US company MCI favoured an alliance with BT rather than with France Télécom largely because of the latter's public sector status (Thatcher 1999, p. 160). Also, equity swaps were a favoured means of forming alliances and this presupposed at least partial privatisation (Bartle 1999, p. 196).

12. This was designed to reinvigorate Germany's information and communication technology sector, suffering a crisis of confidence as a result of certain key weaknesses, notably in microelectronics, office equipment, and in consumer electronics (Lüthje 1997).

13. This was more to do with the promotion of private television than with technological innovation. The network's prime technology – copper coaxial cable – was not designed for advanced telecommunications services (see Humphreys, 1994).

14. Waesche's book argues that this delay in reforming telecommunications was a major factor for the comparatively disappointing development of Internet entrepreneurship in Germany.

15. The Commission approved the alliance, called 'Global One', which included the US company Sprint. The conditions were accepted by the incumbents as the price to be paid for their international expansion

3. Liberalisation and Europeanisation of telecommunications – the emergence of an EU policy framework

This chapter documents the major events which shaped the emergence and growth of telecommunications policy at EU level, culminating in the creation of a body of legislation whose implementation committed the vast majority of EU Member States by 1998 (and all of them by 2003) to complete liberalisation of their telecommunications sectors. It explains the significance of this unprecedented series of events in European telecommunications by reference to our theoretical framework detailed in Chapter 1. Here, several elements can be combined to provide an explanation for the growth of EU telecommunications policy.

First, it illustrates the role played by powerful global political and economic structural forces in influencing policy makers' decisions at the national and EU levels, which promoted the development of a European regulatory approach to the telecommunications sector to be pursued. This process has been heavily underpinned by an ideology of market liberalisation and globalisation, promoted by a range of governmental (e.g. US, UK) and private business interests. Second, it provides evidence of the importance of institutional factors, most outstandingly, the role played by the European Commission, in shaping policy developments. The Commission, by dint of its remit, tends to play a lead role in stimulating policy action, though the telecommunications policy case provides an important example of the need to secure the agreement of Member States in the process. Third, it shows how the EU level, once established as a significant locus for telecommunications policy, became a venue for the promotion and transfer of new liberal policy ideas and best practices and acted as a policy 'transfer platform' (Radaelli 2000a).

Finally, the chapter illustrates how the Commission skilfully employed a combination of, on the one hand, 'coercive' powers based on its legal authority in the field of competition policy and, on the other hand, a 'softer' approach relying on persuasion and the careful building of support, not least through emphasising the external challenge and through the strategic use of reviews and subsequent consultations. As will be explained, the Commission took pains to secure consensual decision making. The history of the creation of a liberalisation framework at EU level also illustrates the different perspectives which were apparent at the national level and how these changed over time. However, agreement on a common European level legislative framework did not signal the abandonment of national telecommunications policy styles and goals as is apparent from an analysis of the short history of the implementation of the new EU regulatory framework(s) for telecommunications, the subject of Chapters 4 and 5.

THE SEEDS OF EUROPEAN UNION TELECOMMUNICATIONS POLICY

From the beginning of the 1980s, telecommunications emerged, increasingly, as a sector of strategic importance for the European Union to such an extent that it has been claimed that it became something of an issue of 'high' politics for the EU (Schneider and Werle 1990). This is no more clearly illustrated than by the efforts made by the European Commission to project telecommunications as a sector of strategic economic importance to the EU. Changes occurring in the European telecommunications sector were, according to the Commission, 'a quantum leap that will wreak a qualitative change on the type of services available to businesses and individuals and transform the means of production, the pattern of consumption and lifestyles. Europe must stake its all on a Community response to these events' (European Commission 1984, p. 7). The situation was portrayed in terms of industrial, economic and political drama (Dang Nygen 1986) which helped the swift transformation of telecommunications policy from, essentially, a series of technical options, to strategic political economic choices upon which the security of Europe's industrial future would be dependent. It was claimed by the Commission that 'Europe's potential resides in its ability to use the Community framework and instruments' (European Commission 1984, p. 13) and telecommunications companies, users and PTTs were urged to unite under a European banner. Telecommunications was noted for its important spin–off effects on the economy as 'the essential vector for information flows and new services which help to create industrial and commercial activities' (ibid., p. 3).

Across Europe, the acute need for massive investment in the sector to modernise the infrastructure was stressed, a challenging task in the face of the growing demands of international competition, shorter innovation cycles, increased obsolescence rates of equipment and the difficulty of achieving economies of scale, all faced by Europe's firms. These factors were aggravated by the heterogeneous nature of the EU's nationally compartmentalised telecommunications markets, within which incompatible telecommunications standards had been developed historically. Another prominent theme in early policy deliberations was the Commission's emphasis on the US–Japanese commercial challenge, bolstered by aggressive political noises emanating from the USA itself where the National Telecommunications Industry Association (NTIA) and the US government were concerned about what were considered the protectionist trade practices of Europeans in telecommunications. The Commission highlighted the comparative weakness of the EU vis-à-vis the USA and Japan in several areas of telecommunications, in particular its lower density of telephone installation and slower growth in telecommunications equipment markets. Commercially, it was noted that US firms were hungry to exploit European markets (see Schiller 1999) for which they were well placed given their experience of a liberalised, non–fragmented domestic market. The Japanese Ministry of International Trade and Industry's (MITI) and the Japanese PTT's (NTT) efforts at developing an advanced integrated services digital network (ISDN) were also viewed with concern (European Commission 1984, p. 10).

This broad rationale for an EU policy drive in telecommunications was soon endorsed by national Member States in the European Council of Ministers which highlighted six areas for the future policy action: the creation of a Community–wide market for telecommunications equipment and terminals; the accelerated development of advanced telecommunications services and networks; the launch of a research programme to create new broadband networks; the improvement of access to new telecommunications services for poorer regions of the EU; the co-ordination of European negotiating positions within international organisations on telecommunications issues.

Institutional resources, essential in any case of Europeanisation, to promote the development of EU telecommunications policy were forged in the early part of the 1980s. Within the ranks of the European Commission, an Information Technology and Telecommunications Task Force was set up in 1983, whose main role was to oversee the progress of the IT–focused European Strategic Programme for Research in Information Technology (ESPRIT), though it soon became important in the telecommunications policy making sphere. In 1983, the Council of Ministers agreed on the formation of the Senior Officials Group on Telecommunications (SOGT) composed of national industry ministers, industry representatives and PTTs. The Group d'Analyse et de Prévision (GAP) was formed in 1984 to assist the SOGT with policy development. Though both SOGT and GAP were merely advisory groups, they formed important epistemic communities within which thinking and exchange of ideas on regulatory innovation could be developed in conjunction with the Commission. In 1986, the then Directorate General XIII (Information Market and Information Services) was absorbed by the IT&T Task Force. Henceforth, DGXIII became the hub of EU telecommunications policy formulation (Stevers 1990).

The type of the political networking occurring within and between the different levels of the Commission was very important for the development of a new policy area, such as telecommunications. This became particularly salient once the EU widened its focus on telecommunications from initial industrial policy concerns to those of competition and regulation. The eventual growth to primacy of competition policy considerations drew the Commission's Competition Directorate–General (DG IV) increasingly into the telecommunications policy arena. It was keen to break up the monopolistic and inherently uncompetitive stranglehold of the PTTs (European Commission 1985a) and took the UK incumbent, British Telecom, to the European Court of Justice over its attempt to exclude a UK message forwarding agency from the telecommunications market (European Court of Justice 1982). It also advocated liberalisation of public procurement in the telecommunications terminal equipment market. By contrast, it regarded with suspicion the corporate rationalisation via merger and acquisition increasingly evident in telecommunications and symptomatic of the transitory nature of the sector. The Competition Directorate–General was concerned that the old monopolistic PTT dominated sectoral structure would merely be replaced by a similarly uncompetitive series of reorganisations. As we illustrate below, however, the Commission was prepared to sanction such international deals as a quid pro quo for domestic liberalisation.

The first concrete steps of an extension of the EU's focus on telecommunications to liberalisation occurred as early as 1986 in the shape of the European Commission's expression of support for policy activity in areas related to 'the organisation and regulation of telecommunications' (European Commission 1986b, p. 18). The Commission partly justified its position by noting that the USA and Japan were already taking action in this area and the threat of the EU losing ground if a re-regulation of the sector did not occur was, thus, made very real. It was around this time, too, that the EU launched its Single European Market (SEM) initiative which, broadly, resolved to remove the considerable barriers to the free movement of goods, services, labour and capital which existed across the EU at the time and from which, it was argued, many of Europe's economic ailments stemmed. The initiative was highly significant for the telecommunications sector in a number of respects. It provided strong evidence of the diffusion of the liberal 'regulatory state' philosophy to (and at) the European level: the SEM heralded the further spread of market liberalisation strategies, albeit with specific European characteristics. The timing of this renewed effort towards European economic union coincided, deliberately, with the early developmental years of Commission telecommunications strategies. The first major legislative pronouncement on the matter was in the form of a white paper from the European Commission (European Commission 1985a) and around the same a Commission document noted that creating a single European telecommunications market would provide 'one of the major infrastructures

needed to complete the establishment of the internal market by 1992'
(European Commission 1986c, p. 92).

The white paper, in dealing with telecommunications, placed emphasis on
mutual recognition, particularly in relation to telecommunications terminal
equipment, noting that 'sales bans cannot be imposed on the sole argument
that an imported product has been manufactured according to specifications
which differ from those used in the importing country' (European
Commission 1985a, p. 12). The paper gave strong indirect support to
forthcoming telecommunications legislation, particularly in the area of
common conformity testing. Here, it noted that 'a major initiative will soon be
launched to bring about mutual recognition of tests...so as to coordinate
wasteful duplication of tests, which in some sectors is the rule rather than the
exception'. A second important area where the white paper gave support to the
EU's re-regulatory efforts in telecommunications was public procurement,
where legislation to decompartmentalise national member state markets was
called for. In particular, there were 'certain services in the new technology
area need[ing] a large market of continental dimensions in order to realise
their full potential'. Finally, the White Paper claimed that new technologies
had led to 'the creation...of new cross border services which are playing an
increasingly important role in the economy' (ibid., p. 112). Both the drive
towards the SEM, viewed with suspicion by its major trading competitors, and
the re-regulation of the telecommunications sector, espoused the common goal
of combating the USA–Japanese challenge by creating a European response in
a market large enough to compete at the global level in technological and
commercial terms.

As shown in Chapter 2, the traditional telecommunications system
presented virtually no choice of alternative service providers to its users.
However, technological change and convergence, coupled with commercial
pressure from new 'telematics' players (providers of new hybrid
IT/telecommunications services) presented telecommunications users, both
corporate and private, with a whole new variety of services. However, the full
benefits of these changes could not be accrued, it was argued, without
significant re-regulation of the sector to create a liberalised market
environment. As a result, the traditional pattern of European
telecommunications policy making was both destabilised and expanded by the
creation of an important policy axis between reformers at the national
government (notably the UK) and EU levels (notably the European
Commission). The alignment between the Commission and business user
interests is particularly striking and was an important source of support for the
Commission in the latter half of the 1980s when most of the EU's powerful
PTTs and many national governments still approached the topic of
telecommunications liberalisation with caution and even antipathy in certain
cases.

THE 1987 GREEN PAPER ON THE SINGLE EUROPEAN MARKET IN TELECOMMUNICATIONS

The publication in 1987 by the Commission of a landmark green paper on telecommunications reform laid plans for an unprecedented re-regulation of the sector across the EU. The broad acceptance of the substance of its proposals by the national Member States, publicly manifest through a 1988 Resolution (European Council of Ministers 1988) meant that the dominance of PTTs in different national markets would gradually and steadily wane. The strong political underpinning of the paper was clear from its resolve 'to set off a dynamic process that [would] give the political, economic and social actors involved a better understanding of their own interests' (European Commission 1987a, p. 10). This was an early indication of the Commission's intention to move the liberalisation agenda forward through promoting policy learning among the Member States. The stipulations of the green paper represented a move by the European Commission, through notable policy entrepreneurship, to catalyse a comprehensive reorganisation of the telecommunications sector in Europe.

The paper's main proposals centred around a series of proposed positions and action lines (see Table 3.1). The central element of the green paper was its declared intention to put 'the establishment and implementation of basic principles and guidelines concerning the regulatory aspects of telecommunications' (European Commission 1987b, figure 13) on the EU telecommunications policy–making agenda. However, to achieve progress, the European Commission was aware of the need to tread a fine line between ground breaking liberalisation and providing reassurance to those very substantial interests who were at this stage sceptical and reticent about radical reform of their telecommunications sectors. Thus, the green paper, a masterpiece of Commission diplomacy, was a classic example of a document with the aim of restrained liberalisation clearly reflected in its proposals.

The paper declared that there should be 'acceptance of continued exclusive provision for the telecommunications administrations, regarding provision and operation of the network infrastructure' (European Commission 1987a, p. 70) though this was counterbalanced by acknowledgement of the right of Member States to diverge from such a system if so desired. The Commission cited Article 122 of the Treaty of Rome to justify its position[1] though this attempt to legally safeguard the position of the EU's PTTs was nonetheless tempered by the proviso that such exclusive network infrastructure provision needed to be narrowly defined. A very important aspect of the paper was its treatment of the future regulatory status of telecommunications services. Whilst the right of PTTs to maintain exclusive provision of a number of basic telecommunications services was accepted, it was also advocated that all other services should be freely and competitively provided across the EU (European Commission 1987a,

p. 34). The disagreement which existed at the time over which services should be classified as 'reserved', and thus not subject to competition, was acknowledged and regarded as something to be closely monitored in the future.

Table 3.1   Green paper proposed action lines

To ensure the long term convergence and integrity of network infrastructure in the Community

To achieve full mutual recognition of type approval for terminal equipment.

To progress towards opening up access to public telecommunication procurement contracts

To reinforce the development of standards and specifications in the Community

To define an agreed set of conditions for open network provision to service providers and users

To develop common Europe–wide services

To define a coherent European position regarding the future development of satellite communications within the EC

To define clearly telecommunications services and equipment with regard to the EU's relations with other countries

To analyse the social impact and conditions for a smooth transition to advanced telecommunications services

---

Source: Adapted from European Commission 1987 green paper

The green paper also displayed early efforts by the EU to address the mechanics of a more liberalised telecommunications environment. The necessity of having clarity and transparency in tariffs and any conditions which incumbent operators might impose on new competitors, notably regarding access and interconnect arrangements, through open network provision (ONP) legislation, was underlined. The Commission suggested that unless an ONP directive was passed, a whole series of legal wrangling would ensue. The paper advocated the creation of a European Telecommunications Standards Institute (ETSI) to be formed on the basis of negotiations with the European Conference of Postal and Telecommunications Administrations (CEPT), the 'club' of European PTTs, and experts from across the telecommunications industry. ETSI and other such organisations would prove important epistemic communities within which policy ideas could be developed and transferred in the new competitive paradigm.

Perhaps the strongest indication of the Commission's determination to launch a reform of the competitive structure of the telecommunications sector in Europe was its willingness to address head–on the dominant position occupied by PTTs in the system. Very importantly, the paper stipulated that there should be separation of regulatory and operational activities of the telecommunications administrations as a 'fundamental pre-condition' for a re-regulated European telecommunications sector where it would be impossible for the PTT to continue being 'both regulator and market participant' (European Commission 1987a, p. 73). This concerned activities such as licensing, control of type approval and interface specification, allocation of frequencies and surveillance of network usage conditions. Drawing on anticompetitive provisions in the Treaty of Rome, notably the then numbered articles 85, 86 and 90, the Commission highlighted its determination to scrutinise for and eradicate predatory pricing and excessive cross–subsidisation which might thwart competition (ibid., p. 78).[2]

Even before these declarations in the green paper, there was evidence of the Commission's willingness to act on this issue. In 1982, it received a complaint from a UK message forwarding agency against British Telecom, concerning prohibitions imposed by the then Post Office regarding the transmission of messages between third countries. The Commission produced a decision which claimed that this prohibition created abuses of dominant commercial position. This decision was challenged by the Italian government in the European Court of Justice. Here, an interesting alliance took place between the UK government and the Commission, the former supporting the Commission's defence before the Court. For the UK, there was a workable trade–off between the increased political profile for the European Commission which a victory against BT would create and the UK government's desire to open up its telecommunications market. The Court of Justice found ultimately that UK message forwarding agencies were being prevented by BT from offering a service to customers in third countries. Equally, it found that BT subjected telecommunications equipment to 'obligations which were neither technically nor commercially necessary'. The Court rejected the plea that the application of (what was then) article 86 of the Treaty of Rome[3] infringed article 222 of the Treaty since it impinged upon a Member State's right to maintain a monopoly. It was argued that, in this instance, such a monopoly was unnecessary, as BT's legally imposed commercial obligations 'were not in jeopardy from the economic point of view' (European Commission 1987a, pp. 123–4).

In the area of terminal equipment, the Commission had acted against Germany, Belgium, Italy, the Netherlands and Denmark. In the German case, the Commission objected to government plans to extend the Deutsche Bundespost's monopoly to the area of cordless telephones (European Commission 1985c). It saw the plans as an infringement of article 37(1) of the Treaty of Rome. Furthermore, it considered abuse of the Bundespost's dominant position as network operator as being contrary to article 86 of the Treaty of Rome. The Commission threatened to use article 90(3) – now article 86 – of the Treaty to issue a decision making the German government's attempted move illegal though in June 1986, agreement was reached with the DBP to 'amend the law which made the Bundespost the sole distributor of modems in Germany' (European Commission 1987a, p. 125). Yet again, the Commission successfully complained against special rights given to the Belgian telecommunications authority to import and supply low speed modems and first telex terminals and took similar action against the Italian government. It also challenged the existence and exclusive rights on importing and sale of terminal equipment in the Netherlands and Denmark. Finally, the Commission attempted to ensure that the US company, IBM, made suitable disclosure on the technical specifications of its proprietary network standard, Systems Network Architecture (SNA). It initiated proceedings against the company in December 1980 under former article 86 of the Treaty of Rome. This was followed by an important series of negotiations between the two parties, networks also maintained with large European corporate business interests. The green paper revealed that during negotiations with IBM 'some major European computer manufacturers expressed concern that IBM's interface disclosure practice was also having an adverse effect in the European market for data communications products' The Commission succeeded in getting a unilateral undertaking from IBM to provide other manufacturers with the information necessary to 'permit competitive products to be used with IBM's most powerful range of computers, the System/370' (ibid., p. 127).

The green paper was open to criticism from pro–liberalisers for lacking any concrete re-regulatory proposals in terms of times and dates though this was not its paramount role. Primarily, it aimed to establish a platform from which the future, major re-regulatory measures would be launched. It represented a clear articulation of the Commission's resolve to ensure that the telecommunications sector operated within the legal stipulations of the Treaty of Rome or put another way, that the Treaty could become a legal weapon for the Commission to draw on subsequently. The results of months of debate, instigated by the Commission, after the publication of the green paper were, arguably, selectively interpreted by the Commission, which concluded at the time that 'the broad consensus apparent...seems to give a strong basis on which to define a further determined campaign, to develop the Community's telecommunications market' (European Commission 1988b, p. 32). The next phase of this campaign was soon to follow in controversial circumstances.

THE TERMINAL EQUIPMENT DIRECTIVES

The Commission proposed two re-regulatory approaches to this important area of the burgeoning telecommunications market, involving directives concerned with mutual recognition of type approval for telecommunications terminal equipment (European Commission 1985a) and the liberalisation of terminal equipment markets across the EC (European Commission 1988b). In the case of the former, a 1986 directive authorised Member States to create the conditions for mutual recognition of conformity with Common Conformity Specifications (CCS) (Allen and Overy 1991). The Commission agreed to compile annually a list of international standards and specifications to be harmonised and terminal equipment for which CCSs should be drafted (European Council of Ministers 1986). The CEPT would then draw up a list of CCSs known as NETS (Normes Européenes de Télécommunications) to be used across the EU by regulatory authorities for type approval of terminal equipment. This system was considered to be merely the first stage in the creation of full mutual recognition through the creation of a system of 'one stop' approval.

The Commission also put forward a second directive on the mutual recognition of type approval (European Commission 1989a) though Member States disagreed on how exactly this should be implemented. The more pro-competitive states, such as the UK, wished to 'avoid the onerous requirements for type approval being applied unnecessarily to IT equipment on in–house systems which do not interact with the public network, whilst retaining type approval for devices which through connection or indirect networking, could have an effect on the network and thus potentially cause harm to it' (Department of Trade and Industry 1990, p. 1). On the other hand, some Members States felt that too loose a directive would allow inferior quality terminals to be sold in their markets under the pretence that they were not intended for connection to the network, even though this could be done by the purchaser. In the end, a compromise was reached whereby any equipment capable of connecting with the network, but marketed for in–house use only, had to carry a warning mark and a statement that connection to the network was a violation of national law.[4] This process provided an early example of the EU's problem solving mode of policy–making in a technical area of telecommunications with significant commercial resonance. It also indicates how the formation of epistemic communities to deal with the mechanics of a more liberalised sectoral environment were proving vital.

The Commission approached the liberalisation of EU terminal equipment in even more forthright fashion. Contending that PTTs were 'commercial undertakings, since they supply goods and services for payment' (European Commission, 1987a, p. 181) it drew on former Article 90 (now 86) of the Treaty of Rome which deals with the eradication of anti–competitive abuses by public undertakings or enterprises which have been granted special or exclusive commercial positions and which requires the Commission to 'ensure the application of the provisions of this article *and...where necessary address appropriate Directives or Decisions to member states*' (our emphasis). The Commission interpreted its remit as a requirement to issue a directive, bypassing the normal EU decision–making process whose effect would be to require competition in the terminal equipment market which was, at the time, foreclosed to competitive entry because of the exclusive competitive position granted to PTTs. After announcing its decision to take this action in a communication on the implementation of the green paper (European Commission 1988a) a directive soon followed. The directive stipulated that all 'economic operators...[should]..have the right to import, market, connect, bring into service and maintain terminal equipment' (European Commission 1988b, article 3) which required removal of the exclusive rights granted to PTTs. An important part of the directive concerned the creation of an independent body in each Member State to draw up technical specifications and type approval procedures which amounted to the first piece of Commission action reinforcing commitment to the separation of regulatory and operational functions espoused in the green paper.[5]

Justifying its position, the Commission highlighted the abuse by PTTs of their dominant position in terms of a violation of article 86 of the Treaty of Rome in conjunction with article 30. This, coupled with a violation of article 90(1) necessitated, it was argued, direct Commission action. Though controversial, the politics of the move were highlighted at the time by an interviewee at DGXIII who noted that, 'it is not a matter of choice as to whether or not the Commission applies article 90, because article 90 is part of the Treaty which gives instruction to the Commission' (authors' interview, European Commission, December 1989). In language which painted itself as a mere servant of the Treaty of Rome, the Commission pleaded in the directive that 'the only instrument therefore, by which the Commission can efficiently carry out the tasks and powers assigned to it, is a Directive based on article 90(3)' (European Commission 1988b, paragraph 10). The directive caused political controversy which ranged beyond the confines of the telecommunications policy–making arena. There were a few recalcitrant liberalisers, most notably Italy, who were opposed to both the detail of the directive and the Commission's use of article 90 to pass it. By contrast, there were those who agreed with its substance but were fundamentally at odds with the Commission's use of article 90. The latter were the majority of EU members which considered the Commission's action as undemocratic and a challenge to their national sovereignty.

The political storm in the directive's wake resulted in the Commission being taken to the European Court of Justice (ECJ) over its use of article 90. Significantly, in the action brought by France, with Belgium, Italy and Greece intervening (i.e. supporting), the substance of the directive went unchallenged reflecting the fact that the new commercial possibilities of telecommunications were by now being considered in an economically liberal light by even the most ardent of the traditionalist governments. Objecting to four articles of the directive, it was contended that the Commission had acted without due competence, infringed essential procedural arrangements by failing to give adequate reasons for its actions, infringed the principle of proportionality and misused its powers (European Court of Justice 1988). In February 1990, the Advocate General of the ECJ delivered an opinion on the case, coming down in favour of France et al. against the Commission.[6] However, in its final judgment in March 1991, the Court upheld the Commission's use of article 90 to issue directives without formal approval of the Member States (European Court of Justice 1991) though in the judgment, the Court did strike out a number of provisions of the directive.[7]

THE TELECOMMUNICATIONS SERVICES DIRECTIVE

In a similar vein to its efforts to liberalise the terminal equipment market, the Commission proceeded to attempt to open up the market for the provision of value added network services in 1989. In the directive, Member States were required to publish details of any licensing or declaration procedures for packet and circuit switched data services by the end of 1992 (European Commission 1989b). EU members still allowing public operators special control rights over the public telecommunications network had to declare to the Commission, by the end of 1990, steps to ensure objective and non–discriminatory access to it. Furthermore, from July 1991, measures such as 'the granting of operating licences, control of type approval and mandatory specification, the allocation of frequencies and surveillance of usage conditions' (ibid., article 4) were to be undertaken by a regulatory body independent of PTTs, effectively pursuing, once again, the Commission's policy goal of the separation of regulatory and operational functions in telecommunications.

In the Commission's opinion, the continuation of provision of exclusive rights for PTTs constituted a breach of article 90 of the Treaty of Rome in conjunction with article 59. The legal basis for the directive was further sustained by article 86, which prohibits abuse of dominant position by undertakings in the EU. A legal basis for exempting voice telephonic services from the directive was highlighted, namely that Article 90(3) allows derogation from application of articles 59 and 86, where application of the latter would obstruct the performance of tasks allotted to the telecommunications administrations. Furthermore, the evolution of telex services necessitated an individual approach, which meant that it was not covered by the directive. The Commission explained its use of the article with the justification that 'article 90(3) assigns clearly defined duties and powers to the Commission to monitor relations between member states and their public undertakings and undertakings to which they have granted exclusive rights'. As such, the Commission needed to take a 'comprehensive approach...to end the infringements that persist in certain member states' (European Commission 1989b, p. 12). An authors' interviewee at DGIV at the time (December 1989) noted 'it has to be stressed that the situation prevailing in most Member States is [was] presently infringing the competition rules of the Treaty...as well as those governing free provision of services across international borders'.

In an illustration of the battle lines being drawn between the reformists and traditionalists, the powerful business–user lobby threw their political weight behind the directive arguing that it was 'likely to improve the performance of the PTTs'. Full implementation of the directive would 'remove cross–subsidies which are [were] largely borne by users' creating 'realistic prices for circuits in Europe (INTUG 1989, p. 7). Certain Member States, notably France, Italy, Spain and Belgium (the 'southern camp' of liberalisation 'laggards') were opposed to both the substance of the directive and the principle under which it was put forward. Others, notably the UK, Germany and the Netherlands (the pro–liberalisation 'northern camp') agreed with its content but, as with the terminal equipment directive, disagreed with the use of the article 90 procedure. The PTTs were alarmed that an important lucrative future revenue base might be eroded. Furthermore, they feared that their obligation to provide a universal voice telephonic service would hamper their ability to compete with new private operators, who could 'cream–skim' profitable areas of the new service markets.

The controversy surrounding the services directive threatened to spill over into an embarrassing political 'dogfight' between the Council of Ministers and the Commission. The Council anticipated the release of the directive in June 1989. On April 28th, it unanimously declared its opposition to the proposed use of article 90. The Commission attempted to defuse the situation by postponing the entry of the directive into force. The reason given for such action was that it wished to give the Council of Ministers time to implement an ONP directive (European Commission 1989c), which it hoped would enter into force simultaneously with the services directive since the two directives were seen as complementary to one another. The period of delay was one of policy networking between the Council of Ministers and the Commission where it became clear to the latter that certain elements of the initially proposed directive would have to be changed. Consequently, in December 1989 the Commission agreed to modify certain aspects of the directive (European Commission 1990a). In June 1990, as part of what become known as the 'Open Network Provision Compromise' (see below), the Council of Ministers agreed that all telecommunications services would be opened to competition across the EU except public voice telephony and basic data transmission services. In a concession to the more reluctant liberalisers, Member States could continue to impose public service obligations on private service providers which operated through leasing lines on the public network, albeit subject to EU competition rules (Humphreys and Simpson 1996, p. 112; Woolcock et al. 1991, p. 69).

The Commission issued the revised directive to this effect in June 1990 (European Commission, 1990b). Nonetheless, national Member States still pursued three separate challenges to its use of the article 90 procedure in the European Court of Justice taken by Spain, Belgium and Italy (European Court of Justice, 1992). However, around the beginning of the 1990s, a number of events meant that the denouement of these legal challenges was less controversial than at first seemed would be the case. First, the decision of the Court upholding the Commission's right to use Article 90 meant that a precedent had been set which was repeated when the Court came to consider its judgment in respect of the VANS cases. Equally important, in terms of the substance of the directive, the rapproachment pursued and quite rapidly obtained during the detailed period of negotiations in 1989–90 was intertwined with policy developments in the area of open network provision.

THE OPEN NETWORK PROVISION DIRECTIVE AND 'ONP COMPROMISE'

ONP concerns the conditions referring to open and efficient access to public telecommunications networks and public telecommunications services and the efficient use of those services. The Commission realised that to create a generally more competitive environment in telecommunications new commercial players in the areas of terminal equipment sale and value added network services provision needed to be capable, technically and commercially, of utilising the established network which would require non–discriminatory (i.e. non restrictive), transparent and cost–oriented behaviour by incumbent PTTs towards them. An initial proposal for an ONP directive was drafted in January 1989, the proposed action being in the form of a framework directive, in which a subsequent series of directives dealing with various aspects of ONP were to be implemented throughout 1989–90. From the outset, the Commission intrinsically linked the areas of ONP and the establishment of a more competitive EU market for telecommunications services, deeming that 'the full establishment of a community wide market in telecommunications services can only be achieved by the rapid introduction of harmonised principles and conditions for Open Network Provision' (European Commission 1989c, paragraph 4).

A 'common position' on the ONP directive, in tandem with negotiations undertaken to secure a compromise on the VANS issue, was adopted involving a weakening of the harmonising power of the Commission's original proposal. In the proposed ONP directive, it was noted that in 1992 the Commission would 'review any remaining conditions for access to telecommunications services which have not been harmonised' (ibid., paragraph 8). In the 'common position' however, the Commission stipulated that these standards would only be voluntary (European Commission 1990a). The Commission could make ONP service standards mandatory if it was strictly necessary to ensure interoperability. However, it was also noted that there were unlikely to be any mandatory standards for value added services, reflecting the feeling that the Commission had been subjected to considerable political 'wing clipping'. The framework directive was adopted on 28 June 1990 in tandem with the proposed Services directive and was immediately ratified (European Commission 1990b) since the absence of article 90 problems and the adoption of a compromise position had rendered it politically uncontroversial. An important stipulation of the directive was the creation of an ONP advisory committee to assist the Commission in the implementation of the directive which was obliged to liaise with a range of interests spanning telecommunications operators, users, and manufacturers. As a consequence, it proved an important epistemic forum for policy learning and problem solving to occur between Member States on issues of best practice in future years.

The ONP compromise can be viewed as a pivotal moment in the history of EU telecommunications policy development. From a Commission perspective, there was a clear desire to broker a compromise out of the realisation that in a delicately balanced political construct like the EU, the achievement of consensus is vital. Whilst the Commission's actions to some extent appear on the surface bold and even relatively outlandish, closer scrutiny of the situation reveals that in taking its actions it received at least tacit support from a number of Member States (see Schmidt, S. 1996; Thatcher 2001a) which, by the end of the 1980s, were very much in favour of adopting a liberalised approach to telecommunications. Prominent here was the UK, whose Thatcher administration would have been expected to display outrage at any Commission attempt to bypass the Council of Ministers to pass EU legislation. The reality was, however, that the UK, since the early 1980s had proceeded much further in liberalising its telecommunications sector than even the Commission was proposing at the time. The UK, through its presence in key EU institutions and epistemic communities, as well as through the lobbying and dissemination activities of its key commercial interests played a leading role in promoting the adoption of (i.e. uploading) new liberal policy stances (Humphreys and Padgett forthcoming).

As seen in Chapter 2, other powerful Member States, notably Germany, had, by the late 1980s, begun to be convinced of the merits of arguments for liberalising its telecommunications sector, albeit gradually. As shown, even in France, there were signs of a cautiously developing penchant for liberalisation in the areas of terminal equipment and VANS. These circumstances proved ripe for a compromise to be secured and any further potential embarrassment from a row about the purview of the Commission to be diffused. By this stage, the structural techno-economic changes affecting the telecommunications sector globally were presenting ever clearer opportunities and challenges to telecommunications policy makers across the EU and their responses were increasingly to be reflected in the further development of telecommunications policy at EU level. In many respects, the EU provided a useful 'alibi' for certain of the more traditionalist Member State governments allowing them to justify regulatory changes in telecommunications resisted by key domestic interests (Thatcher 2002b).

The ONP directive proved an important counterweight to the use of article 90 by the Commission, as well as a practical enabler of the developing compromise between Member States which allowed the process of liberalised re-regulation to proceed further across the EU. The ONP framework would become the context within which a series of future directives, harmonising various aspects of telecommunications provision, such as licensing, interconnection and universal service, were negotiated and passed under a combination of Articles 95 (ex 100a, internal market) and 55 (ex 66, freedom to provide services) of the EU Treaties (Humphreys and Padgett forthcoming) (see next section). Within this framework of harmonisation, Member States were able to upload a number of their policy preferences which, in certain cases, tempered the out–and–out liberalising thrust of the emerging EU telecommunications package: most outstanding here was the development of common EU level measures for universal service which imbued EU telecommunications policy with a significant element of the 'service public' so dear to France and other of the more reticent liberalisers.

TOWARDS FULL LIBERALISATION OF EU TELECOMMUNICATIONS

After the at times quite fraught period of the late 1980s, the liberalisation process evolved with comparatively little political controversy in the 1990s. Given the complex character of the EU, the essentially 'negotiated' nature of its policy processes, and a continuing measure of diversity of Member State interests, telecommunications policy in the early 1990s maintained its inherent characteristic of incrementalist development. Yet progress was attained more smoothly and rapidly than in the 1980s. Buoyed by its policy achievements in terminal equipment and VANS, but also aware of the need to proceed consensually, the European Commission launched, in 1992, what became known as the Telecommunications Services Review. This exercise was, like the consultative process in the wake of the 1987 green paper, pluralist in nature, involving representatives from all parties with an interest in the future evolution of the European telecommunications sector, notably telecommunications service providers (mostly ex–PTTs), equipment producers, users, data processing firms and telecommunications unions. It has been argued that in performing sectoral analyses such as this, the Commission acts as a focal point around which the expectations of the Member States on any given set of issues can converge. As a result of the review, the Commission produced a paper offering Member States four possible options for the future of the European telecommunications sector as follows:

To freeze the liberalisation process in its current state;
To undertake extensive regulation of tariffs and investments at EU level to overcome bottlenecks;
To liberalise voice telephony services between Member States of the EU;
To liberalise all voice telephonic services across the EU.

It was, unsurprisingly, the Commission's recommendation that all public voice telephonic services be opened up to competition on an EU–wide basis (European Commission 1992a). This was agreed to by the Council of Ministers through a resolution in July 1993, the date set being 1998 for all EU member states except Luxembourg (which was given until 2000) and Greece, Portugal, Spain and Ireland (which were given until 2003) (European Council of Ministers 1993). Very significantly, this resolution noted that the liberalisation of the telecommunications infrastructure upon which telecommunications services are delivered would have to be addressed as an issue in the longer term. However, the liberalisation bandwagon had gathered such speed by this stage that this issue was addressed much more quickly than the Commission could have at the time predicted. An undoubted stimulus was the white paper produced by the outgoing Commission president, Jacques Delors, on future prospects for creating growth, competitiveness and employment in the EU. In particular, this document noted the important positive role which advanced telecommunications networks could play in this process (European Commission 1993). An indication of the prominence ICT policy had attained on the political agenda was the request made to the Commission by EU heads of state at the European Council meeting in Brussels in late 1993, to establish a group of 'prominent persons' (European Commission 1994a, p. 1) to prepare a report for the subsequent European Council meeting in Corfu, 24–25 June 1994, on measures required for the future construction and operation of information and communications infrastructures. The Bangemann Group, chaired by the then Telecommunications and Industry Commissioner, Martin Bangemann, duly presented its report, which inter alia, advocated the complete liberalisation of EU–wide telecommunications infrastructure (European Commission 1994). The Commission endorsed this conclusion in a key report to the Council of Ministers which formed the basis for an action plan for the Information Society.

The move towards complete liberalisation of telecommunications infrastructure across Europe was given further impetus when, in September 1994, a special telecommunications/industry joint Council of Ministers meeting was convened to discuss the Commission's proposals for infrastructure liberalisation in the Commission Action Plan. Endorsing the proposals, the Council concluded that Part I of a green paper on infrastructure liberalisation, to be submitted by the Commission, would enable its principles, and a timetable for its realisation, to be determined (European Council of Ministers 1994). This green paper was presented to the Council in October 1994. It had two important dimensions to it. First, it advocated the liberalisation of what were termed as alternative telecommunications infrastructures such as cable TV, satellite, mobile and liberalised terrestrial service networks. Second, the paper proposed harmonising the timetable for telecommunications infrastructure liberalisation with that for the liberalisation of public voice telephony. In December 1994, the Council produced a key resolution on principles and timetabling for the liberalisation of the telecommunications infrastructure. This stipulated that the necessary regulatory framework to ensure its liberalisation should be set up by 1 January 1998. However, Member States which were granted and chose to take advantage of the extension period offered for public voice services would also be eligible for an additional transition period of a maximum of five years (European Council of Ministers 1994).

Clearly, this period in the history of EU telecommunications policy development testified to a very significant attitudinal transformation among those formerly reticent Member States of the EU regarding further liberalisation of the telecommunications sector vis-à-vis the position agreed in the 1990 services directive. It is argued here that this was not merely the result of policy entrepreneurship by the European Commission. Rather, it has been principally determined by a number of structural forces which were affecting the telecommunications industry worldwide. First, telecommunications was now one of the few examples of a truly global industry where protectionism was no longer likely to yield commercial success. As Chapter 2 has explained, for France, the fear of losing business to the UK in the lucrative international telecommunications services market was a factor for its volte-face. Second, as shown, liberalisation transformed the corporate strategies of the leading telecommunications service suppliers. In particular, for some of these former PTTs, intransigence towards liberalisation in their domestic markets expressed in the 1980s, was replaced by a desire to be able to spread their influence across Europe and globally. Nonetheless, they were keen to ensure that the transition to complete liberalisation of telecommunications infrastructures and services occurred at a pace which would not diminish their domestic market dominance too severely. This classic dilemma of globalisation which they faced, namely the need to deliver domestic market liberalisation to gain access to foreign markets, with all its attendant risks, meant that the major European telecommunications players were prepared, in the early 1990s, to accept the 1998 liberalisation deadline in the hope that they would be sufficiently competition–ready by then. To some considerable extent, the negotiations which took place at this time between Member States contributed to 'change in the normative yardstick against which domestic actors define[d] their interests and policy preferences' (Humphreys and Padgett forthcoming).

The significance of what was at stake, as well as the political nous of the Commission, is illustrated by its assurance after the 1998 liberalisation agreement, that EU competition law would be altered to allow greater commercial cooperation between EU telecommunications companies, as well as by discussions between the Commission, France Telecom and Deutsche Telekom over a proposed international telecommunications services joint venture between the latter. Here, it was made clear that this would be given regulatory approval by the Commission's Competition Directorate in return for a commitment from their national government to liberalise alternative telecommunications infrastructures by 1996, two years ahead of schedule (Thatcher 2001a, p. 572; Bartle 1999). For them, the lure of the Europe–wide (valued at around $200 billion in 1998) and global telecommunications market could not be resisted. For other Member States and their telecommunications operators, not confident of staking a claim in an internationally liberalised telecommunications market, there was less enthusiasm for opening up public voice services and infrastructure to competition, though the liberalised regulatory framework produced was not an out and out liberalisation but one imbued with enough compromise regarding public service guarantees to win their approval. They also witnessed the undoubted practical gains, in terms of lower prices and quality of service offered to consumers, from competition in early liberaliser markets, notably the UK.

PREPARING FOR THE 1998 LIBERALISED EU TELECOMMUNICATIONS MARKET

In the aftermath of the landmark 1993 Council of Ministers resolution and the Commission's green paper on the process of across–the–board liberalisation, a number of important legislative measures duly followed. The not inconsiderable task facing the EU in the interim to 1998 amounted to construction of the remaining rules by which the post–1998 telecommunications 'game' would be played out in a single, liberalised, EU–wide market. Whilst the process was, compared to the period of the late 1990s, relatively straightforward politically, it was also the case that careful balances had to be struck, and compromise pursued, on occasions. Differences of opinion were in evidence over issues such as the scope of universal service (the 'southern camp' of EU Member States wanting a more far–reaching approach), and the right to insist on licences having to be issued as opposed to less bureaucratically burdensome general authorisations. The Commission was also careful to pace liberalisation of satellite and mobile communications in tandem with domestic reform agendas (Thatcher 2001a, pp. 570–1) and this respect served to 'synchronise the response of the Member States to the very strong sectoral pressures driving change globally' (Humphreys and Padgett 2006).

The proposal, transposition and implementation of a number of important directives duly occurred, not least the 1996 'Full Competition' directive; the 1997 Authorisations and Licences directive and the 1997 Interconnection directive; and the 1997 Universal Service directive. The new 1998 Framework, as it came to be known, contained a raft of measures which were either liberalising and thus enacted through the article 90 (now 86) route or harmonising and thus employing combinations of articles 100a (now 95), concerning the internal market, and 66 (now 55), concerning freedom to provide services – see Table 3.2.

Table 3.2 Main legislation in the EU 1998 telecommunications framework

Liberalisation Measures	Harmonisation Measures
Commission Directive on Competition in the Markets for Telecommunications Services (1990)	Council Directive on the Establishment of the Internal Market for Telecommunications Services Through the Implementation of Open

Commission Directive Amending the 1988 Terminal Equipment and 1990 Competition Directives in Particular with Regard to Satellite Communications (1994)	Network Provision (1990) Council Directive on the Application of Open Network Provision to Leased Lines (1992)
Commission Directive Amending the 1990 Competition Directive with Regard to the Abolition of the Restrictions on the Use of Cable Television Networks for the Provision of Already Liberalised Telecommunications Services (1995)	European Parliament and Council Directive on a Common Framework for General Authorisations and Individual Licences in the Field of Telecommunications Services (1997) European Parliament and Council Directive on Interconnection in Telecommunications with Regard to
Commission Directive Amending the 1990 Competition directive with Regard to Mobile and Personal Communications (1996)	Ensuring Universal Service and Interoperability Through Application of the Principles of Open Network Provision (1997)
Commission Directive Amending the 1990 Competition directive Regarding the Implementation of Full Competition in Telecommunications (1996)	European Parliament and Council Directive Concerning the Processing of Personal Data and the Protection of Privacy in the Telecommunications Sector (1997)
Commission Directive Amending directive 90/388/EEC in Order to Ensure that Telecommunications Networks and Cable TV Networks Owned by a Single Operator Are Separate Legal Entities (1999)	European Parliament and Council Directive on the Application of Open Network Provision to Voice Telephony and on Universal Service for Telecommunications in a Competitive Environment (replacing directive 95/62/EC) (1998)

The 1996 'Full Competition' directive ensured that all telecommunications services and infrastructure would be opened to competition across the EU from the beginning of 1998 (Luxembourg (2000), Greece, Spain Portugal and Ireland (all 2003) were granted extensions to this deadline). Politically, its passage contained some resonance of the controversy of the late 1980s since it required the use of the article 90 procedure due to legal precedent, though at this stage there was consensus amongst all Member States. The main substance of the directive concerned the liberalisation of voice telephony. Oddly, though, the Commission noted that in the 1990 Services directive it had:

granted a *temporary* [our emphasis] exception under Article 90(2) in respect of exclusive and special rights for the provision of voice telephony, since the financial resources for the development of the network still derived mainly from the operation of the telephony service and the opening up of that service could, at that time, threaten the financial stability of the telecommunications organisations and obstruct the performance of the task of general economic interest assigned to them, consisting in the provision and exploitation of a universal network. (European Commission 1996a, p. 1).

It also stated that further reasons for maintaining voice telephony as a reserved service in 1990 were the ongoing process of network upgrading undertaken by incumbent telecommunications operators and also the fact that, until the early 1990s, price structures did not reflect those of cost.[8] As our analysis has shown, however, this was certainly a rather 'revisionist' way of viewing the past since it did not reflect the real extent of ideological and material resistance to the liberalisation of voice telephony which had been evident in the majority of national Member States at the turn of the 1980s.

As a result of the directive, any telecommunications service provider could construct and use their own infrastructure, or use that of a network provider other than (and including) the incumbent telecommunications operator to provide services in any EU Member State. The mechanics of ensuring effective competition in voice telephonic communications were also referred to in the directive. For example, Member States were required to ensure that the terms and conditions of interconnection to the basic functional components of voice services and public switched telecommunications networks were published. They were also required to permit their incumbent telecommunications operator (former PTT) to undertake suitable tariff rebalancing to adapt rates which were not in line with costs (i.e. were below them) and which could, as a consequence, increase the burden of universal service provision. The detailed issues of universal service, licensing and interconnection were addressed individually as part of the raft of directives passed to create the 1998 regulatory framework. The 1990 directive had excluded from liberalisation at EU level the services of telex, mobile communications, and radio and television broadcasting to the public. However, in the light of the EU's decision to create across-the-board competition in all telecommunications infrastructure and services, directives were duly passed to bring mobile communications (European Commission 1996b), satellite communications (European Commission 1994b) and cable TV services (European Commission 1995) under the scope of the 1990 directive. Since each of these were liberalising in purpose and substance, they were adopted using the former article 90 procedure. However, as in the case of the Full Competition directive, they were politically uncontroversial in the main.

As noted, the requirements of the Full Competition directive were underpinned by the implementation of a directive on the creation of a framework for issuing and obtaining general authorisations and individual licences in telecommunications services. An important distinction was made between general authorisations and individual licences where the former refers to permission to provide telecommunications services and networks which does not require the undertaking concerned to obtain explicit permission from the relevant NRA before exercising rights stemming from the authorisation. A licence, by contrast, refers to specific permission granted to provide telecommunications networks and services and which gives a company specific rights and places specific obligations on it. The policy objective of the directive was to encourage the use of general authorisations, making licensing the exception, with a view to enhancing the competitive dynamics of the liberalised telecommunications market. However, considerable power to determine the instances when licences were required was given to the National Regulatory Authorities and, in practice, there is evidence of differential behaviour across the EU (see Chapter 4).

Interconnection and universal service are two key interrelated issues in the creation of an EU–wide liberalised telecommunications services market. One of the contentions of the directive was that universal service should be an evolving concept. In fact, the directive goes as far as to state that, 'it may be appropriate in due course to consider whether ISDN should be part of the universal service' (European Parliament and Council, 1997a, para 8). It sums up the economic aspect of universal service by stipulating that, 'the net cost of universal service should take due account of costs and revenues, as well as economic externalities and the intangible benefits resulting from providing universal service but should not hinder the ongoing process of tariff re-balancing' (ibid.).

The interconnection directive addressed the obligations (incumbent upon public telecommunications network providers, most notably the ex-PTTs) to negotiate interconnection arrangements with each other, which were deemed vital to a competitive telecommunications market. Once again, the regulatory role given to the NRAs was substantial. They were permitted, for example, to limit the interconnection obligation on a temporary basis on technical and commercial grounds. Contributions made towards the cost of universal service could be linked to interconnection payments in the form of a supplementary charge, the determination of which was left to the NRA. It thus soon became clear that whilst unprecedented Europeanisation of telecommunications had occurred, EU national Member States would retain day–to–day operational control of their telecommunications sectors. Around this time, a debate arose on the possible utility of creating a European Regulatory Authority to carry out tasks in the interconnection and other domains better suited to the EU than the national level, though creation of such an organisation was resisted by national Member States.

CONCLUSION

This chapter has charted the emergence and development of EU telecommunications policy from its embryonic form of the early 1980s to the creation, by 1998, of a substantial and detailed policy framework at the European level. This policy journey proceeded along an evolutionary pathway with occasional notable periods of controversy and an element of coercion by the Commission. Overall, though, what has been witnessed was a broadly consensual process which responded to the vital structural changes in the global political economy of telecommunications charted in Chapter 2. As a consequence, the character of Europe's telecommunications sectors promised to be radically transformed. Varying degrees of closely regulated domestic and international competition in all aspects of the telecommunications sector replaced nationally protectionist, uncompetitive, and state–owned arrangements.

These new broad characteristic features reflective of global trends in the sector and arguably strongly influencing the latter (see Chapter 2), have been, nonetheless, developed in a characteristically complex 'European' fashion. The European Commission undoubtedly played an important role in this process showing leadership qualities at times (occasionally in controversial circumstances) but for the most part working with national Member States to develop policy in an incremental, participatory and consensus seeking manner characterised by compromise outcomes which gave considerable responsibility and latitude to the national level (Thatcher 2001a, p. 560). The development of policy at EU level served a number of purposes for Member States. For those, such as the UK, which had already embarked on radical liberalisation, the EU served as a platform on which policy ideas could be promulgated and, this having been successfully achieved, 'learned' by other members. For others, the EU level was utilised as a shield against the harsh glare of global competition under which policy safeguards to establish limited public service concessions or, by contrast, to reorganise and prepare (domestically or in the various new EU level epistemic communities) for the rigours of international liberalisation, could be realised. Such policy activity resulted in mostly deliberative, rarely coercive, transfers of ideas and practices in which resigned acceptance of the new realities of telecommunications mixed with proactive intentions to capitalise on its new commercial opportunities were evident. Nonetheless, the process by which the 1998 telecommunications regulatory package emerged, whilst highly significant, was only the beginning of the new EU telecommunications policy paradigm. Much would hinge on the transposition and implementation of the framework, as well as its development in the light of further technological and commercial possibilities appearing on the horizon. It is to these issues and surrounding events that we turn in the following chapters of this volume.

NOTES

1. The Commission noted that, according to article 122 'the determination of the appropriate ownership of the telecommunications administrations, in particular whether they should be in public or private ownership, falls to the Member States'.

2. Two legal aspects were stressed by the Commission. First, the existence of monopoly 'may be due to domestic laws and government instruction'. Here, articles 37, 90(1) and 90(3) apply in terms of its removal. Second, EU entities involved in 'anticompetitive arrangements or behaviour' infringe articles 85 and 86 of the Treaty 'when they are not simply implementing laws or government instructions but are performing independent entrepreneurial activity'.

3. This article prohibits any conduct by one or more commercial undertakings that involves an abuse of dominant position within the Common Market (the Single Market) or a substantial part of it.

4. The supplier of such equipment had to advise a notified approval body that the product was being sold and had to justify that the product had a legitimate purpose when not connected to the network. An approvals body, known as the Advisory Committee for Telecommunications Equipment (ACTE), was authorised to oversee the implementation of the Directive. Its main task was designated as creating a system of Common Technical Regulations (CTRs). These were the systems against which approval of individual pieces of terminal equipment would take place.

5. The Commission also cited the then Article 30 of the Treaty of Rome which 'prohibits quantitative restrictions on imports from other member states'. Similarly, it was noted that article 37 of the Treaty of Rome stated that 'member states shall progressively adjust any state monopolies of a commercial character so as to ensure...no discrimination regarding the conditions under which goods are procured and marketed...between nationals and member states'. Yet again, article 59 of the Treaty of Rome stating that 'restrictions on freedom to provide services within the Community shall be progressively abolished' was quoted in the directive.

6. The Advocate General's opinions are always seriously considered and, more often than not, followed.

7. It was deemed by the Court that Article 2 should be struck out of the revised directive. In the original directive, this stipulated that Member States must revise their granting of special rights to PTTs, in order to allow 'users...a free choice between the various types of equipment available' to allow them 'to benefit fully from the technical advances made in the sector'. In keeping with this judgment, article 7 of the original directive, which instructed Member States to ensure that the exclusive right of maintenance of terminals sold was abolished, was also struck out of the directive. Finally, article 9, which stipulated that Member States should create an independent body to draw up and apply type approval procedures for telecommunications terminal equipment, was removed for situations in which its provisions applied to articles 2 and 7.

8. This meant that competitors to the incumbent could have targeted highly profitable services alone, such as international voice telephony.

4. The transposition and implementation of the EU's 1998 regulatory framework

If Chapter 2 stressed the state's role as that of 'competition state', actively creating new regulatory structures that would respond better to the demands of international economic competition in globalising markets, this chapter stresses the other face of the state: the 'regulatory state'. The new European regulatory framework is not simply a matter of removing barriers to the internal market and agreeing EU-wide rules for pro-competitive regulation. It is, of course, also about the *activity* of regulation. Accordingly, this chapter examines the 'downloading' – that is transposition and actual implementation – of the European Union's liberalisation and regulatory '1998 package' for telecommunications. As regards implementation, the 'regulatory state' was central to the new paradigm. In every Member State, national regulatory authorities (NRAs) were established to ensure the creation of competition in new market structures that were still characterised by the dominance of the former monopoly operators. In fact, the NRAs were the institutional embodiment of the new 'regulatory state' in the telecommunications sector, just as the PTTs embodied the 'old' role of the state as owner/operator. Indeed, the new 'regulatory state' was just as interventionist as the 'old' service provider state. Rather than retreat, as the rhetoric about 'deregulation' and the privatisation of state-owned former monopoly incumbents might suggest, the state assumed a host of new *regulatory* functions: enforcing economic efficiency, maintaining social efficiency, and protecting privacy (Grande 1994).

The chapter explores the degree of 'Europeanisation' of national telecommunications policy that is to say the influence of the EU on domestic policies and regulatory practices. In this latter connection, the chapter is concerned with the way Member States adopt European policies in ways that reflect their preferences, institutions, state traditions and policy styles ('domestication'). Clearly, national diversity may continue to characterise the new regulatory paradigm to the extent that:

- historically rooted national institutional and cultural differences are conducive to a degree of 'path dependent' persistence of national regulatory 'policy styles';

- the European telecommunications directives (examined in the preceding chapter) allowed for discretion in their interpretation, in their transposition into national rules, and in the design of national-level regulatory institutions;
- national policy makers may implement the new policies with some licence in order to 'claw back at the base what they they lost at the summit (Mény et al. 1996, p. 7), or to provide a 'regulatory subsidy' for national players (Vogel, S. 1997).

PATTERNS OF TRANSPOSITION

From 1 January 1998, as the European Commission's third implementation report (European Commission 1998a, p. 2) was able to trumpet, telecommunications markets were 'fully liberalised in most of the European Union'. This, it claimed, 'culminated' a ten-year legislative process of gradual market opening that had been 'set in train' by the Commission's 1987 green paper. (The process, the Commission noted, was now being 'given added impetus by the WTO agreement on basic telecommunications services on 5 February 1998' – this is examined in Chapter 7.) As seen in the previous chapter, the EU's 1998 regulatory package was shaped by a series of liberalisation directives for different telecommunications markets and regulatory harmonisation directives, the former removing the barriers to trade and competition in the European telecommunications sector and the latter providing common rules and procedures, to be implemented by NRAs, for a new pro-competitive regulatory framework designed to ensure that the incumbent operators (former monopolies) did not abuse their temporarily continuing dominance in liberalised national markets and to encourage the growth of competition. The most important regulatory harmonisation directive was a framework directive in 1990 (with application directives for leased lines in 1992 and voice telephony services in 1995) and an interconnection directive in 1997, providing harmonised rules establishing the conditions for open access to public telephone networks and services (open network provision; ONP). Two main variables relate to transposition patterns: timing; and diversity of regime types arising from national interpretation of directives.

THE TIMING OF TRANSPOSITION

Observers have tended to classify countries into either the 'speedy-liberalisation' northern European camp, with the UK in the 'lead', or into the 'laggard liberaliser' southern European camp, of which group France tended to be viewed as the 'leader'.[1] As seen, this dichotomy does have some broad analytical purchase. The northern European countries – notably the UK and the Scandinavians - were 'first movers' so they encountered less adaptation pressure and were able to comply relatively easily with EU reform; indeed, to no small extent, the UK provided the original liberalisation 'model'. Further, the Scandinavian countries and the Netherlands shared the UK's predisposition to private enterprise and open markets. Although a 'laggard' within the northern camp, once it had negotiated an incremental pace of EU liberalisation to suit its domestic politics (see Chapter 2) Germany's transposition performance was exemplary. The European Commission's third implementation report, looking principally at the transposition of the EU directives, lacked any criticism of Germany. The measures required to tranpose the most important regulatory harmonisation directives were transposed in all cases before the deadlines. With regard to licensing, interconnection, and new voice telephony Germany legislated even before their enactment by the Council and European Parliament (European Commission 1998a).

By contrast, the *étatiste*, interventionist, protectionist state traditions in France, Belgium and southern Europe have often been seen as an obstacle to rapid reform. France has therefore typically been seen as a liberalisation 'laggard'. This may have been true surrounding the earlier negotiations about EU liberalisation, but as seen (Chapters 2 and 3) France's position shifted. Moreover, with regard to transposition of the '1998' package, France did not feature among the countries targeted by the Commission with infringement proceedings in the run up to the 1998 full liberalisation deadline (Commission Press Release IP/97/954, 5.11.97), having met every EU transposition deadline to date. Relatively successful in 'uploading' its own preferences to the EU level, France had then employed its strong central executive capacity to transpose the EU measures smoothly and for the most part substantially. France could best be viewed as a keen liberaliser *under its own terms*. Under the pressure of globalisation and globalising technologies, France actually began liberalising terminal equipment and value added services in advance of the European Commission's liberalisation directives.

For France, the major sticking points were the scope of 'reserved services' (that might be reserved for 'service public' provision), the protection of 'universal service', and the timing of full liberalisation. These issues were settled respectively by the 1990 'ONP compromise' allowing France (and others) to impose certain public-service obligations on private operators using lines leased on the public network, by inclusion in the subsequent EU legislation of a set of minimum services which must be universally available and allowing for the imposition of contribution to a universal service fund on new entrants, and last, by agreement of the 1998 deadline for full liberalisation. These concessions having been achieved, the French 'strong state' duly transposed the the EU's 1998 full liberalisation package in a Telecommunications Law in 1996. However, the European Commission's Third Implementation Report (European Commission 1998a, p. 25) did note several concerns about specific issues, notably about the licensing condition requiring financial contribution to research and training in the telecommunications sector, the delay in introducing legislation about licensing procedures, and the extent of universal service obligations (see next section).

Nor, as already mentioned in the last chapter, could Spain be viewed as a laggard for very long. It certainly started off squarely in the 'laggard southern European' camp, arguing against a too-rapid liberalisation of basic telecommunications services. Along with Ireland, Greece, Luxembourg and Portugal, Spain negotiated for itself an extension period on implementing the 1998 full liberalisation package. However, with domestic economic interests fearful of losing out in international competition Spain subsequently speeded up its liberalisation pace and accepted a markedly reduced extension. Telefonica's reorientation (under international competitive pressures) was, along with that of France Télécom and Deutsche Telekom, of pivotal importance to sustaining the pace of EU reform (interview in the European Commission, in 2000).

Although Spain was among the countries targeted by the Commission with infringement proceedings in the run up to the 1998 full liberalisation deadline, for failing to lift all restrictions on the establishment of new infrastructures for providing liberalised services (Commission Press Release IP/97/954, 5.11.97), the European Commission's third implementation report (European Commission 1998a) was confident that a law then being discussed in the Spanish Parliament would lead to substantial transposition of the new regulatory package. An independent regulatory authority had operated since early 1997 and by 1998 it had already awarded a second nation-wide licence and was in process of granting a third (European Commission 1998a, p. 9). The European Commission's fifth implementation report (European Commission 1999a, Annex 2, p. 8) recorded that Spain had substantially transposed all regulatory harmonisation directives, making it by now one of the most compliant in this regard. As in the French case, Spain's 'majoritarian' governmental features facilitated smooth executive action, once policy makers and key interests supported full liberalisation.

Italy, by contrast, 'only reluctantly complied with EU requirements...the dominance of status quo-oriented interests and the fragmented political decision structure created too many obstacles for a swift structural adaptation. Major inertia could only be overcome through pressures from Brussels' (Schneider 2002, pp. 40–1). In late 1997 Italy finally enacted a regulation for the implementation of Community directives designed to ensure the transposition of the main contents of the EU's 1998 package. However, in November 1997 the Commission opened infringement proceedings against Italy on two important counts, namely for not ensuring full liberalisation of new and the use of existing infrastructures by the EC's 1 July 1996 deadline for this, and also for not yet having specified the financial obligations which would be imposed upon new entrants in order to share the net cost of universal service burdening Telecom Italia, Italy being the only Member State other than France to have adopted a universal service fund (Commission Press Release IP/97/954, 5.11.97).

In 1998, the European Commission's third implementation report (European Commission 1998a, p. 27) recorded that Italy had by now complied substantially with most transposition measures. However, the Commission still harboured similar concerns to the French case about onerous licensing conditions, notably the condition requiring financial contribution to research and training in the telecommunications sector. Moreover, the Interconnection Directive had still only been partially transposed. Here the Commission's concerns related to 'the lack of implementing measures on universal service contributions, interconnection and numbering and to the fact that the principle of non discrimination [had not been] imposed sufficiently widely'. Most poignantly the report (European Commission 1998a, p. 9) noted that 'no additional operator [to Telecom Italia] ha[d] been authorised to date'. Italy was in fact the only Member State without a derogation that had yet to authorise new market players for the provision of voice telephony and public telecommunications networks. Approaching two years after the 1 January 1998 full liberalisation deadline, Italy had still to transpose the 1997 directive (amending the 1992 one) on leased lines and the new voice telephony directive of 1998. Moreover, Italy had only partially transposed the 1997 licensing directive and the 1998 directive on numbering (European Commission 1999a, Annex 2, p. 8).

By January 1998, the European Commission's third implementation report (European Commission 1998a, pp. 5–6) noted that five countries had still failed to notify some transposition measures for liberalisation; Belgium, Greece, Ireland, Luxembourg and Portugal. All except Belgium had received derogations on full liberalisation; nonetheless, the derogations for the specific measures identified by the Commission had expired by now. These countries also featured prominently regarding delayed or only partial/non-conforming transposition of regulatory harmonisation directives, although the Commission noted that measures were under way to achieve subtantial compliance on most matters. By October 1999, according to the European Commission's fifth implementation report (European Commission 1999a, Annex 2, p. 8), Luxembourg had still only partially transposed the 1997 directive (amending the 1990 one) on ONP, the 1997 interconnection directive, and the 1998 new voice telephony directive.

The Commission was also examining most transposition measures by Greece and some by Portugal, these having only recently been enacted. By now, Ireland ranked among the most compliant in terms of transposition. However, Belgium – a country that had neither requested nor been granted any derogation – was singled out by the Commission for its late transposition of the new regulatory package (*Telecom Markets*, 12.03.1998, p. 5). Its attitude to telecommunications liberalisation was at best 'lukewarm' with little or no domestic support. Like France, its main reservations centred on the 'service public' and employment implications of EU legislation. Like Italy, policy making in Belgium was rendered complex by its (in Lijphartian terms) 'consensual' political system, including in this case a federal system of government. A minimalist approach to transposition was reflected in the number of 'formal notices' issued to Belgium by the Commission. In November 1997, less than two months before the January 1 full liberalisation deadline, the Commission identified no fewer than seven infringements. Among these was even failure to adopt the necessary measures for liberalising voice telephony (Commission Press Release IP/97/954, 5.11.97). Two years later, Belgium still stood apart from most other EU Member States in having only partially transposed a number of regulatory harmonisation directives (leased lines, new voice telephony, licensing, and data protection, while recent interconnection legislation was under examination) (European Commission 1999a, Annex 2, p. 8).

DIVERSITY OF REGULATORY REGIMES

After the third one, the EC's implementation reports switched their main focus away from transposition towards effective implementation. They duly contained much more full reporting on the *actual* extent of market opening on the basis of data supplied by the NRAs. Later in this chapter, these reports will be drawn upon to construct a schema of diverse patterns of implementation. First, however, it is necessary to say something about the diversity of regulatory regimes that emerged from the transposition process. Overall, the 1998 package provided for a quite prescriptive regime. NRAs were required to ensure that interconnection tariffs did not distort competition. The incumbents' cost structures had to be transparent, with clear accounting for different market segments to reveal any cross subsidies. So prescriptive were the rules that Levi-Faur (1999, p. 189) commented: 'if these regulations do not suggest a supranational structure, it is doubtful if such an "animal" exists at all.' Nonetheless, while prescriptive about the principles of regulation, the directives allowed for a significant degree of national discretion in 'downloading'. Notably, the 1998 package allowed for regulation at the national level by diversely designed NRAs and also considerable scope for varied regulatory practice.

The 'domestication effect' at the 'downloading' stage meant that the EU's 1998 telecommunications regime still had a distinctly 'pluralist' element, a state of affairs that has been overlooked by Commission-centred analysts who have stressed the 'supranational' nature of EU telecommunications reform. The distribution of regulatory powers between the core elements of the regulatory regime, namely the new sector-specific NRAs, the competition authorities and the relevant government ministries, varied considerably.

Regulatory strategies varied; thus, the UK prioritised infrastructure competition more enthusiastically than some others, allowing cable systems to carry voice telephony at the start of the 1990s, while almost a decade later the Germans still appeared to be dragging their feet in structurally separating cable systems from the incumbent.

Further, licensing regimes and authorisation procedures varied from 'light' in some Member States (notably, the Scandinavian Member States) to 'onerous' in others (notably France and Belgium). Licence fees were high in some countries (e.g. Germany).

The national regulatory regimes and NRAs differed, too, in the relative weight they give to considerations of equity *vis-à-vis* efficiency. Thus, Coen and Héritier (2000, p. 31) point to the UK's 'push for greater efficiency in the market – via the introduction of pricing models like RPIminusX', whereas 'in Germany regulation has also strongly emphasised equity and public service provision' (though Germany certainly embraced the British concept of price cap regulation as well). 'Service public' was emphasised even more strongly in the case of France, which introduced a universal service fund into which new entrants were compelled to pay in order to compensate the provision of universal service by the incumbent, France Télécom. In the UK, Oftel had actually proposed introducing a universal service fund in 1995; however, by 1997 it was backing away from such a measure (*Telecom Markets*, 27.02.1997, pp. 1, 12).

Moreover, with regard to privatisation – intimately related to liberalisation, if not actually mandated by the EU package – the UK model of complete privatisation of the incumbent was rarely imitated to its full extent. In France, for instance, the state was obliged by law to retain at least 51 per cent of France Télécom; in Germany, the state still retained 31 per cent in 2002; in both cases the personnel retained their civil servant status.

Finally, it has been a general rule that compliance with EU regulatory policy has tended to vary significantly across the Member States (Wilks 1996) and the telecommunications sector was no exception to this rule.

'DOMESTICATION': DIVERSE REGULATORY AUTHORITY MODELS

The principal responsibility for actually implementing the 1998 regulatory package rested primarily with the NRAs. A major decision was taken not to centralise regulation at the EU level but rather to locate regulatory power at the national level, with the Commission 'policing' national regulators in order to ensure that regulators in the Member States adhered to EU regulatory policies. The 1998 regulatory package allowed for a diversity of NRAs; it did not attempt to harmonise their institutional form. As a result, they varied in terms of their institutional powers, procedures and resources. The establishment of specialised regulatory agencies, set apart from ministries, was a new departure for Western Europe, though it was of course a core feature of the archetypal 'regulatory state', the USA.

There were various rationales for Europe's embrace of the new 'regulatory state' model (Majone 1997). Most obviously, liberalisation and increasingly privatisation clearly required the establishment of new regulatory structures, in order to promote and ensure fair competition. The particular character of the telecommunications sector, a network industry with former state-owned monopoly incumbents enjoying market dominance, necessitated sector specific pro-competitive regulation. It was seen as important too to establish independent regulatory capacity, in such a way that judgements would be made according to neutral criteria and would be fair to all players. Thus, the ONP directive (90/387/EEC) required Member States to ensure that the historic regulatory functions of the former public monopolies were now vested in independent bodies. Where governments retained some degree of ownership or control over them, the regulatory function had to be structurally separate from activities associated with ownership or control (European Commission 1999c, p. 11). Also, as Thatcher (2001b, p. 6) notes, specialist regulatory agencies could relieve politicians and general civil servants of the relatively unrewarding and often risky business of performing highly technical and complex tasks. In the telecommunications field, questions of the costs and terms of interconnection, price controls, long-run incremental costs and tariff baskets were all matters that were 'far from exciting for generalist civil servants and ministers'.

All Member States imitated the UK model by establishing a regulatory authority that was organisationally separate from central government and not just merely independent from the sector as required by EU legislation. A degree of policy transfer undoubtedly occurred. According to Thatcher (2001b, p. 9), 'the creation of Oftel was strongly influenced by the example of the Federal Communications Commission' in the USA, and 'in turn, Oftel served as an example for the spate of national telecommunications regulators that were established even in countries with little tradition of such bodies (for instance, Italy)'. Thatcher (2001b, p. 9) notes too the transfer brokerage role of the European Commission 'which brought together national regulators and encouraged cross-national fertilisation of ideas, aiding the spread of the new "model" of independent regulators.' However, it is also clear that the transfer effect was at best 'influence', hardly 'copying'. Across the EU-15, institutional design of the NRAs was adapted to different state traditions, national regulatory cultures and pre-existing regulatory models: in a word, 'domestication'.

'Domestication' is clearly illustrated by the establishment of the German case. In order to underpin the political independence of the new regulatory authority, the Regulierungsbehörde für Telekommunikation und Post (RegTP) was modelled on the Federal Cartel Office, the Bundeskartellamt (interview in the German Economics Ministry, 2001) with independent decision-making chambers covering the various functional areas of the RegTP's operation (network access and interconnection; universal service; licensing; allocation of scarce frequencies). Characteristically for Germany, the chambers' mode of regulation was legalistic. The benefit may have been to increase the neutrality and legitimacy of regulatory decision-making. However, Coen, Héritier and Böllhof (2002, p. 24) suggest that the tendency for business–regulator exchanges to be played out in the courts created cost barriers to new entrants. 'Domestication' was also reflected in the residual influence granted to the Länder in the new regulatory structure (representation on the RegTP's Advisory Council), since in the old order they had enjoyed a significant voice concerning telecommunications policy through their representation on the Bundespost's 'corporatistic' Administrative Council (Verwaltungsrat). The Länder, particularly the more rural ones, were concerned to protect universal service provision. Another continuity with the past was the direct transfer of staff from the former Posts and Telecommunications Ministry and the Federal Office for Posts and Telecommunications, the agency responsible for technical regulation and standards, to the new RegTP with its regulatory headquarters in Bonn and a large technical outpost at Mainz (Werle 1999, p. 114). This was politically expedient, saving a large number of civil service jobs, and it also resulted in Germany having a comparatively large NRA.

To take another example, in France 'domestication' was equally apparent. The Autorité de Régulation des Télécommunications (ART), established by the 1996 reform law, was modelled on the country's pre-existing regulatory authority for broadcasting, the Conseil Supérieur de l'Audiovisuel (CSA) (interview in the European Commission, 2000; interview in the telecommunications branch of the French Industry Ministry, 2001). Rather than opt for the UK model centred on a single expert regulator (the Director-General), the French custom was to prefer collegial bodies of experts. Accordingly, the ART was headed by five members, three of which were government nominees, the others being nominees respectively of the National Assembly (lower house of parliament) and the Senate (upper house).

There was also a characteristically 'French' division of regulatory powers between the PTT Ministry and the new regulatory authority. The regulatory role of the telecommunications branch of the Industry Ministry (DiGITIP) remained very prominent. It was solely responsible for regulatory decision-making (réglementation), that is the issuing of all decrees and rules, as well as the licensing of public networks and public voice telephony services, and also the determination of rules and conditions and cost evaluation pertaining to universal service.[2] Regulatory implementation (régulation) was the ART's specific task. As in the German case, a degree of continuity with the past was assured by the simple transfer of the former staff of the DGT into the ART and the Agence Nationale des Fréquences, separately responsible for spectrum management (interview in the telecommunications branch of the French Industry Ministry, 2001).

The relationship between the sector-specific NRAs and the general competition authorities varied, too. In France, the Conseil de la Concurrence played a relatively strong role in telecommunications regulation, cooperating with the ART and imposing fines on the France Télécom on occasion. Italy's Autorita Garante della Concorrenza e de Mercato was very strong, as indicated by its imposition in May 2001 of a fine totalling approximately 115 billion lire (£37 million) for abusing its dominant position in the local loop market. By contrast, Belgium's Conseil de la Concurrence, was not proactive. In the UK, the 2000 Competition Act provided for stronger powers of intervention, including hefty fines and the power to raid premises, than telecommunications legislation. However, Oftel preferred to rely on its weaker[3] sector-specific authority, since under the Telecommunications Act listed clear objectives that an operator was expected to fulfil in order to maintain its licence and therefore cases were easier to prove. In Germany, competition laws were frequently invoked, but also challenged in the courts. The Dutch competition authority worked very closely with the NRA. In 2003, the competition authority imposed the largest fine ever for a violation of competition law in the Netherlands on mobile operators (*CommunicationsWeek International*, 27.01.2003, p. 6).

Although they were all primarily concerned with regulatory implementation, some NRAs were far more influential than others in the regulatory policy decision-making process. Some attended Council (of Ministers) working groups. Oftel for example, became an increasingly active partner of the ministerial representative in the negotiations (interview in the DTI, 2001).[4] The French ART was allowed to attend Council working groups, but not speak. The German RegTP did not attend them at all (interview in the ART, 2001). This was also the case with the Dutch.[5] Another indicator of the status of the NRA is membership of the EU regulatory committees. If the agenda were 'purely regulatory', as it increasingly became perceived in the UK, DTI practice was to allow Oftel to represent the UK on the ONP and Licensing committees. As a leading DTI official in the telecommunications field explained: 'it is both a waste of tax payers' money and arguably politically unwise for the ministry to baby-sit'. While the ministry clearly retains the ultimate authority over political matters, Oftel takes care of the technical matters, 'provid[ing] 75 per cent of the UK's line'. In the case of France, by contrast, it would be 'inconceivable' for the ministry not to attend a meeting of these committees (interview in the DTI, 2001).

THE INDEPENDENCE OF THE REGULATORY AUTHORITIES

The degree of the NRAs' independence varied. Two related aspects of independence are important, independence from government, and independence from the regulatees. Political independence per se was not an EU stipulation. As suggested above, the central purpose of the EU reform was to establish regulatory capacity that was independent of the industry, allowing judgements to be made according to neutral criteria. However, it is fair to say that as a general rule political independence increases the credibility of regulation (Majone 1997, pp. 152–5). More important, these two aspects of independence could become blurred where the state retained a stake in the incumbent telecommunications operator, as was generally the case in the EU-15. The UK incumbent was exceptional in being wholly private by 1991. Although over the course of the next decade most other EU countries followed suit in privatising their incumbents, the state often retained a significant stake in the 'national champion' companies.

A distinction must also be made between formal autonomy and independence in praxis. The degree of formal political autonomy enjoyed by the NRAs varied considerably across the EU-15. The mode of nomination (and dismissal) of the NRAs was a significant variable. In the majoritarian UK, the regulator was a single person, the Director-General of Telecommunications, who stood at the head of a non-ministerial office called the Office of Telecommunications (Oftel) established under the auspices of the Department of Trade and Industry (DTI). The Director-General was appointed by the Secretary of State for the DTI. In Spain, which could also be seen as relatively 'majoritarian' (Lijphart et al. 1988), the Commission of the Telecommunications Market (CMT) was governed by a council composed of a president, vice-president and seven counsellors, all appointed by the government on the proposal of the Ministry of Development.

By contrast, in Western Europe's more 'consensual' (Lijphart et al. 1988) countries the regulators were more politically representative. In Italy, for example, the Autorità per le Garanzie nella Communicazioni (AGCOM) was a nine–member collegial body with its chair chosen by the prime minister and four members elected from each of the houses of parliament. Similarly, in Germany the regulators were nominated by the federal government on the proposal of an advisory council composed of nine members each from the two houses of parliament (Thatcher 2001b, p. 13). Even in France, with its strong state tradition and its majoritarian semi-presidential executive, only three of the five members of the collegial ART were appointed by the President, the others being appointees of the National Assembly and the Senate.

Formally, the 'majoritarian' UK and Spanish cases therefore appeared to be more in tune with traditional hierarchical structures of control (Jordana and Sancho 2002). However, formal structures could be deceptive. As Thatcher

(2001b, p. 15), has observed, formal controls may have been generally relatively weak, but control could be exercised nonetheless by less formal influence and linkages. The UK regulators were actually rather exceptional in being non-political experts (e.g. Sir Bryan Carsberg, a former academic, or Don Cruickshank, a former businessman). On the Continent the allocation of posts tended to be party political appointments. Thatcher notes that 'in many countries, government officials and regulators [were] in continuous dialogue,...with governments maintaining control and/or well-established relationships between regulatees and governments continuing – for instance between large suppliers such as France Télécom or Telecom Italia and their governments.' However, Thatcher suggests, too, that over time this pattern changed, as the regulatory authorities became more independent and acquired 'expertise, reputations and political weight'. Indeed, in a later study, Thatcher (2002b) found little evidence of party politicisation.

Regulatory structures and performance were certainly influenced by national state traditions and policy styles. In a number of continental countries – including France, Germany and Italy – the regulators' autonomy and scope for discretionary decision making was in praxis more restricted than in the majoritarian UK case. The NRAs varied considerably in terms of their resources, independence and discretionary powers. For example, the UK telecommunications regulatory authority Oftel, in common with other UK sector-specific regulators like Ofgem (energy) and ORR (rail), stood right at the centre of the regulatory process for the sector and 'established a high degree of autonomy, discretion, political independence and transparency in the decision-making process' (Coen and Héritier 2000, p. 30).

In Germany, on the other hand, the RegTP 'found itself restricted by firms, courts, and the Cartel Office, while occasional government interventions have limited its autonomy and discretion' (Coen and Héritier 2000, p. 30). Just weeks before the RegTP became fully operational on 1 January 1998, its vice-president, Volter Schleder, resigned. He was believed by some analysts to have been upset about the close links between the head of the new regulatory authority, Klaus-Dieter Scheurle, and the government. Previously Scheurle had been a member of the supervisory board of T-Mobil, Deutsche Telekom's mobile telephone branch (*Telecom Markets*, 04.12.1997a, p. 3). Coen et al. (2002, p. 24) refer to the RegTP as an 'institutionally constrained quasi-independent regulator', suggesting that it 'was an "open secret" that the BMWi [Economics Ministry] closely monitor[ed] the RegTP and interfere[d] where necessary'. According to their research, 'new entrants [were] especially unhappy with this [alleged] influence, claiming that the ministry influenc[ed] decisions in favour of Deutsche Telekom AG (DTAG), in which the German state still own[ed] 43 per cent of the stakes.' The interest group of new entrants, the VATM, certainly complained that the RegTP was still too weak and politically pressured (interview, VATM, 2001). Against this, the sixth implementation report by the European Commission (2000a) judged the

RegTP to be a comparatively effective and independent regulatory agency. Moreover, a study by Bartle et al. (2002, p. 18) observed, 'the constant legal battles between the regulator and Deutsche Telekom in the first years of liberalisation indicate[d] that the regulator ha[d] resisted a ...bias towards Deutsche Telekom'. The latter researchers concluded that the decision-making chambers *were* 'highly independent, but they [were] constrained by an aspect of regulation endemic in Germany: a high level of legalisation'.

In France, the independence of the ART was quite strictly circumscribed. The shared role of parliament in appointing its membership (see above) might appear to reflect a concern for representativeness and independence, compared to the UK where Oftel's (single) Director-General was a government nominee. Moreover, the fact that the ART members' appointments (for six-year terms) could not be revoked and also that the ART's first president was nearing the end of his career (and therefore more inclined to resist pressure) might point to its independence (interview in the telecommunications branch of the French Industry Ministry, 2001). However, in France the division of responsibilities between the ART and the PTT Minister were less sharply defined than in the UK, while the 1996 laws were more specific and detailed. The UK regulator therefore enjoyed greater discretion in the actual implementation of regulation, including the ability to alter licences, a power denied to the ART (Thatcher 1999, pp. 169–170). The French regulatory agency model could even be characterised as being 'of a primarily technical character ...conditioned by the fact that the ministerial structure retained a strong capacity for regulating the sector' (Jordana and Sancho 2002, p. 28).

Links between certain national regulatory authorities and the domestic incumbent through state ownership was an area of concern identified by the Commission's sixth report on the Europe-wide implementation of its regulatory package released in December 2000 (European Commission 2000a). Belgium was singled out as still having too close a relationship between the regulator and the incumbent, since the minister with responsibility for the state's shareholding in the incumbent operator was also the head of the regulatory authority.[6] In France, too, new entrants had expressed concern that the Industry Ministry was responsible for the state shareholding in the incumbent and for regulatory functions relating in particular to licensing and tariff approval. The Commission noted, too, that the Industry Ministry's powers were delegated to the minister responsible for telecommunications in a way that allowed the latter to exercise his regulatory tasks independently. However, the Commission also concluded by observing generally that 'lack of clarity as to the separation of regulatory functions from the operation of the incumbent, even where independence is in fact guaranteed by the mechanisms put in place, appears to act as a strong market disincentive' (European Commission 2000a, p. 12).

DIVERSE IMPLEMENTATION OF THE 1998 REGULATORY PACKAGE

The diversity of NRAs had 'large implications for the speed of liberalisation in each member state and the degree of competition' (Coen and Doyle 2000, p. 23). As seen, all of the EU-15 adopted the broad 'Oftel-style' independent NRA model of regulation, but the NRAs' organisational design and practices reflected indigenous regulatory policy path dependencies (national state traditions, 'policy styles', institutional isomorphism within countries), and some NRAs were more independent and effective than others. Coen and Doyle (2000, p. 24) note that the Commission has rarely initated investigations into infringements of EU rules, preferring to encourage the NRAs to intervene, and only intervening itself if the NRAs take unreasonably long to do so themselves (approximately 6 months) or if there is a substantial Community interest. Coen and Doyle are scathing about the result: 'the existing regulatory procedures [of the 1998 package] score badly in terms of speed of enforcement and procedural clarity that place unfair pressures on new entrants.' They cite, for instance, the European Commission's fourth implementation report, according to which new entrants complained about the excessive length of time for producing interconnection agreements in Austria, Belgium, France and Germany. In Austria, France, Germany, Greece, Italy and Luxembourg, new entrants complained about the inadequacy of the Reference Interconnection Offer. Even in Sweden and the UK, countries that were generally accepted to have been in the vanguard of liberalisation, substantial interconnection disputes were reported.

'Domestication' resulted in a range of licensing regimes, from light (e.g. Sweden, UK) to relatively onerous (e.g. Belgium, France), reflected in a variety of practices regarding application procedures and timing, level of fees, and the scope of obligations (though the new 2002 framework now mandates an EU-wide light regime – see Chapter 5). Incumbents' market shares, accounting practices, pricing and interconnection tariffs continued to vary. Some countries (e.g. France, Belgium, Italy) placed more emphasis on 'service public' obligations than others. 'Domestication' was very sharply illustrated by the manner in which different countries introduced universal mobile telecommunications service (UMTS) licences. Characteristically, the UK opted for a market-based procedure, an auction, a method that the Thatcher government had already pioneered in 1990 with independent television (ITV) franchises. Equally true to character, the French opted for a 'beauty contest', a typically dirigiste procedure for choosing the licensees.

Just as with national transposition of EU-agreed directives, the 'northern liberaliser' and 'southern laggard' camps dichotomy has some analytical purchase, yet the reality was considerably more nuanced, with some Member States changing their position over time. Thus, the UK's 'model' character became somewhat tarnished by some shortfalls, while Germany moved into the vanguard of liberalisation by some criteria. For analytical purposes, nonetheless, the following study will group countries into *liberal, étatiste,* and *intermediate* regimes.[7]

LIBERAL REGIMES

In 1998 the *liberal* northern European camp could be said to comprise of the UK, Sweden, Finland, Denmark and the Netherlands. These countries' implementation of the 1998 regulatory package resulted in the establishment of strong, independent NRAs, comparatively light licensing procedures and efficient management of regulatory issues, including interconnection. Competition was generally more developed than in the rest of the EU. These countries were all highly receptive to 'Anglo-Saxon' liberalisation norms, while they nonetheless endowed domestic reforms with a national character of their own ('domestication'). Sweden provides a particularly interesting example. It was a 'first mover' like the UK, liberalising ahead of the EU and before it joined in 1995. Competition was progressively introduced in terminal equipment and infrastructure during the 1980s and early 1990s, and a new legal framework of pro-competitive asymmetric regulation was introduced by the 1993 Telecommunications Act. By now Sweden already had one of the most liberalised telecommunications sectors in the world. Like the UK, Sweden therefore had to do comparatively little to transpose most EU rules.

The UK clearly served as a broad model, but Swedish reform nonetheless reflected a characteristic Scandinavian mix of economic liberal and social democratic values. In contrast to the UK, the state was reluctant to relinquish ownership of the incumbent operator,[8] though it did corporatise Televerket into the state-owned Telia AB in 1993. The social democratic government that presided over the process of corporatisation and liberalisation was careful to protect social and regional goals (Karlsson 1998, p. 308). Also, the Swedish approach to UMTS allocation was typically social democratic, the state deciding against a UK-style auction in favour of more public service oriented considerations. Yet, as a result of its early and enthusiastic liberalisation, by 1998 Sweden could boast one of the highest Internet penetration rates in the world, 27 per cent compared to the USA's 29 per cent (cf. the UK's 10 per cent, Germany's 8 per cent and France's 4 per cent) and was leading Europe in Internet venture development (Waesche 2003: 197).

Although Britain has been seen as the leader of this group, and the main liberalisation 'model' for the EU, it should be noted that the Scandinavian countries all had conspicuously light licensing regimes (class licences were the norm, fees if any were low, relatively few conditions), whereas Britain's was actually somewhat less liberal (Roy 2000, p. 16). Also, Oftel was comparatively slow to introduce number portability, which was not achieved for fixed services until May 1996. Don Cruickshank, (then) Oftel Director-

General, admitted that action should have been taken before 1994 to take control of numbering away from the incumbent, BT (*Telecom Markets*, 04.12.1997b, p. 13). However, once introduced, it was done in such a way as to boost competition which was not always the case. In the Netherlands, for instance, small operators complained that the system of number portability adopted there disadvantaged them unfairly by requiring them to instal expensive software to access the system. In the UK model, by contrast, the cost of the call-forwarding system were related to the number of ported customers; if few numbers were ported, the costs were minimal (*Telecom Markets*, 03.06.1999, p. 1).

The UK was also a comparative laggard in implementing the EU's model of carrier preselection (CPS) as prescribed in the EU directive on numbering, agreed by the Council of Ministers in December 1997.[9] The UK was the only one of the 15 Member States that had opposed the Commission's favoured 'equal access' approach of moving towards mandatory CPS for all operators with significant market power, namely 25 per cent or more of the relevant market (*Telecom Markets*, 03.07.97, pp. 1, 11-12). The UK preferred to retain its own 'easy access' system of carrier selection, requiring the dialling of a three-digit number before each call, in order to route a call via a long-distance carrier other than BT; otherwise the call would automatically be routed by BT. The Commission wanted all countries to move to a system of carrier preselection whereby customers would subscribe to a particular carrier, having equal access to the incumbent's network, for a given period. The British position reflected the view of Oftel's (then) Director-General Don Cruickshank that CPS would discourage new operators (e.g. cable operators) from building their own infrastructure. Oftel subsequently came in for criticism for the UK's failure to meet the 1 January 2000 deadline for introducing CPS (*Telecom Markets*, 30.07.1998, p. 2). However, it should be emphasised, the UK position was most definitely not based on a reluctance to liberalise. Rather, the UK government's and Oftel's stance reflected the UK's more competitive market structure, with well-established infrastructure-based competitors, and the UK's policy emphasis on promoting infrastructure competition (*Telecom Markets*, 13.03.1997, p. 13). Moreover, in the event relatively few of the Member States actually met the CPS deadline (*Telecom Markets*, 11.02.2000, pp. 1–2). However, a third area in which the UK was a conspicuous laggard was local loop unbundling (LLU), though, again, it partly reflected the UK's priority to infrastructure competition.

ÉTATISTE REGIMES

In 1998, according to Roy (2000, p. 14) the *étatiste* camp could be said to comprise of France, Belgium, Luxembourg, Portugal and Greece. On the one hand, these countries' regulatory regimes were characterised by a bureaucratic regulatory style and doubts about the independence of the regulators; in particular, ministries continued to exercise a supervisory role over – while the state retained a significant stake in – the incumbent operator. New entrants were burdened with relatively restrictive licensing regimes (with detailed requirements) and in some cases the regulator appeared reticent, tardy or unable to intervene in a pro-competitive manner. On the other hand, the 'model' was characterised by a strong commitment to social and public service goals ('service public'), for which there are strong arguments especially in the context of liberalisation. However, some critics claimed that this was less conducive to competition and potentially favourable to the 'national champion' incumbent operator (Roy 2000).

To take the case of France, licensing was subjected to a burdensome two-stage approval process, first by the NRA, then by the Ministry. Also, new entrants were obliged by their licence conditions to commit 5 per cent of turnover to research and development. A distinctive feature of its legislation was a strong emphasis on 'service public', this being an area where the directives allowed national legislators a fair degree of discretion. One reason put forward to explain this emphasis on public service is the traditional French concern for geographical averaging of charges in a large country with a significant number of remote population pockets, something that would hardly concern the Netherlands for example (interview in the ART, 2001). Clearly, however, the strong interventionist French state tradition is also a very important factor. Measures, such as the provision for other operators to pay a levy into a universal service fund to compensate France Télécom's provision of 'service public',[10] were 'typically French' ('franco-français' - interview in the telecommunications branch of the French Industry Ministry, 2001). However, the fund could also be seen as as a regulatory subsidy to the 'national champion' incumbent and an anti-competitive burden placed on new entrants. In 1999, UK telecommunications minister Michael Wills complained to the Commission about the level of contribution required of new entrants into France's universal service fund (*Telecom Markets*, 06.05.99, pp. 7–8).

However, France's regulatory authority fulfilled its functions increasingly impressively, measured by the steady increase in competition and also the relatively rapid development of new technologies, notably broadband. By contrast, Belgium, a relatively small country which nonetheless constitutes a very important telecommunications market due to its concentration of international businesses and organisations, has been a comparative implementation laggard. Belgium's regulatory provisions confronted new entrants with comparatively high obstacles. Belgacoms's interconnection charges were set far higher than the European average (*Telecom Markets*, 12.03.1998, pp. 5–6). Also, Belgium featured alongside France for the onerous nature of its licensing application procedures and requirements. In Belgium, new entrants even had to submit a 15-year business plan (*Telecom Markets*, 06.05.1999, p. 9). In 2002, Belgium and Luxembourg still lagged behind other Member States in the choice of fixed operators offered to consumers. In Belgium and Greece, the incumbent completely dominated the local call market (European Commission 2002a, pp. 10, 16).

INTERMEDIATE REGIMES

The *intermediate* regimes exhibited a mixture of *liberal* and *étatiste* features, with significant movement from the latter toward the former. In 1998, according to Roy (2000, p. 12) this camp could be said to comprise of Germany, Austria, Ireland, Spain and Italy. Germany provides a good example. Licensing procedures were more complex than in *liberal* countries. Before the RegTP became operational at the beginning of 1998, Germany's pace of progress in actual liberalisation (as distinct from transposition of the directives) came in for some tough criticism. Don Cruickshank, Oftel Director-General between 1993 and 1998, remarked upon Deutsche Telekom's comparatively high interconnection charges, because the incumbent's costs had not been properly analysed, and noted the tendency for decisions to be made by lengthy court proceedings. Reportedly, he observed that Germany was a comparative laggard in Europe (*Telecom Markets*, no. 328, 04.121997c, p. 14). In 1999, UK telecommunications minister Michael Wills complained to the Commission about the unreasonable obstacles to entry encountered by UK telecommunications operators in a number of continental markets, in particular Germany (*Telecom Markets*, 06.05.1999, p. 1). Indeed, German legalism was not conducive to quick remedies. Legal disputes surrounding such matters as the level of licence fees levied on new entrants and interconnection charges for access to Deutsche Telekom's network tended to drag on and on. The implementation of local loop unbundling, mandated by the German Post Ministry in May 1997 (well in advance of the EU Regulation on LLU of December 2000- see Chapter 5) to force through competition in the 'last mile', was delayed by court appeals and hard negotiation between the RegTP, new entrants and DTAG over pricing, which was set relatively high, so that at first it was slow to take off (Waesche 2001, pp. 186-201; interview, Bundeskartellamt, 2001).[11] Thus, until the turn of the century local calls in Germany – and Internet access, which DTAG had hitherto supplied on a metered basis – remained costly in international comparison as DTAG made the most of the last bastion of its former monopoly.

The European Commission's sixth Implementation Report, (European Commission 2000a), looking at the application of the principles contained in the directives, noted a number of remaining concerns in relation to regulatory practice over cost-accounting, licence fees, and the powers of the NRA with regard to interconnection issues. On the other hand, the report confirmed the rapid expansion of German telecommunications services and infrastructure market and the competitive pressure created by new entrants leading to a reduction of prices in nearly all market segments and a sharp reduction of long-distance and international prices, a market in which the DTAG's aggregate share of call minutes was now less than 60 per cent. Germany was second only to the UK in the number of local operators authorised to offer public voice telephony, and 100 per cent of the population now had a choice of operators for local calls even if at the end of 1999 the incumbent's share of the local call market still stood at about 95 per cent (European Commission 2000a Annex 1, pp. 12, 15). Over time, however, it would appear that regulation became increasingly effective. By 2001, Germany – with nearly half a million unbundled local lines, was far in advance of any other Member State, and with a wholesale flat-rate interconnection tariff introduced since 2000 (Roy 2002) - was at last assuming a vanguard position in the liberalisation stakes.

Italy represents an interesting case of movement, too. As seen, Italy was very much a foot-dragger during most of the 1990s. However, as Natalicchi (2001, p. 154) has noted: 'After full liberalisation in 1998, Italian telecommunications policy became increasingly similar to that of its major partners [the UK, France and Germany], and, in some cases, as with privatisation of the PTO, it was actually more radical', at least than France and Germany. Natalicchi (2001, p. 166) points out that Italy's NRA (Agcom), established in 1997, proved to be an active regulator and in the wake of liberalisation market entrants quickly multiplied. With regulatory competence over both telecommunications and broadcasting, Agcom could be seen as promoting the kind of regulatory convergence that the Commission's Information Society DG strongly favoured (see Chapter 6). Moreover, Italy's main PTOs, STET and Telecom Italia, were soon merged into Telecom Italia, which was quickly privatised in October 1997, though the state retained a 'golden share' (a mere 3.46 per cent) for three years. The Commission's fifth implementation report (1999a, Annex 3, p. 12) noted that the 'NRA ha[d] acted independently of the incumbent ...and of the other operators' and it had 'been entrusted with most of the powers in the regulatory domain.' The interconnection and access regime was 'not restrictive' (p. 47). However, Italy still had a distance to go before it could be deemed 'liberal'. In particular, the licensing regime was 'still onerous and heavy' (p. 29). In terms of numbers of operators authorised to offer public telephony it still lagged behind France and Germany, and far behind the UK, though in the number of operators of mobile telephony (4) it was actually ahead of France (3) (Natalicchi 2001, p. 168).

Spain, too, had moved from the 'laggard' camp and was distinctly intermediate on the liberal-étatiste spectrum; Spain could be seen as a 'liberal *étatiste*' country. Its NRA (Comisión del Mercado de las Telecomunicaciones – CMT) commenced operation in 1997. In the same year the incumbent, Telefonica, was fully privatised, though as in Italy a small 'golden share' allowed the government to veto changes in control for a period of 10 years.

The Spanish government also put much effort into building up a communications company from the radio and TV sector, Retevision, capable of competing with Telefonica. In 1999, this company too was fully privatised. Moreover, as noted already, full liberalisation began in December 1998 rather than 2003 as originally envisaged (Jordana et al. 2003).

CONVERGENT TRENDS IN REGULATORY PERFORMANCE BY 2002

Over time the overall trend was convergent. In 2002, the eighth European Commission implementation report deemed that 'after four years of liberalisation of telecommunications services, the regulation put in place at national level [was] very substantially compliant with the EU framework. Licensing and interconnection regimes ha[d] permitted large-scale market entry' (European Commission 2002a, p. 6). Despite the persistence of institutional and procedural differences in regulation between the Member States, there had occurred considerable convergence with regard to the guiding principles and core requirements of the 1998 regulatory framework. Compared to other liberalised public utility sectors (e.g. energy, post, railways) the degree of competition in telecommunications markets was impressive. The telecommunications services market was estimated to be growing at between 5 per cent and 7 per cent in 2002, compared with an estimated EU average GDP growth of 1.0 per cent. Carrier preselection had proven to be a particularly successful means of increasing competition in the fixed market, with twice as many (224) operators using it to provide local calls to residential users as during the previous year and 27 per cent more using it to provide long-distance and international calls. Between 2001–02, there had occurred a marked increase (42 per cent) in the number of infrastucture-based fixed access operators. Prices to consumers were steadily falling. Prices charged by new entrants were significantly lower than those of incumbent operators. The rate of growth in the number of subscribers to mobile services continued to grow, and the mobile penetration rate in some Member States had almost reached saturation level. The market share of incumbent operators continued to fall in long-distance and international calls; however, worryingly, the incumbents' share of the local call market appeared to have stabilised at nearly 90 per cent of the market in terms of retail revenues (European Commission 2002a, pp. 4-5).

The incumbents' continued dominance of the 'local loop' was so worrying that the Commission took the exceptional measure of drawing up an EU Regulation, with direct effect,[12] quickly enacted by the Council and European Parliament in December 2000, mandating the introduction of LLU. Yet, several years later, progress in LLU still remained limited (see Chapter 5).

REGULATORY NETWORKS

One of the factors for the degree of convergence that had occurred was undoubtedly an element of policy transfer of best regulatory practice. In this, regulatory networks were important. As seen in the prosecution of its liberalisation agenda during the 'uploading' stage the Commission had promoted EU-level policy forums – notably the 1992 Telecommunications Services Review – designed to bring the European telecommunications policy community together and to foster consensus. A comparable approach was adopted at the 'downloading stage'. In order to improve the harmonisation of regulatory implementation, the EU regulatory framework established a number of formalised regulatory committees. Thus, the Council established the High Level Regulators Group in 1992 as an official EU-level forum for ministerial representatives. It was complemented by the more specialised and technical ONP and Licensing committees. In part this formal telecommunications comitology was designed to underpin the Member States' ultimate control of regulatory policy *vis-à-vis* the Commission. At the same time, the comitology served as regulatory networks, an 'epistemic community' of regulators committed to professional technocratic problem-solving and the international exchange of 'best practice' with regard to regulatory instruments and procedures. In addition, beyond the realm both of formal EU comitology and also of national ministerial purview, the NRAs formed under their own initiative, with the Commission's blessing, their own Independent Regulators Group (IRG) in 1997. These committees 'served the function of policy learning' (interview in the European Commission, 2000).

With regard to depoliticised technocratic policy learning, the IRG played a particularly important role since it was a forum where information could be exchanged and free discussion could take place, safely removed from the purview of either the Commission or national ministries. If an NRA had a particular question about a particular problem it could circulate it around the other IRG members to see if they could draw on their experience. One or two individuals from each NRA collectively constituted the IRG's 'contact network' (interview in the ART, 2001). Importantly, the IRG produced 'principles of implementation and best practice' (PIBs), each focusing on a specific aspect of policy, for example local loop unbundling or long run incremental cost accounting (Roy 2002). Although they were not legally binding, they were designed to assist in the process of harmonising implementation [of EU law or recommendations] in IRG Member States (the EU-15 plus the EEA and Switzerland). According to their varying resources, expertise and priorities, different regulators took the lead in different matters. Thus, Germany as a 'first mover' was influential in developing LLU, opening up to competition the 'last mile' from the local exchange to the household, which is imperative for promoting the rapid diffusion of broadband Internet access (LLU was made mandatory by a Council and EP Regulation of December 2000).

The UK's Oftel promoted Flat Rate Internet Access Call Origination (FRIACO), namely a wholesale flat-rate interconnection tariff for unmetered Internet access, which was subsequently imitated by others including the Germans (interview in the RegTP, 2001). The IRG – with Oftel playing the lead role within it – was influential in coordinating the thinking of the NRAs on the issues raised by the 1999 Communications Review, examined in the next Chapter (interview, DTI, 2001). Oftel appears to have been influential in developing the IRG's collective response to the Commission's 'New Regulatory Package' (interview in the ART, 2001). The very light Scandinavian licensing regime, and Britain's relatively light licensing regime, appear to have been influential on the New Regulatory Package (Humphreys 2002 p. 73).[13]

In November 1999 the Commission proposed the establishment of two new regulatory committees: namely, the communication committee (COCOM) composed of the Commission and representatives of the Member States; and a High Level Communication Group (HLCG) composed of the NRAs and the Commission, which would replace the High Level Regulators Group (European Commission 1999b). The COCOM would ultimately decide new regulatory measures, while the HLCG would provide its expertise, build consensus among the NRAs, and mediate with sectoral and social interests like the ERT and European consumer groups. This reform, it was hoped, would improve the harmonisation of implementation and regulatory practice. These committees, serving as regulatory networks, would hopefully lead to a gradual convergence of regulatory procedures and improve the exchange of information between Member States. 'By avoiding hard political choices and conflicts, the networks [would] allow for the development of trust and understanding'. In the due course of time, they might 'gradually evolve into more formalised European regulatory bodies' (Coen and Doyle 2000, p. 25). While the proposed COCOM proved uncontroversial, since it would simply streamline existing telecommunications comitology (the ONP Commiteee and the Licensing Committee), the HLCG became the object of suspicion on the part of the Member States, since it was widely seen as an attempt by the Commission to increase its influence over national regulators. The next Chapter explores the actual course that the development of regulatory committees and networks subsequently took.

BENCHMARKING: DG INFORMATION SOCIETY (DG XIII) IMPLEMENTATION REPORTS AND DG COMPETITION (DG IV) INQUIRIES

Another factor for convergence was European Commission benchmarking, which involves the transfer of knowledge about the performance and basic characteristics of policy in other jurisdictions. The European Commission's regulatory unit in DG Information Society (DG XIII) has a special section whose main purpose has been the production of regular implementation reports (ten to date). In addition, DG Competition (DG IV) had conducted its own inquiries into specific competition issues, such as the charges levied on calls between fixed and mobile telephone networks. In 1999, it embarked on its first major review of the entire sector, covering both fixed and mobile sectors.[14] Although the 'naming and shaming' of poor regulatory performers in the Commission's implementation reports tends to be 'subtle' rather than 'harsh', national policy makers still do not like to see their own jurisdiction revealed in an unfavourable light by such exercises, and the reports therefore serve as a spur to reform (interview in the European Commission, 2000).[15] Moreover, the knowledge transferred thereby has resulted on occasion in policy makers' and regulators' drawing lessons about regulatory 'best practice' from other jurisdictions (e.g. interconnection pricing).

Specific benchmarks are typically arrived at on the basis of reports on particular issues (e.g. prices charged for leased lines, or interconnection charges) commissioned by the Commission from consultants (e.g. Eurodata or KPMG), the raw data being collected and provided by the NRAs. The approach to establishing 'best current practice' was pioneered in European Commission Recommendation 98/511/EC on Interconnection Pricing. Accordingly, benchmarks are typically derived from the three lowest retail prices charged in Member States. (This is held to provide a range that accommodates justified differences in costs between them). Although only recommendations, the benchmarks strengthen the resources of new entrants, which can use the figures as the basis of challenges to the prices charged by incumbents. There is evidence, for example relating to prices charged for leased lines, to suggest that the public discussion of such reports in Commission-organised workshops and the establishment of EU benchmarks themselves have contributed to a significant annual decline in prices (*Telecom Markets*, 07.10.1999, pp. 9–10).

COMPETITION AND INFRACTION CASES

Finally, despite its greater reliance on 'soft' coordination and the encouragement of voluntary policy transfer (e.g. through regulatory networks and benchmarking), it is very important to remember that the Commission has occasionally wielded its direct powers of coercion to highly significant effect. New entrants (in both telecommunications and broadcasting) have looked to the European Commission's Competition Directorate and the European Court of Justice as powerful allies (Coen and Héritier 2000, p. 35). In the field of competition policy, these institutions rule with direct effect. Quite simply, they can 'coerce' Member States and other actors. On key occasions, specific competition rulings have been deployed to add momentum to the Commission's broader projects. Repeatedly, DG IV (now called DG Competition) made approval of mergers and alliances conditional on market opening. Most famously, in 1995 EU Competition Commissioner Karel van Miert made clear that he would only approve the Atlas international alliance between DTAG and France Télécom (FT), the focal point for their international strategies, on condition that the French and German governments support early liberalisation of existing alternative telecommunications infrastructures (Bartle 1999, p. 171; Schmidt 1997, p. 17; Schneider and Vedel 1999). This distinctly coercive kind of leverage was employed on a number of further occasions. For instance, in October 1999, DG IV granted conditional approval of the proposed merger between Sweden's Telia and Norway's Telenor – to create a Nordic telecommunications rival to the big players of France, Germany and the UK – after the two incumbents agreed to far-reaching divestments and market-opening measures (*European Voice*, 14.10.99).

On a number of occasions, the Commission's competition authority has taken legal action against Member States for failing to implement particular EU measures to open up markets. EU non-compliance proceedings constitute the worst kind of 'naming and shaming'. As one well placed UK official put it: 'We pride ourselves in not being infracted...and if you are infracted you get the Cabinet Office breathing down your neck...' (interview, DTI, 2001).

It is important, too, to note that pressure has been applied in the shadow of coercion. DG IV could also wield 'softer' instruments at its disposal that were nonetheless capable of being very effective, given that they were deployed under the shadow of coercion. Thus, in 1999 DG IV instigated an inquiry into anti-competitive pricing across the telecommunications sector. In each market segment (leased lines, mobile roaming charges, local loop termination charges, etc.) DG IV aimed to establish and achieve a 'fair price benchmark' charge (*Telecom Markets*, 21.10.1999, pp. 9-10). Competition authority pressure could also be applied through the simple possibility that it might take up complaints brought to it by competitors complaining about an incumbent's abuse of a dominant position. In exactly this way, the Commission pressured Deutsche Telekom to divest its cable network in such a way as to promote competition in the voice telephony market as well as the cable market (*Telecom Markets*, 28.01.1999, p. 4).

The Commission has published guidelines within the 1998 package on the application of EU competition law in the telecommunications sector. These clarify behaviour likely to fall foul of EU competition rules. The Commission has also issued a notice on the application of competition rules to access agreements.

THE COSTS OF REGULATORY 'PLURALISM' AND THE COMMISSION'S DRIVE FOR A NEW PACKAGE

Clearly, the story of the transposition and implementation of the 1998 regulatory package is a mixed bag, from which different interpretations might be drawn. National (historical) institutionalists could certainly find considerable evidence of path dependence and institutional inertia; 'domestication' was plainly rife. The regulatory package accommodated more national regime diversity than allowed by those who have viewed the EU's telecommunications regime as a triumph of 'supranationalism'. Plainly, Europeanisation has not resulted in anything approaching uniformity of regulatory regimes across the Member States. Partly reflecting this pluralism of regulatory regimes and practices, partly reflecting compliance shortfalls, a 'substantial gap between theory and practice' could be detected (Cave 2000, p. 50). On the other hand, structuralists could claim that the degree of convergence – driven by globalisation and technological change, but helped along by Europeanisation – was far more impressive than any residual national institutional diversity, considering the great distance travelled from monopoly to market (Humphreys 2002, p. 74; Thatcher 2004a).

Nonetheless, despite the Commission's formidable competition and regulatory enforcement powers, the lack of a centralised EU-level regulatory authority for telecommunications certainly entailed some costs. Some countries were laggards with regard to a number of liberalisation issues. Others were laggard in only a few specific but nonetheless significant instances, as in the UK's lateness in implementing CPS and also local loop unbundling. Second, there was a 'learning burden'; businesses wanting to operate across Member State borders had to learn about national regulatory differences. Third, licensing regimes varied considerably and were often burdensome, posing particularly serious problems for small companies with relatively few resources. Would-be pan-European operators were compelled to undergo different licence application processes in every EU Member State. Fourth, dispute resolution and enforcement procedures varied considerably. The Commission's seventh implementation report drew attention to the lengthy and cumbersome procedures for enforcement of NRA decisions on incumbents in France, Italy, Austria and Portugal, while in Ireland and Germany enforcement was hampered by low penalties. In Germany, Greece,

Spain, Italy, Ireland, Austria, Finland and Sweden, incumbents appealed systematically against NRA decisions, which – though such appeals were seldom successful – contributed to excessive delay. New entrants were concerned about lengthy appeals procedures in Belgium, Germany, the Netherlands, Austria and Finland (European Commission 2001a, p. 15).

Finally, some countries' application of the 1998 regulatory package allowed for lifting the regulatory burden as markets became more competitive; others were far more bureaucratic and heavy handed. Thus, as network competition increased in the UK, Oftel moved away from detailed licence conditions and reduced the scope for retail price regulation. In France, by contrast, no equivalent framework for regulating competition was developed, 'leaving future entrants very dependent on the detailed decisions of the …ART' (Thatcher 1999, p. 225). The next chapter will now examine the EU policy process, which actually commenced in 1997, towards streamlining the regulatory package in order to take account of increased competition and technological change.

NOTES

1. A number of our interviewees pointed to the existence of these two 'camps'. An interviewee in the UK Department of Trade and Industry (2001) portrayed the UK and France as their respective 'leaders'.

2. All the incumbent's tariffs were approved by DiGITIP in cooperation with the Competition Authority. The regulator, ART, gave the ministry advice only. A 1999 study produced by the new entrants lobby, the Association des Opérateurs de Services de Télécommunications (AOST), which included BT and MCI Worldcom among its members, complained that France Télécom failed to provide adequate price information (*Telecom Markets*, 01.07.1999, pp. 2-4).

3. Not counting its ability to confiscate a licence, a power it is not usually likely to actually deploy.

4. A leading DTI official explained: 'it would be almost impossible for me to tell Oftel not to come…if Oftel were excluded they would kick up a fuss' (interview, DTI, 2001).

5. The same DTI official explained this in terms of an absence of trust on the part of the politicians, since the Dutch regulatory authority was in his view one of the best in Europe (interview, DTI, 2001).

6. The Commission noted in its eighth implementation report (European Commission, 2002a: 18) that this state of affairs would at last be satisfactorily rectified as a result of the adoption of new legislation – transposing the EU's new 2003 regulatory package for electronic communication networks and services (see next chapter). This would confer on the NRA powers currently held by the minister responsible for the state shareholding in the incumbent operator.

7. The following draws on the detailed analysis of the European Commission's Fifth implementation report (European Commission 1999a) conducted by Roy (2000) for the ESRC policy transfer project mentioned in the Acknowledgements.

8. Though, it should be remembered that privatisation of the incumbent was not actually part of the EU regulatory package.

9. CPS allows customers to use an alternative carrier without having to dial a prefix. Without it, alllternative carriers lose revenue every time a customer cannot be bothered to dial their prefix.

10.   To cover the cost to FT of, for example, providing lines to everyone who wants one at the same cost regardless of geographical location, and covering loss-making services such as the 'social tariffs' (reduced rates for certain social categories).

11.   There was a chorus of complaint from new entrants over (German regulator) RegTP's announcement in February 1999 that it was raising the price of access to Deutsche Telekom's local network from DM 20–65 to DM 25–40 per month until March 31 2001. The RegTP rejected competitors' suggestions that the rate should have been set at DM12 per month, arguing that the rate had to be a price low enough to promote competition, but high enough to prevent inefficient operators from easily entering the market (*Telecom Markets*, 17.06.1999, p. 7)

12.   It did not require transposition into national law, as a directive would.

13   In March 1998, close on the heels of an European Commission investigation into the cost of fixed-to-mobile calls, Oftel referred the issue of fixed-to-mobile charges to the UK's Monopolies and Mergers Commission (MMC). Don Cruickshank, then Oftel Director-General, had become frustrated with the 'tedious' negotiations with BT and other cellular operators and is reported to have described BT's fixed-to-mobile charges as a 'rip off'. Oftel's decision looked likely to set a European trend (*Telecom Markets*, 12.03.1998, p. 13).

14.   This competition inquiry was prompted in part by overpricing concerns first raised in a 1997 report by the International Telecommunications Users Group (INTUG) which highlighted the high prices charged by incumbents for international leased lines (*Telecom Markets*, 25.03.1999, pp. 1 and 10)

15.   An interviewee in the UK DTI (2001) observed: 'it is a public naming and shaming exercise and we take it very seriously' .

5. A new EU regulatory package for converging electronic communications networks and services

This chapter explores further the implementation of the EU's liberalising regulatory framework for telecommunications, with particular emphasis on two themes already touched on: namely, digital 'convergence' and the 'regulatory state'. To take convergence first, it has already been explained how the convergence of data-processing, a private activity, and telecommunications, formerly a public one, provided the spur for a paradigmatic transformation of the governance structures of the telecommunications sector. The old PTT model, with the state as owner/service provider, was replaced by a new 'regulatory state' model, with the state relinquishing ownership and instead providing pro-competitive regulation of a free market in telecommunications services. During the 1990s, these two sectors converged with broadcasting too, since digitalisation meant that data, sound and images could all be transmitted over the same networks.

New communication services were not so easily categorised as in the past as 'information', 'telecommunications' or 'broadcasting'. This posed difficult questions for regulatory policy. Moreover, this 'convergence' in the 'electronic communication' sector assumed a more explicitly expressed strategic dimension: the central importance for Europe's economy of having a competitive telecommunications infrastructure and markets in the emerging 'global information society'. The growth of the Internet in the USA transformed perspectives on the importance of telecommunications. During the 1990s, telecommunications liberalisation came to be seen as being absolutely vital for the development of a dynamic European 'information society' (Bauer 2002, p. 110). While detailed policy preferences varied, the common concern – of the Commission, national policy makers, the industry, users – was now that regulatory policy should cater in an appropriately 'technologically neutral' and 'pro-competitive' way to the digital convergence of electronic communications networks and services in the global information society. In particular, effective implementation of telecommunications liberalisation was deemed to be crucial to Europe's uptake of the Internet and its competitiveness in the new (knowledge-based) economy.

The other principal theme of this chapter is that of the 'regulatory state'. The liberalisation of the communications sectors – both telecommunications and broadcasting – during the 1980s and 1990s was accompanied by much rhetoric about 'deregulation'. Neo-liberal political declarations and much journalistic comment may have stressed how, following 'deregulation', the disciplines of the market would replace state intervention. However, as the preceding chapter has already demonstrated, the reality was very much that of 'liberalising re-regulation', characterised in particular by the emergence of distinctly interventionist 'regulatory state' structures. In certain respects, a deregulation did occur: notably with respect to type-approval of terminal equipment ('fewer rules, freer markets'). However, with regard to the most important aspects of the new regulatory framework, interconnection and access, regulatory intervention became more, not less, necessary ('more rules, freer markets') (Levi-Faur 1999). In a sector like telecommunications, competitive markets in networks and services had to be created from scratch. Regulatory intervention was required to ensure effective market entry of new network operators and service providers.

After liberalisation, the former monopoly incumbents continued to enjoy a dominant market position; they needed strict regulation to prevent them abusing this dominance, for instance by setting discriminatory interconnection conditions and charges for their competitors. Yet special sector-specific interventionist pro-competitive regulation for the electronic communications sector was widely regarded as a temporary state of affairs. Once markets became fully competitive, so official discourse anticipated, regulation could be rolled back and fair competition ensured by reliance on generic competition rules. The implication was that the regulatory state would become a 'light touch' rather than a heavily bureaucratic edifice. Of course, the 'regulatory state' was not simply about promoting economic goals like market making and ensuring fair competition, it was also about pursuing social goals, such as safeguarding universal service and the protection of privacy. As will be seen, these issues continued to divide opinion between the 'de-regulators' and the 're-regulators'.

THE 1997 GREEN PAPER ON CONVERGENCE AND THE 1999 COMMUNICATIONS REVIEW

The Commission took the initiative in refocusing regulatory thinking on the issue of the growing convergence of telecommunications, broadcasting and the Internet by publishing in December 1997 a green paper on the regulatory implications of the convergence of the telecommunications, audiovisual and IT sectors (European Commission 1997a). This green paper was highly analogous to the 1987 green paper on telecommunications that had provided the early road map towards what became the 1998 regulatory package (see

Chapter 3), since the 1997 green paper was the prelude to what in due course emerged in 2002 as a new, streamlined regulatory package for all 'electronic communication' networks and services. The 1997 green paper was a typical example of the Commission's employment of consultation to set a radical new agenda and it sparked off an intense Europe-wide debate about the implications of convergence for broadcasting regulation in particular, which will be explored in the next chapter. The convergence debate was further enriched by the Commission's 1999 Communications Review. The latter could be seen as the 'third key review point in the history of EC telecommunications policy'. If the 1987 green paper 'had set forth an initial market integration and liberalisation program' and the 1992 services review 'had completed and accelerated the process', the Commission's 1999 review 'dealt with post-liberalisation issues more than with liberalisation' (Natalicchi 2001, p. 71). The theme of the regulatory implications of convergence for telecommunications featured strongly in the 1999 review, organised by the Commission (DG Information Society and DG Competition) to take stock of the sector following its full liberalisation on 1 January 1998.

The 1999 review concentrated on three main themes. First, it explored the extent to which the 1998 regulatory package was showing success in promoting competitive telecommunications markets. Second, it considered areas in which telecommunication markets might now be becoming competitive enough to merit a lightening of the 'regulatory burden'. Both Bangemann and his successor as European commissioner responsible for the Information Society, Erkki Liikanen, were concerned about the dangers of over-regulation, as well as by the need for liberalisation.[1] Third, as suggested, it considered the regulatory implications of convergence of telecommunications, broadcasting and the Internet. It was clear that convergence called into question existing sector-specific approaches to regulation. The 1999 review culminated with the Commission's publication in November 1999 of proposals for a new regulatory framework for 'electronic communications'. These were presented to Member States for consultation before being tabled as legislative proposals in July 2000 (see p. 99).

As the 1999 Communications Review drew to a close, the new Information Society Commissioner Liikanen (replacing Martin Bangemann) made a number of remarks at an industry gathering, Telecom 99, in Geneva that indicated his frustration with 'red tape' in the licensing of telecommunications services (see previous chapter). He also pointed to the remarkable growth of the Internet and the need for the EU to develop the 'right tools' to regulate the emergence of the Information Society (*Telecom Markets*, 21.10.1999, p. 9). A major concern was the lack of competition in the 'local loop' (the 'last mile to the home') and the impediment that high local call charges presented to Europe's take-up of the Internet. Affordable and fast Internet connections were seen as vital if Europe was to catch up with the USA in Internet use generally and e-commerce specifically. Telecommunications reform was a key part of the economic modernisation agenda of the Lisbon Summit in March 2000, at which heads of government announced a package of measures to make the the the EU 'the most competitive and dynamic knowledge economy in the world'. Further liberalisation of telecommunications was seen as crucial to the accelerated uptake of the Internet and the development of e-commerce. Shortly thereafter the Commission produced a proposal for the urgent enactment of a Council and Parliament Regulation to mandate the Europe-wide LLU.

UNBUNDLING THE LOCAL LOOP

In July 2000, the European Commission (2000b) unveiled a proposed EU regulation to mandate LLU[2], to ensure that alternative carriers gained (physical) access to the incumbent's 'local loop' – the 'last mile to homes and offices' – for the purpose of offering DSL (or ADSL) services. Accordingly, operators would be able to rent access on the incumbent's metallic loop (copper cable) without having to pay for a 'bundle' of services (e.g. payment towards the cost of operation of local exchanges).[3] This regulation would require incumbents by 1 January 2001 to provide other carriers with full or shared access (i.e. access to high frequency capacity only) to their local loop on a fair and non-discriminatory basis, in other words on the same terms of access as enjoyed by the local loop's owner or by the latter's subsidiaries. Article 3 mandated the operators to open their local loop, while Article 4 obliged the NRAs to ensure that unbundled access would be cost-oriented. Having direct effect, the regulation would allow carriers with complaints against incumbents to have direct recourse to legal action in their national courts under EU law. The Commission's choice of a regulation had a major advantage over a directive. It necessitated no transposition by the Member States. A regulation would therefore permit a much quicker adoption process than a directive (*Telecom Markets*, 28.07.2000, pp. 1–2).

The Commission regarded LLU as a matter of critical urgency. In its view, lack of competition in the local loop and the consequent high local call charges presented a major impediment to Europe's take-up of the Internet and, in turn, the development of e-commerce. Opening up the local loop would spur technological innovation and enable Internet service providers (ISPs) to offer business and home users low-cost Internet access and high-speed broadband services. The Commission's sense of urgency about the need for speedy action over this key issue was shared by the Member States and the European Parliament. The main conflict centred on the objections of the German government (supported by its NRA and incumbent). Although Germany had adopted 'full unbundling' in 1998, it now objected vigorously to the Commission's provision for 'shared access' and 'bitstream access', arguing that these additional measures amounted to over-regulation, entailing more bureaucracy and technology- and pricing-related costs (*European Voice*, 13.07.2000).[4] In October 2000, telecommunications ministers approved, and the EP voted through in a single reading, the Commission's recommendation on the regulation, which, ratified in December, came into force on 1 January 2001 (European Parliament and Council 2000a). Last minute reworking of the regulation saw a compromise that some were inclined to see as an indicator of 'regulatory capture' and an invitation to delays on technical grounds (*Telecom Markets*, 27.10.2000, p. 5). The final wording of the regulation specified that '[r]equests shall only be refused on the basis of objective criteria, relating to technical feasibility or the need to maintain network integrity' (Article 3, para. 2). It was left to NRAs to settle disputes over such excuses, and judge their legitimacy.

Unsurprisingly, the European Telecommunications Network Operators Association (ETNO), representing predominantly European incumbents, was unenthusiastic about the LLU regulation, describing the Commission's timetable as unrealistic. Broadly, however, the industry welcomed the Commission's initiative, while expressing some scepticism about how it would work in practice. The European Competitive Telecommunications Association (ECTA), the pan-European trade association for new businesses within the industry, called for the establishment of monitoring arrangements with the possibility of financial penalties (*Telecom Markets*, 28.07.2000, pp. 1–2). ECTA worried that incumbents would look for excuses to delay unbundling in order to protect their historically protected and profitable leased line, integrated services digital network (ISDN) and digital subscriber line (DSL) businesses from competition. ECTA's chairman, Kevin Power, observed that 'failure to meet the deadline would rob the EU's 16 million small and medium-sized businesses of the high speed Internet and electronic commerce links they need to compete....The new economy in Europe [was] under threat from old attitudes.' He looked to the Commission to ensure that '[a]ny delaying or market spoiler tactics by incumbent companies should not be tolerated. These incumbents [and their subsidiaries] should not be allowed to use their dominant market positions to control the products and services being offered to customers, or to dictate the speed and location of service roll-out' (*Financial Times*, 21.06.2000, p. 27).

As the 1 January 2001 deadline approached, a problem had become apparent from those countries – Austria, Denmark, Finland, Germany, the Netherlands, and Sweden – that had already opened the local loop to competition. This was the incumbents' slowness in providing co-location (literally physical 'space') in their exchanges to alternative carriers. Complaints from new entrants led the Commission to press NRAs to closely monitor the space allocation process (*Telecom Markets*, 19.12.2000, p. 5). Another issue became apparent upon the passing of the deadline, namely concern among regulators and new entrants over the pricing structures proposed by the incumbents. In France, for example, the alternative carriers

Cegetel and Tele2 threatened legal action against France Télécom (FT) unless – as was likely – the ART required the incumbent radically to reduce its prices. FT proposed to levy a €162 installation fee and charge operators €17 per month for a fully unbundled line, well over the EU average price of €13.7 per month. Yet another issue was uncertainty over which exchanges were going to be opened and when. In the UK, for example, operators complained over the pace and market value of the exchanges opened up by the incumbent, BT (*Telecom Markets*, 16.01.2001, pp. 3–4).

Within months of the passage of the deadline, the major international Internet service provider AOL Europe was complaining that LLU was a 'massive disappointment'. The Member States, it alleged, were failing to ensure implementation of the regulation (*European Voice*, 01.03.2001a). The EU's seventh report on the Europe-wide implementation of its telecommunications regulatory policy deemed LLU 'very disappointing'. Germany, having mandated unbundling in 1998, stood out with over half a million fully unbundled lines. Denmark and Finland, each with 40,000, came next. Elsewhere, progress had hardly gone beyond the publication of reference unbundling offers. Full unbundling agreements had been concluded in ten Member States, involving more than two hundred operators, but half of these were in Germany (European Commission 2001a, pp. 19–21). By July 2002, there were calls for a more radical measure than regulatory intervention: namely, structural separation. At a public hearing on LLU in Brussels, instigated by Competition Commissioner Mario Monti at the end of the second year of a competition directorate inquiry into LLU, the chief executives of six competitive operators (alternative carriers) from four Member States declared the local loop unbundling regulation to be a failure and urged the Commission to consider more radical measures that might include divesting the incumbents of their fixed line local networks. However, US-style divestiture in Europe remained unlikely.[5] The European Internet Service Provider Association (EuroISPA) called for more incentives for incumbents and regulators. One suggestion, from the secretary-general of the Association of Spanish Internet Service Providers (AEPSI) was to make the incumbent's own provision of ADSL to the retail market conditional on LLU (*CommunicationsWeek International*, 15.07.2002, p. 4). By now, however, the new entrants' lobby ECTA was settling for 'second best', focusing on competition in services. An ECTA policy paper urged regulators not only to pursue full LLU (installation of equipment by alternative carriers in the incumbent's exchanges) but also to ensure that incumbents provided competitors with DSL (and ADSL) wholesale and interconnection products on a cost-oriented basis (*CommunicationsWeek International*, 06.05.2002, p. 3).

UK telecommunications regulator Oftel pioneered another way of improving European take-up of the Internet: by mandating non-discriminatory flat-rate, un-metered Internet access tariffs. In a landmark decision of May 2000 Oftel ruled first that as the incumbent BT had started to offer retail

Internet access services on an unmetered basis, the company should offer the same interconnection terms to competitors allowing them to provide the same service under non-discriminatory conditions (Roy 2002, p. 111). Later, in February 2001 Oftel required BT to provide 'single tandem' flat rate Internet access call origination (ST-FRIACO) at the regional level, in order to make it easier for new entrants to establish FRIACO-based services covering rural and business areas. A number of other European countries soon followed suit (*Telecom Markets*, 31.07.2001, pp. 4–6), providing a classic example of policy transfer. Disappointed with the poor progress on LLU, AOL Europe now pressed the Commission to promote this UK pioneered model of Internet access (*European Voice*, 22.03.2001).

COMMISSION LEGISLATIVE PROPOSALS FOR A STREAMLINED REGULATORY FRAMEWORK FOR ALL ELECTRONIC COMMUNICATIONS

In July, 2000, along with publishing its recommendation for unbundling the local loop, the Commission published its legislative proposals – developed by DG Information Society (ex DG XIII), now under Commissioner Erkki Liikanen – for 'streamlining' the 1998 telecommunications regulatory framework. The proposed new package reduced the number of sector-specific legal measures from 20 to six (seven if the aforementioned Local Loop Unbundling Directive is counted). Essentially the telecommunications regulatory framework was to be extended to all electronic communication networks and associated services, a prime aim being to cater to the digital 'convergence' of the telecommunications, broadcasting and Internet sectors. The new package would provide a 'technology neutral' framework covering all kinds of communication network, including fixed and mobile telecommunications networks, cable TV networks, networks used for terrestrial broadcasting, satellite networks and Internet networks. Another major aim was to allow for the progressive reduction of the 'regulatory burden' of the 1998 package as markets became increasingly competitive and technologically convergent. An urgent concern was to lighten licence/ authorisation conditions. As seen, telecommunications authorisation regimes varied across the EU-15, from onerous (e.g. France, Belgium) to light (e.g. Sweden, Denmark, Finland). Would-be pan-European operators were currently compelled to undergo often exacting licence application processes in every EU Member State. During the consultation exercise that preceded publication of the draft legislation, there had been little expression of dissent. ETNO welcomed 'the Commission's apparent determination to ensure that the current structure of sector-specific regulation does not develop into a self-perpetuating mechanism' (*European Voice*, 14.10.1999). The most controversial issue was the future scope of the European Commission's competence, not simply over broadcasting, but also with regard to its role of supervising and coordinating the telecommunications NRAs.

Table 5.1 Legislation providing for the 2002 Electronic Communications Regulatory Framework

EU liberalisation legislation	EU harmonisation legislation
2000: Regulation on Local Loop Unbundling (Regulation 2887/2000/EC)	2002 European Parliament and Council Access and Interconnection Directive (2002/19/EC
2002: Commission Competition (Liberalisation) Directive (2002/77/EC)	2002 European Parliament and Council Authorisation Directive (2002/21/EC)
	2002: European Parliament and Council Framework Directive (2002/21/EC)
	2002 European Parliament and Council Universal Service and Users' Rights Directive (2002/22/EC)
	2002 European Parliament and Council Data Protection and Privacy Directive (2002/58/EC)

A new competition directive aimed to replace, by a single text, all existing telecommunications liberalisation directives: notably the 1990 Services Directive (90/3888/EEC), and its five subsequent amendments in the form of the Satellite Communications Directive (94/46/EEC), the Cable Directive (95/51/EC), the Mobile Directive (96/2/EC), the Full Competition Directive (96/19/EC) and the Cable Ownership Directive (1999/64/EC). The Directive was to be adopted under Article 86 (ex 90) by the Commission, but – in line with the practice adopted for the 1998 package – its enactment would be accompanied with the enactment by the Council and Parliament of a package of five new regulatory harmonisation directives, which would effectively streamline the regulatory framework. The key aim of reducing the regulatory burden in the 'converging' communications sector was to be accomplished by allowing regulators to apply ex ante regulatory obligations only where competition was not effective and by lightening authorisation conditions. Article 15 (14 in early drafts) of the framework directive set out the procedure the NRAs had to follow when deciding whether to maintain or withdraw obligations on specific telecommunications companies. In accordance with Commission guidelines, the NRAs would have to conduct a market analysis to assess the level of competition. Where competition was deemed to be effective, obligations would have to be removed.

THE DEFINITION OF SIGNIFICANT MARKET POWER

In negotiating the new package, there was some tugging and hauling over the criteria and procedures for identifying significant market power (SMP). The June 1997 Interconnection Directive (97/33/EC) had presumed that an operator, whether fixed or mobile, had SMP if it controlled 25 per cent or more of a particular market. However, generic competition laws had much less restrictive market share thresholds for dominance. The German Cartel Office set the threshold at 33 per cent. In EU competition law 50 per cent could be taken as the usual threshold, though it was recognised that dominance could occur at lower levels depending on the characteristics of the particular market. For competition law, markets therefore had to be carefully analysed, with factors other than market share taken into account (Cini and McGowan 1998, p. 87). The strictness of the 1998 package's sector-specific regulation, with its 25 per cent threshold for the imposition of regulation, reflected the special need to create competition in a network industry with a former monopoly structure. It was central to the concept of ONP that network operators, both old and new, be required to offer cost-oriented interconnection rates and meet all reasonable requests for access to their networks. However, as competition increased, the number of telecommunications providers and as convergence opened up new network possibilities (e.g. Internet), the question presented itself: was the 25 per cent definition of SMP still appropriate? Or should it be aligned with the competition law concept of dominance?

In a consultation paper published in November 1999, Commissioner Liikanen had suggested that only operators with a 50 per cent market share should in future be compelled to offer cost-based interconnection. Those with 25–50 per cent could in future be allowed to negotiate their rates. During the consultation period leading up to publication of the draft legislation in summer of 2000, this mooted regulatory reorientation towards an EU competition law concept of 'dominant position' came in for considerable criticism. International telecommunications users group INTUG complained that it would allow some operators to escape regulation and squeeze rivals out of the market. Moreover, the more flexible approach could lead to Member States and national courts defining dominance in different ways, undermining regulatory harmonisation. New entrants, on the other hand, criticised the draft proposals for not giving national regulators enough discretionary powers to police their markets. Some NRAs, including the UK's Oftel, were worried about the lack of teeth in the new proposals (*European Voice*, 08.06.2000).

While some regulators and Member States favoured aligning telecommunications regulation with a lighter touch competition–based approach, others wanted to retain stricter sector-specific regulatory intervention. This issue cut across the classic 'north/south' cleavage. Germany and the Netherlands were keen to align with competition policy. However, the UK and France were of the strong opinion that there was not enough competition case law or legal precedents in the relatively immature telecommunications sector for competition law to be easily enforceable (*Financial Times*, 06.04.2001, p. 8). The UK was particularly concerned that the Commission's proposals did not cater adequately for 'collective dominance', a highly relevant concern in the mobile telephony market. In the end, a political deal was brokered principally by Monti, the competition commissioner, and the Ministers of the UK (Patricia Hewitt, DTI Secretary) and France (Christian Pierrot, Economics Secretary) (interview, DTI, 2001).[6]

The concept of 'collective dominance' was sufficiently clarified, and a long list of criteria was produced that would help decide whether companies (singly or collectively) dominated a particular market. At the Telecommunications Council of April 2001 the Member States broadly agreed to the Commission's proposal to align the definition of SMP with competition law, replacing the previous strict threshold of 25 per cent market share with a set of guidelines. The Council agreed that an undertaking should henceforth be deemed to have SMP if 'either individually or jointly with others, it enjoys a position of economic strength affording it the power to behave to an appreciable extent independently of competitors, customers and, ultimately, consumers'. Also, a carrier might trigger ex ante regulatory intervention if it was deemed to leverage SMP from one market to another closely related market (*Telecom Markets*, 10.04.2001, p. 7).

CENTRALISATION: WHETHER OR NOT TO STRENGTHEN THE EU'S REGULATORY ROLE?

The issue that generated most heat, however, was about the scope for national regulatory discretion vis-à-vis the centralising authority of the Commission. As seen, the 1998 package had not created a central EU regulator. Instead, its supranational regulatory framework was implemented by national regulatory structures, notably ministries and the new NRAs, operating according to principles and prescriptions specified in directives. However, as seen in the last chapter, these directives had allowed for considerable 'domestication' of

EU-agreed rules. This state of affairs may have brought the advantages of subsidiarity, notably regulation close to the market, but it also led to the problem of national regulators behaving more like 'locals' than 'cosmopolitans', contributing to a 'credibility crisis of community regulation' (Majone 2000). There had been calls, particularly from new entrants, for the establishment of a central EU regulatory authority. First mooted by the 1994 Bangemann report (European Commission 1994a), the idea stimulated a serious policy debate but also strong Member State resistance (Bartle 2001). By the end of the 1990s the Commission had abandoned any idea of a European regulatory authority (Michalis 2004 p. 290).

Nonetheless, during the 1999 Communications Review and the drafting of the new regulatory regulatory package, the Commission produced new proposals that bore clear features of an attempt at 'regulatory clawback' (Coen and Héritier 2000, p. 36). The Commission plainly wanted to gain more influence for itself, in order to ensure greater regulatory harmonisation than had been achieved by the 1998 regulatory package. It now sought to formally institutionalise at the EU level, and bring much more under its influence, the 'transnational regulatory network' (Majone 2000) which it saw emerging in the shape of the Independent Regulators Group (IRG). The Commission now proposed the establishment of two new committees. The first, called the Communications Committee, proved uncontroversial, since it would simply streamline the telecommunications comitology by replacing existing committees, notably the ONP Committee and the Licensing Committee. The second proposed committee, to be called the High Level Communications Group, was controversial since it was plainly intended to be the Commission's 'own coordinating body of national regulators' (Michalis 2004, p. 291). This latter proposal was resisted by Member State governments, jealous to protect subsidiarity. In the end, a compromise solution emerged in the shape of the European Regulators Group (ERG – see later), in which the scope for Commission direction was less clear.

Controversy now came to focus on the issue of the Commission's powers of veto of national regulatory decisions. The Commision's original reform proposals had suggested that it would issue a legally binding 'decision' identifying a 'hit list' of markets where regulation might be needed. If Member States wanted to impose regulations in other areas, they would require its consent. This proposal was strongly challenged by a proposal from France in November 2000, during the French presidency, suggesting that the Commission's decision on relevant markets be replaced by a recommendation which would not be legally binding. The French paper also removed the requirement for NRAs to receive the consent of the Commission before employing their own market definitions (*European Voice*, 23.11.2000). In due course, the Commission accepted that it would adopt a recommendation only on relevant markets, following public consultation and consultation with NRAs (Article 15 of the Framework Directive).

The principal conflict now came to centre on the 'consultation and transparency' procedures in Article 6 of the draft liberalisation directive. This specified that NRAs should inform the Commission and other NRAs about any decision to remove ex ante obligations on a telecommunications undertaking based on an evaluation that the market was competitive and gave the Commission the authority to veto, that is require the amendment or withdrawal of the decision, in the event of disgreement. This article – with the Commission veto at its core – was fiercely contested. Broadly, the NRAs and the Member States wanted to maintain devolved national regulatory powers, while the Commission and the European Parliament wanted to increase supranational authority, in the cause of harmonisation.

The Member States and NRAs were all adamant that there should be no European regulatory agency, and that the Commission's supervision of the NRAs should not become overbearing. Instead, ways should be found to improve the 'regulatory culture between regulators'. The Council position was that the Commission should rely mainly on its 'naming and shaming' (i.e. 'soft') power, but that the NRAs should retain their sphere of discretion (interview, DTI, 2001). Doubtless, motives varied. One reason was functional. Despite liberalisation, at this stage, there were in reality still fifteen national markets, some at very different levels of development. It was argued that a European regulatory authority would not be able to command the detailed information required properly to regulate this diversity. It would be 'like having a European Central Bank without having convergence of economies' (interview, DTI, 2001). Another motive was the Member States' concern to retain regulatory 'sovereignty'.[7] The NRAs saw themselves as best equipped to provide 'near-to-the-market regulation'. Through the IRG they expressed concern about the proposed 'consultation transparency' measure's addition of another layer of approval that would be overly bureaucratic and cumbersome; this, the IRG argued, would impede the growth of competition (*Telecom Markets*, 03.07.2001, p. 1; *European Voice*, 05.07.2001, 29.11.2001).

The European Parliament broadly approved the Commission's legislative proposals in March 2001, but also proposed some amendments. The Parliament was actually in favour of increasing the regulatory autonomy of the individual NRAs (within the Member States); they would be responsible for undertaking the assessments of SMP – the key basis for determining whether continued sector–specific regulation was necessary – in their respective markets. At the same time, aware that NRAs had been criticised for favouring incumbents, the Parliament favoured a fail-safe mechanism whereby individual NRA decisions to intervene in the market would be subjected to the Commission and to the other 14 NRAs for approval as part of a 'transparency and consultation' process (*Telecom Markets*, 27.03.2001, p. 7). However, at a meeting of the Telecommunications Council in April 2001 the Member States, led by Germany, Austria and Spain, voiced their opposition to a Commission veto on national decisions, afraid of the emergence of an EU-wide regulator. The Council proposed that, instead of a veto or power of amendment, the Commission should merely be given two months in which to voice objections to any NRA decisions.

ETNO voiced disappointment at this move by the Member States to weaken the Commission's bid for more authority (*Telecom Markets*, 10.04.2001, p. 7). By and large, telecommunications operators favoured strengthening the Commission's role in limiting the scope for 'arbitrary' national regulation (*European Voice*, 01.02.2001). Liberalisation during the last decade had seen many operators, including the former incumbents, moving out of their home markets to compete in other Member States. They perceived the hand of government interference behind many of the perceived barriers they encountered as new entrants. As an ETNO representative observed, '[i]f the Commission has no final veto or a failsafe check on decisions by national regulators, we may see the development of a very uneven market' (*Financial Times*, 02.02.2001, p. 8). Likewise, the alternative operators body, ECTA, saw a Commission veto as being vital for achieving the EU's goal of being in the 'vanguard of the e-economy'. Lack of regulatory harmonisation discouraged them from doing business across the EU (*European Voice*, 05.07.2001). The industry was united as never before in seeing the Commission as the guarantor of fair market access across the Union (*European Voice*, 29.11.2001). For his part, following the April 2001 Telecommunications Council, and emboldened by the strong support of the European Parliament, Commissioner Liikanen (DG XIII) appeared unwilling to concede the loss of its veto over NRA decisions (*Financial Times*, 06.04.2001, p. 8).

Various compromise solutions were bandied around, including the possibility that the IRG itself might even be officially institutionalised as a joint European regulatory authority, possibly with the Commission exercising a supervisory role within such a body. However, this would transform the IRG's 'voluntary' and relatively 'informal' nature.[8] Moreover, as indicated, the carriers – new entrants and incumbents alike – harboured suspicions about the NRAs' neutrality and favoured a strengthening of the Commission's authority (*Telecom Markets*, 23.10.2001, pp. 1–2). However, the Member States were unanimously and implacably opposed to this. In the Council working groups, national officials tried to 'water down the Commission's role or even eliminate it' (*Financial Times*, 02.02.2001). In the end, though, the dispute was resolved without recourse to a Conciliation Committee of the EP, Council of Ministers and Commission, which would have significantly delayed the legislative process.

In December 2001, the EP and Council of Ministers were able to approve a compromise according to which the Commission would only have the power of veto if there was an EU dimension (*Telecom Markets*, 18.12.2001, p. 5). Accordingly, Article 7 of the final Framework Directive allowed the Commission to veto certain NRA decisions, notably about which operators had SMP in particular markets, and also about markets not identified by the Commission as clearly requiring regulatory review and possible regulation.[9] However, in order to prevent any regulatory bottlenecks the Council had inserted the stipulation that the Commission had only one month to review each notification, before losing its right to veto. Moreover, the Commission would have to justify each exercise of the veto to the NRAs collectively.[10]

UNIVERSAL SERVICE

The new package also saw some debate over universal service. In the event, however, the issue was not as contentious as many expected.[11] The liberalisation of telecommunications during the 1990s plainly had not led to a 'de-regulation' of universal service requirements. In fact, 'the introduction of competition in telecommunications [had] led to the codification of [universal service] regulation', a field of activity that was an ideological pillar of the old system but one that had also been largely ill–defined, at least in Europe where the state telecommunications monopolies had been supposed to have acted 'in the best interests of all citizens' (Michalis 2002, p. 83). The NRAs found themselves responsible for a sensitive regulatory balancing act. The EU's 1998 regulatory framework recognised the importance of ensuring a minimum level of service at an affordable price for all users regardless of their geographical location, but at the same time sought to ensure that universal service provisions were not allowed to distort the market. It therefore defined universal service at the European level to include: the provision of the public fixed telephone network, supporting voice telephony, fax and voice band data transmission via modems (enabling basic Internet access); the provision of fixed public telephone service; the provision of operator assistance and directory services; the provision of public pay phones; and the provision of services under special terms and special facilities for customers with disabilities and special social needs. The 1998 framework also defined the bounds of permissible universal service funding schemes. Provision was made for sharing the cost of universal service amongst market players and, as seen, the French availed themselves of this scope in order to compensate the incumbent France Télécom for its universal service provision. The 1998 framework allowed Member States to extend the definition of universal service at national level, but it also forbade them from funding such provision via contributions from market players (European Commission 1999c, p. 12).

When Information Society Commissioner Liikanen's proposals for the new regulatory framework were debated by EU telecommunications ministers in May 2000, the French, Italian and Spanish telecommunications ministers called for an updating of the concept of 'universal service', to include new broadband services such as ADSL (*European Voice*, 04.05.2000). However, after some debate, broadband was not included in the final 2002 regulatory package, the scope of which remained essentially the same as before. There was one very significant modification. The Universal Services and Users Rights Directive (2002/22/EC) specified that Member States might impose 'must carry' obligations for specified radio and TV broadcasts on undertakings under their jurisdiction which provide communications networks. This particular provision resulted from widespread concern, and indeed a very serious policy debate, about the impact of convergence on public service broadcasting (this will be examined in the next chapter).

The issue of universal service retained the potential to become more controversial in the future. At the end of 2003 both alternative telecommunications carriers and incumbents found themselves in an unusual measure of agreement over the possibility that the European Parliament might recommend that the Commission should develop legislation that would classify telecommunications among 'services of general economic interest' (SGEI). ECTA, the alternative carriers' interest group, and ETNO, the network operators' association, were united in opposition to a proposal that they were agreed would increase the regulatory burden. Incumbents were particularly concerned that such a step might result in the universal service obligation being extended to include mobile telephony and broadband, while alternative carriers feared that it could lead to incumbents benefiting from state aid and being exempted from competition rules for performing functions such as rolling out rural broadband (*Telecom Markets*, 16.12.2003, pp. 4–5).

DATA PRIVACY

Controversy actually delayed the passage of the Data Protection Directive (2002/58/EC) until several months after the rest of the regulatory package had been enacted. This latter directive essentially extended to the 'electronic communication' sector the data protection and privacy provisions that had been incorporated into the 1998 regulatory package for telecommunications (Directive 97/66/EC). In the emerging 'information society', the issue of data protection assumed a new poignancy, yet in the early 1990s there had existed considerable disparity between Member States' provisions. The 'southern' camp – Greece, Italy, Portugal, Spain, and Belgium[12] – had no national law on data protection. In drafting the directive (97/66/EC) on data protection, the Commission had recognised 'that the effective protection of personal data and privacy [was] an essential precondition for social acceptance of the new digital networks and services'. However, issues such as storage of connection data by network operators and automatic call identification led to 'severe conflicts between the operational requirements and commercial interests of the network operator and the data protection norms and privacy concerns of the user'. Such conflicts demonstrated how commercial interests and legal norms 'ha[d] to be balanced by public regulation' (Grande 1994).

At the end of the decade, the issue of data protection and privacy was still a subject of conflict during the negotiation of the new package for electronic communication networks and services. The key issue of how long data (such as customer billing information, Internet usage, and e-mail traffic) should be retained – for combating criminal or terrorist activity – divided the Council of Ministers and the Parliament, the former – under pressure from national law-enforcement agencies and security services – in favour of data retention for an indefinite period, the latter arguing for a defined period of time, that should be applicable across all Member States. The UK even wanted to specify a seven-year period for data retention. The issue served, unusually, to unite all telecommunications carriers (incumbents and alternative operators) because of the cost that data retention imposed on all of them. The telecommunications industry argued that existing European data-protection legislation, which required carriers to store data for only a limited period, was sufficient.

On this issue, the industry had its way, Article 15 of the directive (2002/58/EC) specifying that data might be retained 'for a limited period'. Other issues that caused controversy in the draft directive were what to do about unsolicited e-mail, 'spam', and website cookies (*Telecom Markets*, 07.05.2002, pp. 3–4). Many market players – particularly the direct-marketing industry – had been infuriated by proposals that they would have to seek customers' permission before sending them commercial e-mails (*European Voice*, 14.09.2000). The directive (Article 13) stipulated that users should give their prior consent before commercial electronic communications are addressed to them (the 'opt-in' principle), and that (Article 5) they should have the opportunity to refuse to have a cookie on their terminal equipment, and that they be informed clearly and precisely about its purpose.

THE REGULATORY STATE AND THE 'REGULATORY BURDEN'

The new regulatory package was supposed to lighten the regulatory burden. In certain respects, it clearly achieved this aim. It simplified authorisation and lightened the regulatory burden for most new entrants. Also, the move towards ex post competition rules, based on a higher threshold of SMP, was unsurprisingly generally welcomed by incumbents (*Telecom Markets*, 22.05.2001, p. 3), though not unequivocally. Michael Bartholomew, director of ETNO, the European telecom network operators lobby, observed that the package would actually increase regulation in certain areas, such as mobile telephony (*European Voice*, 06.12.2001).[13] Belgacom chief executive John Goosens pointed to the irony that while no attempt had been made to harmonise at the EU level the costly process of issuing 3G licences,[14] regulatory pressure was now being applied to the day-to-day operations and future profitability of mobile operators (*European Voice*, 05.07.2001).

Incumbents were concerned, too, that the Commission was set on regulating data services like bitstream under wholesale broadband access. Too much, regulation, they argued, would be a disincentive to investment in new infrastructure. Thus, in 2002, the Commission came in for some unprecedentedly heavy lobbying over the issue of regulation of the nascent European broadband market. The incumbents' lobby, ETNO, objected to the Commission's intention to mandate 'bitstream access', interconnection rules for broadband networks, requiring them to offer access to competitors on a regulated cost basis, exactly like other voice and data networks (*Telecom Markets*, 25.02.2003, p. 3). The incumbents argued that full (local loop) unbundling (competitors installing equipment in an incumbent's exchange) and shared access (competitors leasing part of the line on a wholesale basis), were sufficient to create competition in the high-speed Internet access market. The incumbents warned that over-regulation of these new networks and services would deter their investment in 'broadband Europe' (*Communications Week International*, 16.12.2002, p. 12).

By contrast, new entrants and telecommunications users – despite generally welcoming the reduction of red tape brought by the light authorisation regime – were instead concerned that de-regulation might arrive too early. Telecommunications user associations – and the US trade representative – had become impatient at Europe's 'regulatory logjam', over issues such as the cost of leased lines and business mobile calls as well as LLU (*Communications Week International*, 20.05.2002, p. 1). New entrants, too, wanted more regulatory action. According to a 2002 survey by ECTA, the new entrants' Brussels lobby, leased lines in some European countries could cost four times as much as in others. ECTA called upon the Commission to introduce and ensure the implementation (by NRAs) of new benchmarks for cost-orientation (*Communications Week International*, 20.05.2002, p. 14).

However, the interests were not always so clear cut. For instance, disappointing development in Europe of third–generation mobile telephony led operators, already embittered by the costly 3G licence auctions that had occurred in certain Member States, notably the UK and Germany, to place the blame on national regulators for their failure to show flexibility at a time when markets were weak. From Europe the mobile operators wanted deregulation, rather than the threatened imposition on them – under the new regulatory package – of cost orientation for fixed-to-mobile call termination, international roaming and text messaging (*Communications Week International*, 25.11.2002, p. 10).[15] Yet the same operators also wanted more regulatory harmonisation and a larger role for the Commission in order to eliminate the kind of market distortions created by the licence auctions. Thus, they wanted the Commission to have a greater say in spectrum pricing. Spectrum trading would allow consolidation in the market, and it also had the benefit of taking the teeth out of any future licence auctions. The new EU regulatory package did allow for spectrum trading, but at the individual

NRAs' discretion[16] (*CommunicationsWeek International*, 09.09.2002, p. 3). In advance of the European Council meeting in Seville, at which the Commission was due to present its eEurope 2005 action plan, chief executives of Europe's mobile operators lobbied Information Society Commissioner Erkki Liikanen to promote spectrum trading and to help remove other hindrances to the rollout of 3G networks, such as difficulties in obtaining local planning approvals for mast sites (*CommunicationsWeek International*, 03.06.2002, p. 3).

The new framework certainly does not lighten the regulatory burden on the regulators. The new rules make more work for the regulators, who will now have to carry out detailed market reviews across an extended number of markets, and also take into account a more complex range of considerations when determining whether or not a company has SMP. The new package subdivided the sector into far more markets than the 1998 regulatory framework had done.[17] This meant that more detailed information on specific services and infrastructure would be required. Also, reflecting the Commission's long-standing concern about the general lack of transparency regarding cost-accounting, the new package required the NRAs to base their decisions on more detailed cost information. To explore ways of harmonising the many different national models of cost-accounting, the IRG established a working party (*Telecom Markets*, 24.09.2002, p. 3-4).[18]

Another area where the new regulatory package increased the pressure on regulators was dispute resolution, one of the areas that had been identified as an area of remaining fairly general EU-wide concern by the EC's eighth implementation report. In certain countries, deadlines had been exceeded (Netherlands, Austria, Portugal, UK); in two cases, dispute resolution had been particularly lengthy (Finland) or elaborate (France) (EC 2002a, p. 19). Under the new Framework Directive (Article 20), NRAs would from now on have to address disputes within four months.

Moreover, as the representative of the IRG (independent regulators' group) had objected during the negotiation of the new regulatory package, the 'consultation and transparency' requirement in the Framework Directive, requiring NRAs to submit their country-specific decisions to the Commission, added a extra layer of approval that 'would tie up NRA and Commission resources in reviewing "hundreds, perhaps thousands" of decisions a year' (*Telecom Markets*, 03.07.2001, p. 1; *European Voice*, 05.07.2001). It hardly amounted to 'streamlining' regulatory decision making. This new activity would also add to the European Commission's already considerable regulatory load, because the Commission had only a month to review an NRA decision before losing its veto (see above).

At the same time, the Commission's monitoring burden was burgeoning. Since 1997 DG Information Society had produced regular (annual) implementation reports, which had quickly become very comprehensive and detailed, and since 1999 DG Competition had conducted its own investigations, aimed at establishing benchmark prices for different telecommunications markets (*Telecom Markets*, 21.10.1999, pp. 9–10). In the summer of 2002, in addition to concluding the second year of its inquiry into anti-competitive practice in the local loop, the Commission launched new investigations into fixed network ownership, the cost of mobile services and provision of leased lines for business users.

The clearest signal that at least the scope of the 'regulatory state' in telecommunications would expand, not contract, was provided by a European Commission study conducted by the analyst firm Ovum and the law firm Squire, Sanders and Dempsey, the first stage of which was published as *Barriers to Competition in the Supply of Electronic Communications Networks and Services* (Lewin et al. 2003). Looking beyond the new regulatory package, the study's purpose was to identify areas that might require additional regulation by the Commission in the years ahead. LLU and the advent of Voice over Internet Protocol (VoIP) raised possible regulatory issues over such matters as divestiture of the local loop and IP interconnection.[19] Simply, new technologies created new regulatory demands (*Telecom Markets*, 20.05.2003, pp. 4–6). This was reflected in the creation of an EU committee structure to support the new communications package.

NEW REGULATORY COMMITTEES

The new regulatory framework created a number of new committees and working groups in order to help the Commission and facilitate the harmonised implementation of the new regulatory package. These committees partly reflected the new framework's much trumpeted intention to streamline regulation. Accordingly, the ONP Committee and the Licensing Committee, instituted under the 1998 regulatory package, were replaced by a single Communications Committee (Cocom), established by new package's Framework Directive (Article 22). Like its predecessors, it fulfilled advisory and executive functions in support of the Commission's task of implementing the regulatory framework, and it also provided a forum for the exchange of information on markets and regulatory practice. It was composed of Member State officials and chaired by the Commission. It conducted its business according to the Council Comitology Decision. However, the net effect of the changes was actually a proliferation of EU 'regulatory state' committees, in part marking a degree of centralisation by the Commission, in part marking the expanded scope of regulation (see Table 5.2).

The establishment[20] of the ERG – which replaced the High Level Regulators Group of the 1998 package – both increased the independence of the NRAs and subtly increased the Commission's own influence, without extending it voting rights. Composed of the heads of the NRAs and a non-voting representative of the European Commission, with the chair rotating between the NRAs, the ERG's purpose was to help coordinate the NRAs and promote the consistent application of the new framework.

Table 5.2 The committee structures: 1998 and 2002 regulatory frameworks

Formal 1998 package committees	Formal 2002 package committees
ONP Committee	Communications Committee
Licensing Committee	European Regulators Group (NRAs, with European Commission
High Level Regulators Group (mainly ministry representatives).	providing secretariat in Brussels)
	Radio Spectrum Committee
	Radio Spectrum Policy Group
	Working Party on the Protection of Individuals with regard to the Processing of Personal Data (Article 29 working party).
Informal transnational regulatory network	Informal transnational regulatory network
Independent Regulators Group	Independent Regulators Group

As 'an independent body for reflection, debate and advice',[21] serving as a forum for the exchange of information and regulatory ideas, the ERG duplicated the informal IRG, which however continued to exist alongside it. Significantly, the new committee represented the formal EU-institutionalisation of a committee of the NRAs, with the Commission now supplying its secretariat. Unclear how much influence the Commission would wield over the ERG, the NRAs determined to continue to meet as well in the more informal and less bureaucratic IRG for the foreseeable future (*Telecom Markets*, 16.07.2002, pp. 6-8).

Other new committees – and also the ERG – reflected the sheer expansion of the scope of regulation in the 'converged' electronic communications sector. Thus, the ERG differed from the IRG in that it was a committee of regulators concerned with both broadcasting (carriage, not content) and telecommunications, though its membership remained composed overwhelmingly of sector-specific telecoms regulators (the Austrian, Italian and UK 'converged' regulators being the exceptions), this reflecting the limited nature of regulatory convergence in Europe (see Chapter 6). In addition, the new package created the Radio Spectrum Committee (RSC),[22] in order to assist the Commission in ensuring a harmonised approach to the regulation of radio spectrum (licensing, trading, etc.). Like Cocom (see above), the RSC was composed of Member State officials, was chaired by the Commission, and exercised its advisory and regulatory procedures in accordance with the Council Comitology Decision. Alongside it, a Radio Spectrum Policy Group (RSPG) was also set up,[23] to advise the Commission on radio spectrum issues. Its composition was identical to that of the ERG (namely, the heads of the NRAs, a rotating chair, and the Commission providing the secretariat). Article 29 of Directive (95/46/EC)[24] established a Working Party on the Protection of Individuals with regard to the Processing of Personal Data. The function of the 'Article 29 working party' was to serve as an independent EU advisory body on data protection and privacy, providing the Commission with expert opinion from the Member States and promoting the uniform application by the Member States of the principles in the various European directives on data protection and privacy through the cooperation between their data protection supervisory authorities. It was composed of representatives of these national authorities and the Commission. As with the ERG and RSPG, the Commission also supplied the secretariat. Finally, the Commission established an internal task force of its own – comprised of officials from both DG Competition and DG Information Society – to manage the work that it anticipated would be generated by its need to review, under Article 7 of the Framework Directive, NRA decisions about players with SMP and about markets that may differ from those identified by the Commission as requiring review and possible regulation.

MARKET REVIEWS

One of the main provisions of the new regulatory package was the requirement for NRAs to conduct periodic market reviews, major economic analyses of specific product and service markets in the electronic communications sector, in order to establish which fixed or mobile players (if any) had dominance and therefore needed to be subject to regulation under the provisions of the new package's Access (interconnection) and Universal Service Directives. Under the new regulatory framework the NRAs retained discretion to define markets appropriate to national circumstances but – as seen – the consultation and transparency procedures contained in Article 7 of the Framework Directive provided an important check, including the possibility of a Commission veto of key NRA decisions. It was crucial, for smooth and consistent implementation, that the Commission provide detailed guidance to the NRAs.

Already, in 2002 the Commission had produced a set of guidelines for the NRAs setting out the principles for the conduct of market analysis and assessment of significant market power. The guidelines were adopted after consultation with the NRAs and a public (industry, consumers, etc.) consultation exercise. They specifically addressed the criteria and methodology for the definition of markets and the assessment and designation of SMP, and procedural issues relating to these subjects (European Commission 2002b). Later, in February 2003 the Commission published its Relevant Markets Recommendation (European Commission 2003a), listing 18 qualifying specific markets that it considered to be insufficiently competitive. DG Competition, headed by Mario Monti, had applied pressure on DG Information Society to limit the list to between eight and ten markets, in order to achieve a lighter regulatory approach. A first draft, published in July 2002, provided for 12 markets (*Telecom Markets*, 02.07.2002, pp. 6–7). However, DG Information Society was worried that this approach carried the risk that Member States might identify a range of 'submarkets' to suit their particular country preferences, decisions about which the Commission might not have been able to veto since its powers of veto formally only extended to the definition by the NRAs of 'new' markets. This would plainly undermine the regulatory harmonisation that the Commission was seeking from the new package. Therefore, in the end the Commission agreed on a 'long list' of 18 markets, which pinned down the NRAs more tightly (*Telecom Markets*, 25.02.2003, pp. 1–3).

Accordingly, the final Commission list identified seven rather than three retail[25] markets as being 'susceptible to ex ante regulation'. The original market for access to the public telephone network at a fixed location was divided into separate markets for (1) residential and (2) non-residential customers. The market for publicly available telephone services provided at a fixed location was divided into four separate markets: namely, (3) publicly available local and/or national services provided at a fixed location for residential customers; (4) publicly available international services provided at a fixed location for residential customers; (5) publicly available local and/or national services provided at a fixed location for non-residential customers; and (6) publicly available international services provided at a fixed location for non-residential customers. The last element of the retail market remained, as before, the leased line market (7).[26]

The Recommendation identified the following wholesale[27] markets as 'susceptible to ex ante regulation': (8) call origination on the public telephone network provided at a fixed location; (9) call termination on individual public telephone networks provided at a fixed location; (10) transit services in the fixed public telephone network; (11) wholesale unbundled access (including shared access) to metallic loops and sub-loops for the purpose of providing broadband and voice services; (12) wholesale broadband access (covering 'bitstream' access); (13) wholesale local dedicated capacity on leased lines was divided into wholesale terminating segments of leased lines and (14) wholesale trunk segments of leased lines, in recognition that competition varied in different parts of the leased lines in different countries; (15) access and call origination on public mobile telephone networks; (16) voice call termination on individual mobile networks;[28] (17) the wholesale national market for international roaming on public mobile networks; and (18) broadcasting transmission services, to deliver broadcast content to end-users (*Telecom Markets*, 25.02.2003, p. 2; European Commission 2003a, pp. 48–9). In July 2003, the Commission published a Recommendation on notifications, time-limits and consultations (European Commission 2003b), which spelled out in detail Article 7 requirements, rules and procedural arrangements. This document included an outline 'summary notification form', specifying the information – on market definition, designation of undertakings with significant market power, and regulatory obligations – that the NRA had to provide to the Commission when notifying draft Article 7 measures (European Commission 2002b).

REMEDIES

An area that obviously presented scope for excessive 'domestication' was the question of remedies. What penalties should NRAs be able to impose for competition shortfalls? The Commission, naturally in favour of harmonisation, had had to concede its demand for a veto on NRA decisions over remedies during the negotiation of the new regulatory package. The Commission nonetheless determined to produce a set of guidelines by the autumn of 2003, by which time the new package should have been transposed in all Member States, to ensure that the deployment of remedies by the Member State's NRAs would be at least broadly harmonised, overcoming the inconsistency that currently characterised regulatory practice by the EI-15.[29]

The newly established ERG, for which the Commission served as the secretariat, assumed the task of consulting across the industry, including network operators (ETNO), competitive operators (ECTA), and telecommunications users (INTUG). Meanwhile, the IRG – without Commission involvement – worked on its own remedies guidelines, four working groups covering particular areas (fixed, mobile, end-user and implementation). Several differing interests had to be reconciled. Operators sought harmonised regulation for all the markets in which they were operative. NRAs, on the other hand, wanted discretion, free from Commission intervention, to impose the remedies that they judged were appropriate for their particular jurisdictions. The result was bound to be a compromise. Accordingly, the Commission proceeded consensually, drafting the guidelines together with both the ERG and the IRG. Characteristically, though, the Commission declined to rule out the possibility that it would issue its own guidelines (*Telecom Markets*, 15.07.2003, pp. 4–5). Thus, with characteristic subtlety, the Commission still sought to centrally steer the process.

TRANSPOSITION AND IMPLEMENTATION OF THE NEW REGULATORY PACKAGE

Several months after the summer 2003 deadline for the transposition by the Member States of the new regulatory framework for electronic communications, eight Member States had yet to notify the European Commission of their transposition measures. In October 2003, the Commission therefore resorted to opening infringement proceedings against them. Spain promptly notified the Commission of its implementation of the directives. However, the Commission felt compelled to proceed further against the remaining seven Member States, these being Belgium, Germany, Greece, France, Luxembourg, the Netherlands and Portugal.[30] In April 2004, the Commission duly took all these Member States except Portugal, which had in the meantime also largely complied,[31] to the European Court of Justice for failure to implement the new electronic communications package.

The Commission's ninth implementation report, published in November 2003, was the first to look at how Member States were implementing the new package (European Commission 2003c). Unlike earlier reports, it did not name particular Member States, so as not to prejudice any current and future infringement proceedings. However, it did enumerate a host of problems with legislation, both enacted and in draft form. In some countries, effective regulation was imperilled by the dispersion of the powers that should have been accorded to the NRAs among different national bodies, including the government.

The report's failure to identify particular countries' shortfalls could be seen as a major weakness, in that it effectively failed to perform the 'naming and shaming' function of preceding reports. The lack of country profiles detailing Member State efforts to improve competition in specific markets was in the view of ECTA, the body representing alternative operators, a worrying omission: it appeared, for a time at least, that normal regulatory affairs had been suspended (*Telecom Markets*, 04.11.2003, p. 5).

At the end of 2004, the Commission published its tenth implementation report (European Commission 2004a). This time, perhaps in response to the criticism of the ninth report, the Commission provided a detailed country by country review of regulatory implementation in a working document (European Commission 2004b) that was annexed to the tenth report. The report itself provided a broad summary analysis of market data that was provided in greater detail in the attached working document. This time, the report covered 25 Member States, reflecting the fact that 10 countries had formally joined the EU in May 2004. The report was presented by Viviane

Reding, the Commissioner who had recently assumed responsibility for Information Society and Media, following the transfer of responsibility for audiovisual and media policies from DG Education and Culture, a development that clearly reflected the Commission's approach to the convergence of electronic communications (see Chapter 6).

The tenth implementation report noted that the Electronic Communications Regulatory Framework had by now been largely tranposed in most Member States. Only Belgium, Czech Republic, Estonia, Greece and Luxembourg had not yet adopted primary legislation to transpose the framework. Accordingly, European Court of Justice proceedings against the three west European cases remained pending. However, secondary legislation had yet to be adopted in eight Member States; Spain, France, Cyprus, Latvia, Lithuania, Poland, Slovenia and Slovakia (European Commission 2004a, p. 9).

The tenth implementation report indicated that '[t]he e-communications services sector [was] characterised by an increasingly positive outlook. Competition [was] intensifying in most markets'. While overall growth had 'stabilised', it would 'outpace GDP expansion for the EU 25. The key drivers [were] fixed data and mobile services' (European Commission 2004a, pp. 2–3). Mobile phones were now used by 83 per cent of European citizens and third-generation (3G) phones had been launched in most Member States. A significant increase in competition in mobile telephony was illustrated, for instance, by the fact that 'the average market share of leading operators ha[d] dropped from 46.6% [in 2003] to 43.2% [in 2004], a fall greater that that seen in the [previous] three years combined'. Moreover, 'there ha[d] been a welcome reduction in mobile termination rates in many EU countries'. However, 'concern persist[ed] as to the high level of international roaming charges', a field which the Commission was investigating (European Commission 2004a, p. 4). The report observed that 'broadband penetration had increased dramatically', to almost 30 million. The report noted that '[t]he new entrants share of the broadband market [had] continued to rise and [was] now at 43.7%', though 'competition in broadband access [was] still weak in certain countries'. The Commission resolved 'to monitor its development and intervene where appropriate' (European Commission 2004a, p. 5). The report noted positively that there had occurred 'an increase of 110% in unbundled local loops (fully unbundled and shared lines) from 1.8 m in July 2003 to more than 3.8 m in the EU 15 in July 2004'. This was in part due to 'decisive regulatory action' (European Commission 2004a, p. 6). As for the fixed sector, the incumbents' market share had continued to decline, though 'in some Member States the incumbent's share of the local call segment in particular remain[ed] high'. The Commission remarked that there was a 'strong correlation between the timing of liberalisation and incumbent market share', which was unsurprisingly 'particularly evident for the new Member States' (European Commission 2004a, pp. 7–8).

The report highlighted a number of areas where there was room for improvement of regulatory implemenation. The Commission still had 'substantial concerns' about the degree of regulatory independence and impartiality in certain Member States. Another area of 'major concern' was the length of appeals procedures against NRA decisions in some Member States. The Commission noted too that the need to conduct market reviews under the new regulatory package, in addition to the NRAs' routine work on market supervision, dispute settlement and enforcement, had in some cases 'caused severe resource problems'. The Commission intended to examine several cases where the charges for administrative costs of the authorisation of services appeared 'relatively high'. The Commission noted 'persistent problems that ha[d] arisen across the Union' over the granting of rights to install mobile telephony masts, which was in some cases delaying the rollout of 3G infrastructure. The Commission was also concerned about possible abuses of the universal service and must-carrry provisions. In some cases, the Commission was examining concerns about cost accounting and tariff transparency. Also, the ten new Member States were 'replicating' problems experienced under the 1998 package in the EU-15, notably to do with interconnection charges and carrier selection/pre-selection and number portability (European Commission 2004a, pp. 10–13).

As suggested above, the tenth report marked a return to the policy of 'naming and shaming'. Thus the Commission noted continuing concerns, for example, about the extent of the ability of the Belgian government to interfere with NRA decisions and also about whether the NRA commanded sufficient resources, particularly in view of the need under the new framework to conduct market analyses (European Commission 2004b, p. 76). In the case of France, the Commission noted that, despite regulatory achievements such as the speedy development of broadband competition, 'there continue[d] to be a perception of a lack of regulatory independence'. In the French political climate surrounding discussions on the new regulatory framework, it was 'hard to reassure market players that regulatory decisions [were] taken in an atmosphere that is conducive to independence and objectivity' (European Commission 2004b, p. 121). Doubts stubbornly persisted, too, about regulatory independence in Germany. The pan-European trade association for new businesses within the industry, ECTA, had been concerned that German legislation would allow the potential for government influence over key decisions that should under the new package be the preserve of the NRA. Under the 1998 package, regulatory decisions were made by a number of ruling chambers within the RegTP, staffed by career civil servants. Under the new law, the key decisions – over market definition, SMP, and remedies – would be made by a so-called President's Chamber, comprising the RegTP's senior management, which was appointed by the government (*Telecom Markets*, 03.06.2003, pp. 1–4). The Commission (2004b, p. 96) observed that 'the fact that the members of the Presidential Chamber depend on political appointment and that they have annulable public service contracts...could give rise to concern', and promised to 'continue to scrutinize this issue'.

Clearly, in the case of those countries that had only belatedly or not yet even transposed the new regulatory package, the problems were potentially serious. Thus, the Commission noted that 'positive developments in regard to competition in France over the past year, especially with regard to broadband, ha[d] been overshadowed by the fact that France was very late in adopting the laws required to transpose the new regulatory framework'. There was still a need for secondary legislation 'before the new framework [could] begin to be properly implemented'. At least, France seemed to be making 'considerable efforts' on this front, with the relevant decrees that would allow market analysis to proceed in imminent prospect (European Commission 2004b, p. 120). In the case of Greece, however, the situation seemed more worrying because of the failure yet to transpose the new package. The Greek NRA's 'ability ...to intervene in monitoring and regulating the markets ha[d] been restricted because of the lack of transposition', notably there had been delays in conducting market analysis and in applying relevant remedies (European Commission 2004b, p. 108).

CONCLUSION: A RECIPE FOR REGULATORY CREATIVITY OR FOR REGULATORY FRAGMENTATION?

The detailed country reviews in the tenth implementation report confirmed that the transposition and implementation of the new package, just like the 1998 package examined in Chapter 4, carried the possibility of significant – and possibly excessive – 'domestication'. Indeed, Michalis (2004, p. 286) has observed that 'the new EC regulatory framework ...[i]s likely to result in renewed diversity at the national level. The greater flexibility of the European regulatory framework will allow national governments to pursue their own policy objectives but with adverse implications for policy convergence.'

The UK soon provided an example of the exercise of NRA discretion under the new regulatory package. The regulator Oftel, very quick off the mark to conduct its market reviews, identified two markets of its own – wholesale international services and Internet termination – which were not included on the European Commission's list of 18 qualifying markets (see above). This prompted the EU affairs manager of the alternative carriers' body, ECTA, to observe that this could serve as a precedent, tempting other countries to do the same (*Telecom Markets*, 08.04.2003, p. 7). There was an obvious risk that Oftel's actions might encourage an unwelcome degree of regulatory fragmentation and proliferation of new layers of regulation across Europe. However, one of the new markets – for wholesale international services – was clearly of particular importance to the UK, as a major hub for international telecommunications traffic. Oftel was naturally reluctant to see regulation (on SMP operators BT and Cable and Wireless) lifted, though the amount of traffic regulated might be reduced under the new package and market definition (*Telecom Markets*, 25.03.2003, p. 1–2).

In fact, the UK appeared yet again to be providing a regulatory policy model. The Commission's review of the UK in its annex to the tenth implementation report (European Commission 2000b) was largely complimentary. The UK had been very quick to transpose the requirements of the Electronic Communications Regulatory Framework (primarily through the Communications Act 2003). The 'converged' new regulator of telecommunications and broadcasting, Ofcom, was in some respects the very embodiment of the Information Society DG's own thinking about the regulatory implications of 'convergence' (see Chapter 6). Furthermore, it had already conducted the majority of the required market analyses. The Commission was full in its praise, noting that '[w]hether seen from a European or a domestic perspective, the overall perception by market players of regulatory developments over the reference period has been very positive'. Although the number of unbundled lines was still very low in the UK, most market indicators were positive and Ofcom was deemed to 'have shown imagination and creativity in its approach to persistent regulatory problems' (European Commission 2004b, pp. 222–3).

In the future, much would depend on the ability of the new regulatory structures – and in particular the new package's regulatory committees, together with the continuing IRG – to transfer best practice across the enlarged EU. Also much would hinge on the Commission's ability to encourage harmonisation in the challenging context of the EU's more diverse membership. The successful negotiation of the new package – and in particular the compromise over the Commission's veto over NRA decisions – did not mean that the source of tension between Commission and Member States (and NRAs) would evaporate. The compromise itself produced scope for future disagreement. The Commission may have successfully obtained a potential veto over NRAs' decisions regarding SMP and market definitions, but not over other important regulatory decisions, such as remedies.

NOTES

1.   This sub-text had pervaded Bangemann's famous 1993 report advocating extensive liberalisation.
2.   The Commission also published its proposals for a new regulatory framework based on five new directives.
3.   This might involve full unbundling, where the competitor rents complete access to the copper line, or shared access, where the competitor rents high frequency capacity on the line for the provision of high-speed (ADSL or DSL) services, while the network owner continues to provide telephone services. A third possibility was 'bitstream access' which

gives rivals access to customers through interconnection with the incumbent's broadband services.

4. Line sharing was seen by ISPs like AOL as an important alternative to full unbundling because customers were often reluctant to switch from their traditional operator for telephone services.

5. Structural separation of BT's network from supply of telecommunications services was advocated by Lord Currie, the new chairman of Ofcom, the successor regulatory authority to Oftel for the entire 'converged' electronic communications sector.

6. The interviewee suggested that the UK and France were 'leaders' of the northern and southern camps of Member States. Their agreement therefore provided the basis for much telecommunications regulation.

7. Even if, as our DTI interviewee suggested, the comparatively liberal UK had more to gain from national 'regulators being brought into line than …to fear from Oftel or Ofcom being slapped into place' (interview, DTI, 2001).

8. In the event, a committee along these lines did emerge – as will be seen – though the IRG continued to exist in parallel.

9. Though not NRA decisions about remedies for competition shortfalls. The NRAs had to notify the Commission about the regulatory obligations they planned to impose on SMP operators, but here the Commission had no power of veto.

10. NRA decisions had to be notified to other NRAs as well as the Commission. Other NRAs were therefore able to respond directly to the NRA in question and/or to express any concerns to the Commission.

11. 'It hasn't turned out into the political battlefield that we thought it might be' (interview, DTI, 2001).

12. Belgium, though not geographically southern, counts as 'southern' for our purposes; it was certainly a liberalisation laggard.

13. This was because of the implications of joint (or 'collective') dominance. The new package specified fixed to mobile termination and international roaming as areas susceptible to ex ante regulation.

14. Leading European telecommunications companies had paid around €150 billion, in total, for operating licences. Costs were inflated by hugely expensive auctions, notably in Germany and the UK.

15. Some countries, such as Germany, did not have fixed-to-mobile regulation. Roaming had generally avoided regulation so far (*CommunicationsWeek International*, 20.05.2002, p. 6).

16. The new package created the basis for better coordination of spectrum policy (establishing the Radio Spectrum Policy Group and the Radio Spectrum Committee) but essentially left spectrum policy as a Member State jurisdiction

17. The 1998 regulatory framework only identified four (terminal equipment, advanced services, leased lines, voice telephony).

18. Accordingly, some, smaller NRAs, such as the Irish and the Greek ones, appeared to be considering commissioning market analyses from external consultants (*Telecom Markets*, 10.09.2002, p. 1).

19. European ISPs were already testing IP-based voice services that might in future be offered over broadband at a fraction of the price of traditional PSTN-based voice calls. VoIP therefore presented a tremendous challenge to the incumbents' continued dominance of the residential voice market.

20. Decision 2002/627/EC.

21. Its web-site announces its mission as follows: 'The ERG is an independent body for reflection, debate and advice in the electronic communications regulatory field. Composed of the heads of the relevant national authorities, it acts as an interface between them and the European Commission in order to advise and assist the Commission in consolidating the internal market for electronic communications networks and services.' Read at http://www.erg.eu.int/about/index_en.htm on 18.07.2004.

22. Commission Decision 676/2002/EC.

23. Commission Decision 2002/622/EC.
24. Its tasks were laid down in Article 30 of Directive 95/46/EC, in Article 14 of Directive 97/66/EC and in Article 15(3) of Directive 2002/58/EC.
25. The Recommendation defined retail markets as 'markets for services or products provided to end-users'.
26. That is, leased lines up to and including 2Mbit/sec. Above this, the Commission deemed the market to be competitive.
27. The Recommendation defined wholesale markets as 'markets for the inputs which are necessary for operators to provide services and products to end users.'
28. The Commission specifically mentioned voice to make clear that it would not regulate mobile data.
29. To take mobile termination rates as a good example, the UK regulator Oftel had imposed heavy fines on operators, while the German regulator, RegTP, chose not to regulate the market (*Telecom Markets*, 03.06.2003).
30 European Commission press release IP/03/1750, at http://europa.eu.int/rapid/start/cgi/guesten.ksh?p_action.gettxt=gt&doc=IP/03/1750.
31. Though the Commission continued proceedings against Portugal's failure to implement the privacy and electronic communications directive by the 2003 deadline.

6. Regulation of communications content and the EU's Electronic Communications Regulatory Framework

The 2002 Electronic Communications Regulatory Framework (ECRF) became operational in July 2003. As the previous chapter has illustrated, the ECRF is a system which covers, in a 'technologically neutral' manner, the regulation of all 'converging' communications infrastructures and associated services, including fixed and mobile telecommunications networks, cable television networks, networks for terrestrial broadcasting, satellite networks and Internet networks. However, it does not apply to communications content. It is primarily, therefore, a modification (through streamlining) and further development (through the creation of new regulations on market structure and power) of the EU telecommunications regulatory framework whose developmental course has been charted throughout this volume. The chapter complements Chapter 5 by focusing on the EU's consideration of convergence in information and communications technologies (ICT) in the late 1990s. In particular, it examines the key issues and considers the policy–making processes which resulted in the restriction of the ECRF's scope to infrastructural matters ('carriage' as distinct from 'content'), amounting to a rather more modest movement towards convergent governance of the communications sector than some, including the Commission's Information Society Directorate General (DG XIII), had originally envisaged. It begins with an examination of the detailed politics surrounding the European Commission's 1997 green paper on convergence, as well as the process which resulted in the eventual agreement of the ECRF. The remainder of the chapter considers why this outcome has occurred and explores some of its implications.

First, regarding broadcasting content, the chapter highlights the significance of the long established 'gravitational pull' of the national policy context which has ensured that the EU's efforts to develop initiatives, and to regulate, in broadcasting policy have been often controversial and limited in scope (primarily to creation of a single market), the convergence debate serving as yet another example. Second, despite the limited terms of reference of the ECRF to infrastructural issues, by focusing on what have come to be known as 'digital gateways', the chapter illustrates how, in converging communications service environments, it is difficult to differentiate fully between carriage (infrastructural) and content issues, which is likely to present broadcasting and other communications policy makers across the EU with challenges in the future. Third, the chapter turns its attention to content issues related to the development of the Internet. Here in contrast to broadcasting, with its national 'gravitational pull', the chapter argues that EU Member States excluded so-called Information Society services (most notably those associated with Internet commerce) from the ECRF due to the global 'gravitational pull' of this relatively new part of the communications sector. Here, uncertainties about how to create a suitable pattern of governance arrangements for this part of the communications sector, which has been imbued with global characteristics since its popularisation, led the EU to eschew including it in the ECRF, for the time being at least.

THE ORIGINS OF ICT CONVERGENCE

Until recently, broadcasting, IT and telecommunications were largely separate sectors with their own highly specific characteristics in terms of technology, commerce and regulation. However, over the course of the last 30–40 years each of these sectors has undergone considerable transformation, a prominent feature of which is that they have come closer together in number of ways. So significant has this process been, that it is now commonplace to speak of a new hybrid sector: information and communications technologies (ICT). ICT convergence has been defined as a process, involving the coming together of information distribution infrastructures; interactive information storage and processing capabilities; and widespread availability of consumer electronics products, publishing and IT content (KPMG 1996, p. 87). Evidence suggests that such convergence is occurring in technological, commercial and regulatory contexts, and that it is a complex process which is unevenly distributed across countries and regions.

The first seeds of ICT convergence were technological developments that opened up opportunities for commercial players involved in the broadcasting, IT and telecommunications in particular, to create new markets offering customers a plethora of new services. It was envisaged that, ultimately, these services would embody various combinations of voice, data, text and video selected and paid for by electronic means in a high speed, sophisticated, interactive environment. One of the first practical examples was the coming together of certain technical elements of IT and telecommunications, which manifested itself in the digitalisation of telecommunications switching and the application of IT to telecommunications terminal equipment allowing the conversion of voice, data, text and pictures into a form which allowed high quality storage, manipulation and transmission of the data to occur. As noted in Chapter 2, techno-economic convergence provided an opportunity for companies from both sides of the telecommunications/IT fence to capitalise on the creation of new products (e.g. digital switches) and services (VANS). Another development which facilitated early convergence in the 1980s, due to its large bandwidth, was fibre–optic technology, massively increasing the channel capacity of cable TV systems beyond that of copper coaxial cable and introducing the possibility of 'interactivity'. The arrival of digital TV in the 1990s accelerated IT/telecommunications/broadcasting convergence. Players from each industry saw opportunity to diversify into each other's markets.

The new service possibilities brought by convergent ICTs raised considerable expectations of a 'brave new world' of electronic communications, promising the availability of a panoramic array of sophisticated, interactive and affordable services for all. Terms such as 'multimedia', 'Integrated Broadband Communications', the 'Information Superhighway' and the 'Information Society' entered into common parlance. However, this discourse has been viewed as industry and government–fuelled hype in some quarters. Some have even gone so far as to suggest that such terms constitute a political mythology that allows policy makers to provide simplified solutions to highly complex problems (Joseph 1997).[1] In the midst of a wave of enthusiasm about the promise of the 'new media', even the OECD argued that: 'Whereas the marriage between telecommunications and computer technology now seems to have been consummated, the convergence between telecommunications and broadcasting is still in the planning stage' (cited in Joseph 1993, p. 1).

Nonetheless, digital 'convergence' between broadcasting, new electronic media, telecommunications and computing plainly made it more difficult to justify maintaining separate regulatory structures for these hitherto distinct sectors (European Commission 1997a). For example, the ability to play remotely computer games in groups linked to interactive digital services raises the question of the distinction between what is computer software and what is broadcasting (Beat Graber 2004).

A regulatory issue at the very heart of debates about 'convergence' was the possibility that broadcasting might be subsumed into telecommunications regulation. It has been argued that the convergence of technology, allowing all kinds of electronic communication services, including broadcasting, to be provided over the same network (whether cable, satellite or wireless), requires an appropriately converged regulatory framework. Many began to contend that regulating services differently according to their mode of transmission is not justified in the digital era and that, therefore, sector–specific broadcasting rules should be replaced by 'horizontal' technology neutral regulation along telecommunications lines, confined to ensuring non–discriminatory access, fair competition, and a minimum of universal service. In extremis, this argument for broadcasting deregulation could be expressed succinctly by the question: Why keep broadcasting rules, when the Internet, which can deliver TV programmes, is free from such regulation? The counter–argument is that broadcasting remains distinct from telecommunications in that it is point–to–multipoint, one–way, *mass* communication rather than a point–to–point, two–way, *private* transaction and it therefore requires some degree of public service content regulation. However, there are certainly electronic communications services that blur such an easy distinction between broadcasting and telecommunications: What are services that allow the viewer to access information via an interactive menu? How should video–on–demand services be regulated? Ultimately, there is the question: how should a broadcast service provided over a high bandwidth Internet connection and viewed by means of a PC (not a 'TV set') be regulated? As this chapter shows, whilst considerable technological and commercial developments have occurred which promote convergence, there remain significant impediments to complete convergence into a new hybrid sector. These constraints became manifest in the course of the regulatory policy deliberations on convergence which occurred at EU level from the late 1990s, starting with the publication of a 1997 green paper.

THE EUROPEAN COMMISSION'S 1997 GREEN PAPER ON CONVERGENCE

Historically, in Europe the main composite parts of ICT, namely IT, telecommunications and broadcasting, have been, for the most part, highly national–centric in terms of their governance arrangements. As illustrated in Chapter 2, the telecommunications sector across Europe was nationally balkanised. Given the weakness of Europe's IT industry, it was therefore at risk of becoming dangerously uncompetitive in terms of equipment production and, more importantly, service provision in the converging technological and market context. It was also tightly regulated to the extent of being state–owned in most cases and underpinned by the social policy goal of the eventual achievement of universally available, affordable, basic telecommunications services (Steinfeld et al. 1994).

The broadcasting sector was also considered a unique case because of its intrusive, potentially persuasive and thus powerful nature whose negative characteristics need to be guarded against and positive possibilities promoted, for all citizens (Doyle 2002a). In rather more prosaic terms, the technological constraint of bandwidth scarcity for terrestrial broadcasting also contributed to the political decision taken in most EU states to develop a system of tightly regulated 'public service broadcasting' (PSB) which provided viewers with a comparatively small number (by present standards) of channels with a variety of content broadly of an educational, informational and entertainment nature, framed by rules on taste and decency and a requirement on PSB providers to cater for as much of the population as possible (Humphreys 1996, pp. 111–22).

The IT sector developed in a very different way. Largely unregulated, its output and industry structure tended to be governed only by general rules pertaining to all sectors regarding market power, commercial behaviour and consumer welfare. IT was, however, considered to be a strategically vital sector of the economy and it was, as a consequence, the beneficiary of significantly interventionist national government policies, notably in respect of public procurement and research and development.

At EU level, by the late 1990s, a fairly well established pattern of involvement in the ICT sector was discernible. Policy deliberations of the early 1980s on the 'technology gap' between Europe and her global competitors, the USA and Japan, resulted in the launch of a collaborative framework programme in research and technological development in 1984, of which IT was the centrepiece. The ESPRIT policy initiative continued through a number of phases well into the 1990s (Peterson and Sharp 1998). In the strongly national sectors of broadcasting and telecommunications, there also occurred degrees of Europeanisation. In the 1980s, the EU embarked on a process which eventually resulted in the 1989 Television Without Frontiers (TWF) directive which aimed to create the conditions for the establishment of a Single European Market in broadcasting. The EU also launched a (quite modest) initiative to subsidise the European audiovisual industry (Humphreys 1996). It was in telecommunications, however, that the greatest degree of EU involvement was witnessed in terms of research and development, regional aid initiatives and, most significantly, regulation.

Given this track record of involvement in broadcasting, IT and telecommunications, it was natural that the European Commission began to take an interest in ICT convergence policy issues. In 1997, it produced a green paper which was intended to generate a period of deliberation on convergence, and might ultimately have resulted in the development of a new hybrid policy area. The crux of the green paper was its presentation to Member States of three possible future regulatory strategies. The most modest one was to continue with separate sector–specific regulatory treatment of broadcasting, IT and telecommunications with the possibility of some kind of (poorly defined) coordinative mechanism at EU level. More far–reaching was the second option of developing a new regulatory apparatus for clearly defined convergent services to run in tandem with a separate set of independent structures for existing services. The third and most radical option was the creation of a new, all inclusive, horizontal regulatory framework for existing and new ICT services (European Commission 1997a).

The launch of policy initiatives through the release of a green paper had become by the late 1990s a favoured modus operandi of the European Commission. As has been shown already in this volume, it proved particularly useful at critical points in the liberalisation of the telecommunications sector. It had also been employed in the broadcasting domain to launch the Television Without Frontiers policy process (Humphreys 1996, pp. 264–7). The use of green papers to define the policy agenda can be seen as a mark of the policy activism and entrepreneurship (Sandholtz and Zysman 1989) of the European Commission or more accurately of the relevant part(s) of the Commission responsible for a particular policy domain. As one high–placed Commission official put it: 'Once you say to people "You have got to think about this" they start thinking about it willy nilly. Their first reaction is "We don't need to think about it". But they are obliged to think about it' (interview, European Commission, 2001). The ideas contained in the green papers naturally reflect the thinking of the relevant DG(s) and are often a compromise between different DGs which have an interest in the issue (see Christiansen 1997). This process is often very political, since the Directorates–General naturally have different constituencies of interest within their relevant policy areas. These interests, too, feed into the process of drafting the green paper (thus, the pan–European advertising lobby fed into the TWF green paper). This has been a mutually beneficial arrangement for the parties concerned since the relatively poorly resourced Commission can gain valuable information on, and experience of, a new policy area. For their part, the various interests, notably business (Coen 1997), are provided with the chance to air views and preferences on an issue at the vital early stages of the EU policy–making process. This pattern can be clearly discerned in the case of ICTs, where the Information Society DG (XIII) had cultivated a close association with IT and telecommunications business interests while the Information, Communication, Culture and Audiovisual Media DG (X) liaised with, and was lobbied by, the increasingly diverse broadcasting constituency.[2]

All this, however, illustrates the potential institutional complexity associated with the development of policy initiatives in the area. Indeed, the 1997 convergence green paper provides a striking example of how this complexity can lead to blunted policy activism by the Commission, should the issue at stake prove controversial enough. It was the Information Society and Competition DGs of the Commission which, in the first instance, led on the production of the green paper and in the process they took close cognisance of the interests of the telecommunications sector (Levy 1997, p. 35).

The draft version of the paper, produced in September 1997, was striking in its advocacy of the telecommunications policy agenda of liberalisation described elsewhere in this volume. It was underpinned by acceptance of the inevitability of ICT convergence and urged Member States to create a new regulatory framework which would capture the commercial benefits of advances in ICTs. The corollary of this was the expression of scepticism about the other two less radical options for regulatory developments detailed above (European Commission 1997b). This version was intended for circulation between the Commission's DGs rather than in the public domain, but such was its controversial nature that it was leaked via the Internet. At this juncture, it became clear that a range of often opposing views existed on the shape of any possible EU level regulatory framework for ICT. The subsequent input made by the audiovisual DG of the Commission and by (mainly public service) broadcasting interests was effective in introducing a measure of balance into the green paper's final version which was released in December 1997, though the paper was also, as a consequence, much less incisive and, arguably, unwieldy and contradictory (Hills and Michalis 1999). Tellingly, the December version stated that 'there is no assumption that convergence in technologies, industries, services and/or markets will necessarily imply a need for a uniform regulatory environment' (European Commission 1997a, iv).

Thus, the final version was more equivocal in its commentary on the three options presented to Member States and in general terms paid greater attention to the impact of convergence on European citizens. Nonetheless, close analysis of the green paper reveals an underlying theme according to which convergence requires a slimmed down, converged regulatory framework calculated to promote the economic benefits of convergence and conducive to Europe's global competitiveness (Humphreys 1999).

THE GREEN PAPER CONSULTATION PROCESS

The official release of the green paper intensified the energetic debate that had been unexpectedly created over ICT convergence. It was sharpened by the declared intention of the Commission, having taken on board comments arising from the consultation, to publish a convergence action plan by the end of 1998. From the consultation, it was clear that the majority of a miscellany of often powerful and influential respondents were in favour of pursuing a cautious approach to the regulatory treatment of convergence within the EU. In particular, it became evident that the most powerful national Member States of the EU were wary of pursuing a common regulatory approach to ICTs developed at EU level.

As Levy (1999) describes, there were important domestic politics constraints in place. In Germany, responsibility for telecommunications and broadcasting regulation was split between the Federal and *Länder* levels. The French were highly protective of their broadcasting sector and showed no enthusiasm for a convergence framework, let alone one developed at the EU level. The UK was, by contrast, more open to regulatory innovation in ICTs, in part due to its recent history as a policy experimentalist in communications. In fact, shortly after the Commission's green paper, the UK government launched its own green paper and consultative exercise on convergence This eventually resulted in the enactment of the 2003 Communications Act which (transposing the EU's ECRF) integrated telecommunications and broadcasting regulation and established a new 'converged' regulator in the UK, the Office of Communications (Ofcom)[3] with wide ranging powers over all ICT, including broadcasting (see Simpson 2004a). Nonetheless, despite its relative radicalism and experimentation in communications policy, the UK – unlike in telecommunications – has not pressed its model at the EU level. Moreover, it retains a characteristically distinctive national centric approach to the regulation of broadcasting content (Humphreys 2004).

The convergence consultation exercise was perhaps most notable for its illumination of the divergence of opinion between service providers and other commercial interests in IT and telecommunications, on one hand, and broadcasting, on the other. On the whole, telecommunications and IT companies, in line with their perceived interests, expressed support for the creation of a common liberalised regulatory environment for all ICTs in which any framework was as light touch as possible, many advocating a combination of industry self–regulation and general competition policy rules as the way forward. By contrast, broadcasting interests called for caution to be exercised, due to the need to protect, cater for and promote public service goals in ICT. These parties, made up of public service and some commercial broadcasters in the main, were keen to point out the continued relevance of the special nature of the broadcasting component of electronic communications, which would require, more than ever before, specific measures which self–regulation and general competition policy could not provide (see European Broadcasting Union 1998).

Overall, the consultation exercise made it clear to the Commission that it was going to be impossible to reach an agreement on the creation of a common regulatory framework for those ICT services which provide content of any kind, most notably broadcasting but also a burgeoning new array of what the Commission came to call 'Information Society services' delivered across the Internet. In fact, it appeared that the best way of making progress on the issue might be the creation of a classic European compromise package, designed to appeal to the convergence radicals and also to assuage the convergence conservatives.

Thus, the Commission launched a second, more focused, phase of the consultation exercise in which it appealed for views on three matters: (1) how to create a satisfactory system of access to digital gateways (such as conditional access systems and electronic programme guides); (2) the provision of a framework for investment in European ICT content; and (3) how to develop a balanced approach to ICT regulation with the modest goal of determining whether or not it should proceed to develop the convergence policy issue any further (European Commission 1998b). Behind this somewhat rhetorical call, the Commission's true purpose was revealed when it subsequently declared proposals to introduce a common European–wide regulatory framework for all ICT infrastructures and services associated with them in tandem with a series of auxilliary support measures related to both content and infrastructure but with a distinct orientation towards broadcasting.[4] This process was operationalised, most notably, at the end of 1999, with the release by the Commission's DG Information Society of its

Communications Review paper, which focused largely on infrastructural (and associated services) issues and pointedly excluded communications services content regulation (European Commission 1999b).

THE EU AND THE GOVERNANCE OF BROADCASTING REGULATION

It is important to note that, in parallel with telecommunications policy, the EU had been developing several policy strands directly related to broadcasting content issues. However, on the whole these proved to be rather modest in nature and/or controversial on occasions, clearly illustrating the strength of the national level 'gravitational pull' in broadcasting and serving to highlight further why the convergence debate and subsequent ECRF directly excluded issues of broadcasting content. Overall, the substance of the EU's intervention in broadcasting policy has been complementary and supportive rather than 'dirigiste' (Collins 1994). Aside from the very modest audiovisual content production support programme, Measures to Encourage the Development of the Audiovisual Industries in Europe (MEDIA) (Humphreys 1996, pp. 264–78) and its successors MEDIA II and MEDIA Plus, the EU institutions (Commission and European Court of Justice) have been most active in the area of competition policy, where their powers are strong and relatively well developed. By contrast, in the area of media concentration and pluralism, little or no policy ground has been gained (Harcourt 2004).

Regarding matters of competition in the EU broadcasting market, the European Commission has become increasingly active since the 1989 enactment of the Television Without Frontiers Directive. At first, it appeared that the public service broadcasters were the Commission's principal targets (Collins 1994, pp. 147–50), since in the first two noteworthy cases – the ARD/MGM and Screensport/EBU cases – it supported complaints from private broadcasters about the anti-competitive arrangements that public service broadcasters (PSBs) had for access to programme rights (films and sports programme rights respectively). Since then, as complaints from the private sector about the alleged unfair benefits ('state aid') enjoyed by public service broadcasters have piled up in Brussels, there has occurred a lengthy period of uncertainty about the Competition DG's stance on public service broadcasting. Concerned to underpin the future of public service broadcasting and to underline their competence in this matter, the Member States attached a protocol to the 1997 Treaty of Amsterdam, based on a European Parliament resolution, stating that: '[t]he provisions of the Treaty establishing the European Community shall be without prejudice to the competence of the member states to provide for the funding of public service broadcasting in so far as such funding is granted to broadcasting organisations for the fulfilment of the public service remit as conferred, defined, and organised by each member state' (Treaty of Amsterdam 1997).

However, shortly after the release of the 1997 convergence green paper, a Commission Competition DG discussion document caused particular concern amongst public service broadcasters, by suggesting that the continued funding of PSB activities through a combination of public and private financing (the norm in continental Europe) needed to be closely scrutinised, since it could be in contravention of article 92 of the EU Treaty. Controversially, the discussion paper suggested that PSBs in receipt of advertising and licence fee funding could not justify the showing of films, entertainment programmes or most sports coverage as part of their public service remit. The discussion paper angered Member States which, led by Germany, were quick to reassert the basic principle that underlined their right to define public service broadcasting (*European Voice*, 05.11.1998; 12.11.1998), a point affirmed by a Council of Ministers Resolution (European Council of Ministers 1999, p. 1). Subsequently, the Commission adopted a more conciliatory approach to Member State sensitivities. In November 2001, it released a Communication on the application of state aid rules to public service broadcasting (European Commission 2001b). While this communication suggested that state support for public service broadcasters did amount to state aid in the terms of the EC treaty and would 'have to be assessed on a case by case basis' (European Commission 2001b, paragraph 17), it also made very clear that, *so long as the remit is clearly defined by the Member State* (our emphasis), the Commission had principally to confine itself to evaluating the proportionality of that aid.

The EU's efforts to become involved in policy issues of media pluralism, by contrast, were unsuccessful. The initial lead here came from the Industrial Policy Directorate of the European Commission which produced, in 1992, a green paper on Pluralism and Media Concentration (European Commission 1992b). Given the orientation of its author, it was of no surprise that the paper tended to approach the issues from a commercial standpoint, primarily, though the ensuing debate highlighted the existence of interests at EU level, in, notably, the European Parliament and the Commission's Audiovisual DG, which were in favour of developing a non–economic approach to the pursuit of pluralism. It took four years for a draft directive on media pluralism to be produced in 1996, spearheaded by the Commission's Internal Market DG, in which a proposal to measure media concentration in terms of audience share (as a proxy of market share) proved controversial (see Harcourt 2004). Consequently, a re-worked draft directive was produced in 1997 on media ownership, which controversially included a clause which would allow Member States to exempt any broadcaster from designated upper limits on media ownership as long as that Member State had measures in place to promote (content) pluralism. In effect, the directive was now so loose and ill–defined that its goals of creating media ownership rule uniformity across the EU were rendered meaningless (Michalis 1999, p. 157). Despite this dilution, as a consequence of heavy lobbying from national and corporate interests, the draft directive was shelved.

THE ECRF AND THE REGULATION OF 'DIGITAL GATEWAYS'

As Chapter 5 has described, the 1999 Communications Review culminated with the Commission's publication in November 1999 of proposals for a new 'electronic communications' regulatory framework (the ECRF), which excluded content regulation. The 2002 Framework Directive of the ECRF acknowledged explicitly that 'audiovisual policy and content regulation are undertaken in pursuit of general interest objectives, such as freedom of expression, media pluralism, impartiality, cultural and linguistic diversity, social inclusion, consumer protection, and the protection of minors' (European Parliament and Council 2002a, pp. 5–6). It included two very important provisions that responded to the concerns expressed during the convergence consultations by broadcasters, the Member States and the European Parliament about the need to guarantee universal service, cultural diversity and media pluralism in the era of digital convergence. First, the Universal Services Directive (European Parliament and Council 2002b, Article 31), in the new regulatory package, allowed Member States to impose 'reasonable "must carry" obligations', for the transmission of public service channels (the term used is services that meet 'general interest' objectives), on providers of electronic communication networks used for the distribution of radio or television broadcasts. Second, the Access Directive (European Parliament and Council 2002c, Articles 5 and 6 and Annex 1), recognising that competition policy alone would not be an adequate guarantor of cultural diversity and media pluralism, provided some regulatory principles and conditions for the regulation of conditional access systems and other 'gateway' technologies such as electronic programme guides. Thus, here there is clear evidence of the use of 'classic' telecommunications policy regulatory tools in a broadcasting context.

With regard to 'carriage', the key issue for broadcasters is access to the network or platform. The provision in the ECRF's Universal Services Directive (Article 31) for 'must carry' rules for public service broadcasters allows (though it does not prescribe) the Member States to guarantee universal access to public service content. However, this provision only applies to those deemed to be public service broadcasters. Moreover, in the age of digital convergence, there is rather more to the issue of access. As Michalis (2002, p. 91) argues: 'Traditional telecommunications regulatory concerns about interconnection, interoperability and access to gateways are now relevant to broadcasting networks and are pertinent to the future of digital television.' However, as Levy (1997b, p. 661) has explained: 'at a time of increasing awareness of the importance of convergence between telecommunications, broadcasting and computing, the issue of interoperability in digital broadcasting was accorded...much less importance than in telecommunications'.

Levy (1997b, 1999, pp. 63–79) has documented in detail the policy process whereby the Commission, bruised by the embarrassing failure of its past technology policy interventionism in the field of high–definition television (HDTV) and very keen to see industry develop the new technology, was not disposed to regulate for either common standards or access terms for digital TV networks and instead chose to defer to the decisions of the industry grouping – the Digital Video Broadcasting (DVB) project. Leaving the issue to industrial and commercial interests in this way resulted in the agreement only of a common European digital transmission standard. However, no common standards were agreed for conditional access systems, these being the systems which scramble and, through set–top boxes, unscramble TV signals, allowing only those consumers who have paid for a service to access it.[5] Instead, the market operators chose to develop proprietary systems. This resulted in the emergence of a fragmented European digital TV market, characterised by incompatible conditional access systems (CAS) in different national or linguistic areas. By virtue of its first mover advantage, BSkyB quickly established a monopoly in the UK. In Italy, too, a single operator emerged (Telepiu). In Germany, two competing operators (Kirch and Bertelsmann) soon joined forces to share a single CAS. Only in France, where the government chose to support the public service broadcasters' engagement in digital satellite TV, did three operators compete. This fragmentation of the European digital TV market clearly went against the direction of the EU's audiovisual policy, which ever since the Commission's publication of a 1984 green paper leading to the enactment in 1989 of the Television Without Frontiers (TWF) directive, revised in 1997, had been conceived to create a single European market in order to promote a stronger European audiovisual industry (Humphreys 1996, pp. 256– 96).

Plainly, apart from fragmenting the European digital TV market, this state of affairs also raised competition and media pluralism issues. Control of the set–top box presented the opportunity to discriminate (through price or access terms) against potential competitors in the field of pay–TV and new Information Society services (see Humphreys and Lang 1998). As Levy (1999) shows, for a while it seemed that, in their enthusiasm to see rapid development of the new technologies, European and national policy makers would leave the matter to be covered by an industry (DVB) code of conduct. However, at the insistence of the European Parliament, it was finally accepted there should be statutory access provisions. Accordingly, the EU's 1995 Advanced Television Standards Directive (article 4) established some regulatory principles for conditional access regulation. The core principle was that CAS providers should be required to supply access to conditional access services on fair, reasonable and non-discriminatory terms. The directive also obliged national regulators to ensure that CAS operators kept separate financial accounts, published unbundled tariffs, and that they should not prohibit a manufacturer from including a common interface allowing connection with other access systems. However, as Levy (1999) explains, the latter stipulation was a far cry from mandating the inclusion of a common interface, manufacturers being most unlikely to include a common interface against the wishes of such powerful customers. Moreover, the directive was 'so vague as to leave national officials unclear as to what provisions meant, and as to which needed to be written into national law. The result was that national implementation varied hugely' (p. 73).

Clearly, the issues surrounding conditional access lend themselves to classic 'telecommunications–style' regulation, and this was exactly the approach adopted in the UK where Oftel – rather than the broadcasting regulator, the Independent Television Commission (ITC) – issued a class licence for conditional access systems and produced detailed 'telecommunications–style' regulatory conditions (which have been recently modified to conform with the new ECRF). However, in France and Germany, '[t]here was no great enthusiasm either for rapid implementation of the Directive or for seeing how its provisions might be enforced more effectively' (Levy 1999, p. 74). It fell to the broadcasting regulators[6] in the first instance, with the possibility of referral to competition authorities, to ensure fair and non-discriminatory access. Levy (1999, p. 74) suggests that the UK's apparent greater concern about conditional access regulation could at least in part be attributed to the higher political profile of the issue arising from 'the controversial role of News International [the owner of BSkyB] in the UK media industry'. Moreover, by the mid–1990s the UK telecommunications regulator had already acquired a wealth of experience in dealing with telecommunication access issues. The UK 'had a ready–made route through the telecommunications regulator Oftel to deal with the requirement in Article 4e of the Directive for there to be an inexpensive "fair, timely and transparent" disputes procedure'. Finally, national differences in regulatory approach were also the product of 'differing administrative cultures' (Levy 1999, pp. 75–6).

Clearly, the 1995 Advanced Television Standards Directive allowed considerable scope for 'domestication' in national transposition and implementation. This state of affairs does not look likely to change as a result of the EU's new ECRF. The Access Directive of the new framework essentially incorporates the same, arguably rather imprecise, provisions from the Advanced Television Standards Directive. Furthermore, in accordance with the flexible approach of the ECRF, the Access Directive allows for the possibility of relaxing ('amending' or 'withdrawing') CAS regulation if, having conducted a market analysis in accordance with Article 16 of the Framework Directive, the NRA finds that an operator does not have significant market power, so long as this does not adversely affect either radio and TV consumers or the prospects for effective competition in the markets for retail digital broadcasting services and for conditional access systems and other associated facilities (European Parliament and Council, 2002c, Article 6). However, the ECRF has introduced a new EU obligation (not provided for in the 1995 Advanced Television Services Directive) for operators to provide access to application program interfaces and electronic programme guides on 'fair, reasonable and non-discriminatory terms' (European Parliament and Council, 2002c, Article 5 and Annex, part II). How these regulatory principles are implemented is left to the discretion of NRAs, with all the continued scope for 'domestication' that this invites.

However, not all digital gateway regulation has been a matter for implementation by the NRAs (with the possibility of retrospective remedies imposed by the Commission under EC competition law). In the field of merger control, the European competition authority had direct power to approve or reject mergers which have a Community dimension. Indeed, the Competition Directorate General (DG IV) has been increasingly active in the field of convergence mergers and alliances (Pauwels 1998) For instance, two noteworthy occasions when the authority ruled against the potential dominance of a digital bottleneck were the so–called Media Services Gesellschaft (MSG) cases in Germany. In 1994 and again in 1998, DG IV blocked bids to produce a digital TV alliance by the leading German companies, Bertelsmann, the Kirch group and Deutsche Telekom AG. Their aim was that MSG would deliver pay television and other interactive services such as video–on–demand through a proprietorial conditional access system. However, the Commission vetoed the alliance on the grounds that it would pose a threat to an open market for pay–TV – and indeed also for future digital communication services – in Germany. In fact, the Commission held that the alliance would create a dominant position in three markets.

First, such an alliance would leverage the Kirch group's dominant position over German television programme rights and libraries into the pay–TV market. Second, it would create monopoly control over the provision of conditional access and subscriber management systems for pay–TV and other new digital services. The first mover advantage that this conferred on MSG would risk foreclosing of the German market to potential EU new entrants. Third, the alliance would consolidate DTAG's dominance of the German cable market (Humphreys 1996, pp. 285–6).

THE INTERNET AND THE ICT CONVERGENCE DEBATE AT EU LEVEL

Broadcasting content was not the only field of content not catered for by the ECRF. Surprisingly, perhaps, the Internet largely escapes mention in the new framework, other than as 'Internet networks' requiring access. As with broadcasting, Information Society services (primarily those associated with Internet [or electronic] commerce) were excluded. EU regulation developed along another policy stream altogether. If broadcasting content was excluded because the 'gravitational pull' of the nation state was so strong in the media field, Internet commerce was excluded because of the very strong 'gravitational pull' of the global level. The emergence of the Internet through the 1990s from the relative margins of the US academic and computer science communities to become a globally developing communications 'landscape' has called forth the attention of policy makers at the international level. In economic terms, the possibility of using the Internet as an increasingly user–friendly communications tool to conduct (at least partially) commercial transactions attracted the attention of a range of multinational business interests from the IT and communications producer (infrastructure, hardware and software manufacturing), service provider and, very importantly, user constituencies. The Internet is significant in that it developed historically outside the telecommunications and broadcasting sectors, though its continued expansion required the use of the former's infrastructure. As it continued to develop as a resource of strategic economic and social importance, a debate arose at the global level as to how it might best be governed to realise its potential. As Chapter 7 of this volume argues, through the 1990s, a neo-liberal telecommunications policy agenda was propounded internationally by the US and the EU in particular and its success undoubtedly added weight to the view that the Internet, certainly in terms of the way it was organised and the commercial activity conducted across it, should be as liberalised and as lightly regulated as possible, to the extent of developing, where possible, self–regulation (see Simpson 2004). The non–mainstream, libertarian culture that emerged at an early stage of the Internet's development reinforced this view, though for very different reasons.

The Internet is significant in terms of ICT convergence in that it embodies elements of broadcasting, IT and telecommunications. Indeed, in the Convergence green paper, the European Commission went as far as to suggest that it was 'both the symbolic and prime driver of convergence' (European Commission 1997a, p. 6). As such, it would have been logical to assume that the centrepiece of any new convergence regulatory package might indeed have been the Internet. However, when the proposals for the ECRF were introduced in the light of the 1999 Communications Review, Internet services and e-commerce were explicitly excluded from coverage along with broadcasting, since they are classified as content laden.

The reasons why broadcasting content issues were not assimilable into a convergence framework at EU level, as noted above, were largely to do with national gravitational pull as a result of the heterogeneity of well-established broadcasting traditions and systems across the EU. However, by contrast, the Internet was relatively new and, due to its US origins, had not developed within any of the communications policy systems and traditions of EU

Member States. It might therefore have been expected to be more amenable to the development of a regulatory package at EU level, given its intrinsic global characteristics and the fact that the EU has been noted as often capable of acting as both a filter of, and a shield against, globalisation for its Member States (Schmidt 1996). However, it was the still developing global gravitational pull of the Internet, and the commensurate uncertainties over how it should be governed, which ensured that, in the late 1990s, caution was exercised which resulted in the exclusion of the key aspects of its governance from the EU's convergence regulatory package.

In several important ways, the development of the Internet was something that bypassed policy makers at EU level, certainly in the early to mid–1990s (interview, European Commission, 2004). As shown in this volume, substantial policy–making energy was invested in the pursuit of a liberalised telecommunications environment (as well as in efforts to create a broadcasting regulatory package). As the broader economic and social significance of ICT became a topic of some political salience, the EU began to develop policy initiatives in the area of the Information Society (European Commission 1994a). However, until the latter part of the 1990s, these developments showed very little recognition of the importance of the Internet. The landmark Bangemann report illustrated the general lack of awareness, with its quite tentative assertion that the EU 'should consider the evolution of INTERNET [sic] closely, paying a more active role in the development of interlinkages' (European Commission 1994a, p. 25). It has also been argued that, in terms of new communications network technologies, the EU and European computer manufacturers ignored the Internet's Transmission Control Protocol/Internet Protocl (TCP/IP), investing resources instead into Open Systems Interconnect (OSI) standards (Werle 2002), indicating an assumption that new Information Society services would be delivered primarily through the upgrading of the traditional telecommunications network.

There were institutional reasons, too, why the Internet, though relevant, did not figure centrally in the thinking of those interests in the Commission who were the architects of the green paper on convergence. At the time, most policy experts in DG Information Society were concerned with telecommunications regulation, though a small number of key individuals, notably Christopher Wilkinson, did take a lead in putting together an EU response to the green paper produced by the US Department of Commerce on the global management of the vitally important system of Internet naming and addressing (US Department of Commerce 1998). In doing this, they liaised with the internet service provider (ISP) commercial constituency, rather than more traditional ICT commercial interests. Thus, whilst DG Information Society did address issues of Internet governance and in doing so employed the characteristic approach of drawing on the assistance of European business, this occurred beyond the mainstream of the ICT convergence debate and process being conducted at EU level (interview, European Commission,

2004). The negotiations which ensued occurred at the global level resulting in the creation of the Internet Corporation for Assigned Names and Numbers (ICANN) in 1999 all of which was ongoing around the time of the convergence debate at EU level. This policy entrepreneurship of the European Commission has eventually resulted in it playing a significant role in the affairs of ICANN (Christou and Simpson 2004) but can also explain the general tentativeness with which the EU approached the inherently global nature of Internet governance issues around the end of the 1990s.

With regard to the crucial area of electronic commerce, at the time the convergence debate broke out, the EU was arguably only beginning to develop policy expertise in this new area of (primarily) Internet–based activity. In 1997, an Initiative in Electronic Commerce was launched which set out a number of areas to be pursued, such as the creation of appropriate technical standards to ensure interoperability between networks and systems, the global liberalisation of telecommunications infrastructures, data and payment system security, intellectual property rights, privacy, taxation and digital signatures (European Commission 1997c), thereby illustrating the cross–cutting, complex and poorly understood nature of the area. In terms of the regulation of e-commerce itself, the European Commission began work on a draft directive in the late 1990s, which eventually produced agreement between Members States in 2000. The aim of this, arguably rather loose, piece of legislation was to set in place a common legal framework to facilitate the creation of a liberalised single European market in what are termed Information Society services. The directive covers a series of aspects of electronic business, such as codes of conduct for suppliers of services, information requirements, notice and take down procedures and liability and dispute settlement services (European Parliament and Council 2000b).

In institutional terms, it is very important to note that the architect of this Directive was the Commission's Internal Market DG, rather than DG Information Society, which also explains, to a significant extent, why it was not central to the convergence deliberations. Even more important, however, is the uncertainty that existed surrounding how to regulate e-commerce, uncertainty which has still not been resolved at the time of writing (interview, European Commission, 2004). Due to the potentially global nature of commerce conducted across the Internet, the EU, like other governmental organisations and nation states, has been careful to ensure that it does not put in place any regulatory prescriptions which might disadvantage its companies in what is seen as an embryonic, but potentially very lucrative, market (in this context, see Chapter 7). Thus, around the time of the convergence debate and the formulation of the new electronic communications regulatory package, the global gravitational pull of Internet commerce regulatory issues meant information society and e-commerce services were left off the convergence policy agenda and, like broadcasting content, they look set to remain so for the foreseeable future.

Aside from the commercial aspects of Internet regulation, the regulation of Internet content for what might be broadly described as social reasons was, and still remains, a highly problematic area, not only for the EU, but for governments worldwide. On the one hand, there were strong arguments for the imposition of regulatory measures to monitor and restrict the posting and exchange of illegal and harmful content on the Internet, even though they might be very difficult to enforce. Conversely, there are arguments, related to the protection of freedom of expression, privacy and freedom of information which advocate the Internet as a free communications space where excessive regulation is deemed undesirable. The need to develop an effective regulatory system for Internet content in these matters has reasonably been viewed an issue requiring agreement at the global level and the general uncertainties surrounding the issues has meant that the EU has adopted a cautious approach. In 1997, the European Commission launched an Action Plan Promoting Safe Use of the Internet (European Commission 1997d) though no specific regulatory measures have been introduced. Instead, the EU's approach has been to advocate a combination of self–regulation by commercial providers and users (assisted by the development of filter technologies) backed by the legal system in cases where self–regulation fails (Halpin and Simpson 2002). Consequently, like the economic aspects of Internet regulation, these issues remained separate from the ECRF emanating from the convergence debate.

CONCLUSIONS

This chapter has illustrated the rather limited extent to which it has been possible for the EU to develop a convergent regulatory framework for the ICT sector, even though technologies and markets in its composite parts have been coming together for a number of years. The process of Europeanisation of a system of telecommunications regulation described in this volume, by the mid to late 1990s, led telecommunications and competition policy architects in the European Commission to believe that a process could be launched which would result in the development of a new, common, horizontal regulatory framework for all ICTs at EU level, to be underpinned by the neo-liberal values and practices which had developed in telecommunications since the early 1980s (in the case of the first movers). However, as this chapter has shown, such ambitions were thwarted and, rather quickly, had to be reined in for a number of reasons, resulting ultimately in a modest and only partial convergence regulatory framework which was termed, somewhat erroneously perhaps in view of what has been excluded, the Electronic Communications Regulatory Framework.

The oppositional and highly effective reaction of a series of parties with an interest in broadcasting to the more ambitious elements of proposals of the Commission's green paper on convergence powerfully illustrated the relative weakness of the EU as a locus for the regulation of broadcasting (Michalis 2002; Humphreys 2004). This chapter has shown how jealously protective the Member States have been of their primary competence for broadcasting. Thus, the Commission has been conciliatory over the application of EU competition rules to public service broadcasters and has proven distinctly ineffective in its attempts to regulate for media pluralism. This is primarily due to the 'gravitational pull' of the national level where Member States have proved powerfully resistant to any attempts to weaken their capacity to control the evolution of broadcasting in their territories. Nonetheless, the ECRF itself, despite being studiously crafted to avoid regulation of broadcasting content, provides an important example of how infrastructural matters can directly impinge upon the regulation of communications content. Indeed, it is unrealistic to expect that it is at all possible to completely separate content and infrastructural issues, not least in the fast evolving techno-commercial context of ICT. Thus, as shown, certain key provisions of the ECRF's directives on access and universal service will be crucially important in ensuring Member States' ability to maintain fully and develop certain staples of public service broadcasting, for example universality of access and pluralism, in a time of digital convergence.

The convergence policy saga also illustrated the extent to which new, and thus uncertain, policy areas were not ready for inclusion in the convergence framework. Here, the Internet, as a classic embodiment of the convergence of ICTs, had associated with it a series of highly significant and unresolved issues with regard to both its economic and social regulation and thus was excluded from the agreed convergence package. The Internet provides an important and contrasting example to broadcasting, where the 'gravitational pull' of global regulatory issues, at that time, illustrated the ineffectiveness of the EU as a regulatory policy locus.

What are the prospects for a more convergent approach to ICT regulation across the EU? At present, it is significant that the only two EU Member States that have decided to adopt such a framework are Italy and the UK. The latter, has been, since the beginning of the 1980s, something of a policy innovator in communications and the creation of the convergence regulator, Ofcom, which began its work in December 2003, would appear to be consistent with the UK's approach. Whilst UK convergence policy goes beyond the confines of this chapter, and at this stage it is too early to determine whether Ofcom has been successful, there is no doubt that the new system faces an important series of regulatory and bureaucratic challenges (see Simpson 2004a). The extent to which the UK's 'experiment' in convergent regulation for ICT works will depend, ultimately, on whether or not Ofcom performs efficaciously, which, given the range of issues and interests with which it has to deal, is no mean task. Even if the UK model is successful and is more widely adopted across the EU, it is unlikely that any strong convergent regulatory package will emerge at EU level in the short to medium term for two reasons.

First, as witnessed already, there is reluctance among Member States to invest further regulatory authority in the EU and the degree of such investment needed to cope with the complex range of issues arising from ICT convergence, will be too great, for the foreseeable future. Second and related to this, the expansion of the EU in May 2004 to 25 member states creates an even more diverse patchwork of cultural and economic traditions and systems. If the different levels of technological development of the new members' electronic communications sectors is added to this, then an even stronger argument is likely to be voiced for allowing divergent patterns of communications regulation to exist at the national level for the time being.

NOTES

1. Joseph (1997, p. 293) defines a political myth as 'a widely believed set of political beliefs that give events and actions a particular meaning....A political myth can include themes on how a certain society came into being, its present predicament and its likely direction for the future.'
2. ICT issues have also exercised the minds of officials in the broadly pro-liberalisation Internal Market and Competition Policy DGs, as well as the Employment, Industrial Relations and Social Affairs DG.
3. Replacing and combining the functions of Oftel), the Independent Television Commission (ITC), the Radio Authority, the Broadcasting Standards Commission, and the Radiocommunications Agency.
4. Reference here was made to ensuring full implementation of existing EU directives in respect of television programming and transmission standards, as well as to measures to encourage the development of Europe's audiovisual industry through subsidy
5. Levy (1999) describes these CAS as digital 'turnstyles'.
6. In France the Conseil Supérieure de l'Audiovisuel and in Germany the private media regulatory authorities of the *Länder*, following guidelines produced by their directors' conference, the Directorenkonferenz der Landesmedienanstalten.

7. The changing global governance of telecommunications and the EU

Whilst telecommunications developed historically as, overwhelmingly, a national–centric series of markets, the very nature of evolving communications requirements dictated that arrangements needed to be developed and operationalised for the carriage of international telephone traffic as a technical and commercial undertaking. Thus, there has been for many years a system of international, if not global, regulation of telecommunications. However, as part of the ancien regime, this system and the global electronic communications environment in general, have been in recent years the subject of profound changes and it to these and their consequences that we turn our attention in this chapter. In particular, the chapter explores the position of the EU, as an actor with increasingly significant responsibilities in communications governance, in the evolving system of traditional and new services – principally those of telecommunications and electronic commerce.

The chapter commences with a brief examination of the traditional international governance system for telecommunications by considering the role played by the International Telecommunications Union (ITU). Broadly speaking, the ITU was at the centre of an intergovernmentalist, technocratic, system in which epistemic communities of experts focused, for the most part, on the arcane technical (and to a lesser extent commercial) details of facilitating international telecommunications traffic, a system overlaid by a series of bilateral arrangements between the monopoly PTT carriers of most of the world's nation states.

The chapter then explains how the earlier documented series of techno-economic pressures (see in particular Chapter 2) began to be utilised by governments, which had embraced a liberalisation agenda in telecommunications, in order to create a new global governance system in line with the 'logic' of liberalisation. The principal forerunner here was, unsurprisingly, the USA but as we indicate, the EU soon followed suit becoming, in the process, an arch proponent of a global system. The chapter next moves on to a detailed consideration of the new, and as yet evolving, global telecommunications regulatory order. Here, the chapter explores the rise to prominence in telecommunications policy development of the WTO, as well as a simultaneous waning in the influence of the ITU, as trade liberalisation and foreign direct investment regulation have become the new imperatives of global telecommunications. Within this ferment of change, the chapter locates the position and role played by the EU, illustrating how it served as an effective agent of policy transfer not just to its Member States but also other WTO members with its clarion calls for liberalisation. Very importantly, however, it also served as a shield against the out–and–out liberalisation of audiovisual communications content as part of any WTO–based agreement, an issue which has become increasingly important in a technologically blurred–at–the–margins communications environment and which, as shown earlier, has been dealt with in a very 'European' way by the EU as a result of its convergence debate and subsequent policy reform. Equally important, there is evidence from the character of the WTO's Agreement on Basic Telecommunications (ABT), that the EU has been able to upload its policy preferences to the global level.

Finally, and related to this, the Chapter explores the role which the EU has played to date in the evolution of the, as yet embryonic system of global governance for electronic commerce. Chapter 6 has argued that the governance of Information Society services, notably those related to electronic commerce, were excluded from the 2002 ECRF because of uncertainties about the future course which governance of activities conducted through the Internet should take given its inherently global nature. We detail the rationale propounded for devising a governance system for e-commerce, note briefly the major elements of e-commerce regulation which have been promoted in existing and new international regulatory fora to date and consider the role which the EU has played, in particular, in the deliberations on e-commerce trade which have occurred in the organisation most likely to occupy the centrepiece role in any future system of e-commerce trade governance, the WTO.

CHARACTERISTICS OF THE ORIGINAL INTERNATIONAL TELECOMMUNICATIONS REGULATORY REGIME

Historically, developments in telecommunications have served as vital enablers in the opening and expansion of international markets in goods and services, though ensuring that the potential of such technologies is realised to some extent or another has been seen to require – by those at the leading edge of capitalist development – the creation of forms of international organisation able to set stable, predictable, parameters for such systems (Murphy 1994). In this respect, the ITU is the longest established organisation charged with the task of dealing with international telecommunications regulation. Formed initially in 1865 as the International Telegraph Union, to devise and agree arrangements for international wireless (and subsequently radio) telegraph traffic (technical interconnection and standardisation, uniform operating instructions, and common international tariff and accounting rules), it soon expanded its remit, with the advent of the telephone, to telephonic regulation (ITU 2003a). In 1932, existing treaties (covering telegraphy and radiotelegraphy) were merged to create the International Telecommunication Convention and the International Telegraph Union changed its name to the International Telecommunication Union, becoming, 15 years later, a specialised agency of the United Nations (ITU 2003a), now comprising 189 members (ITU 2003b).

The ITU, in a number of respects, represents the traditional order of telecommunications. It was dominated by technical experts from the outset and employed a technocratic approach to organising international telecommunications. Here, the mostly publicly–owned monopoly PTTs played a central role in influencing the direction of the Union, and were particularly important in its work on devising an agreed system of international accounting rates from which international call charges to users were derived. The ITU has been likened to a non–governmental organisation (NGO) in certain respects: its key individuals have tended to play multiple roles and its decisions can be the product of long drawn out debate or, by contrast, a speedily put together compromise (MacLean 1999, p. 150).

In political terms, the ITU has been run upon the basis of classic intergovernmentalism, reflecting the deeply national–centric structure of traditional global telecommunications: international governance arrangements in the 'old order' were a minimalist technical and commercial necessity and in practice, for example in the determination of call settlement rates between countries, bilateralism operationalised the detail of international 'base–line' starting points. Within the organisation itself, however, it has been argued that a federal structure exists in which each of its three policy–making sectors enjoy considerable independence. At the 'federal' level, in the shape of periodic plenipotentiary conferences, policy generalists have tended to accept the work and judgements of the technical elite in each of the ITU's sectors (MacLean 1995, p. 184) in which the determination of international telecommunications tariffing and accounting principles took place in the Standardisation Sector of the ITU (ITU 2003c). As MacLean (1999, p. 151) notes:

Sovereignty aside, it is clear that before telecommunications became a huge, largely private, competitive, fast–moving, global business, there was no compelling practical reason for the ITU to be any more than a place where experts from different countries could meet periodically to develop the standards and regulations needed to enable the growth of 'inter–national' telecommunications networks and services.

CHANGES IN THE INTERNATIONAL ACCOUNTING RATE SYSTEM AND THE RELATIVE DECLINE OF THE ITU

One of the most important and controversial tasks undertaken by the ITU historically has been its involvement in the determination of international call charging tariff rates. Fundamental changes in this system provide a useful example of how the growth of liberalisation and new organisational and commercial arrangements to facilitate its spread, have called into question and ultimately undermined the position of historically lynchpin organisations of the 'old' regulatory system, such as the ITU.

Through its Study Group 3, the ITU produced a series of recommendations (which were, as the name suggests, voluntary, but which turned out to be very influential in practice) forming the basis of subsequent bilateral settlement rates agreed between the PTTs of its member countries. In the calculation of revenue flows between PTTs, the chosen accounting rate (a price agreed between the operators which was usually the same in both directions) was halved and multiplied by the time volume of traffic generated between the two parties in each direction. As a result of this, depending on the nature and extent of telecommunications traffic flows, a net payment was made by the country generating the greater volume of outgoing international traffic (Tyler and Bednarczyk 1998, p. 799). Bilateral cooperation in international call charge settlement was underpinned by commercial cooperation and in line with the traditional system eschewed direct competition. As the liberalisation of telecommunications proceeded in the USA and the EU, in particular, during the course of the 1980s, a number of aspects of this system increasingly became the focus of dissatisfaction among policy makers for two underlying reasons.

First, it was clear that those countries generating a lot of international traffic were accruing large and increasing international telecommunications balance of payments deficits. The US, for historical demographic as well as economic reasons, happened to be by far and away the greatest net out–payer in the system. Powerful EU Member States, notably the UK and Germany, were also prominent in this regard. Second, for many years, users of international telecommunications services had suspected that the accounting rates, upon which the international call charges they paid were determined, were very far above the economic costs of service provision. The well–

documented rise of powerful multinational companies, in need of cost effective ways to spread their productive reach globally, ensured that political influence was exercised by these strategically important business users to urge reform of the system on both sides of the Atlantic initially, and beyond the EU-USA sphere, subsequently. Tyler and Bednarczyk (1998) argue that the traditional system has been challenged in the five key respects of commercial negotiations, regulatory pressure from net payer countries, new technical–commercial modes of international service supply, negotiations in multilateral bodies and finally, the conclusion in 1997 of the WTO's Agreement on Basic Telecommunications.

A vital role in dismemberment of the old system has been played by the US Federal Communications Commission which undertook unilateral action to reduce rates by specifying a series of conditions to its domestic and foreign companies to facilitate the reduction of call charges. These relate to obtaining operational authority by foreign carriers from the FCC and post–entry conditions on foreign carriers, both conditioned by the unilateral setting by the FCC of benchmark accounting rates to which particular foreign carriers should work towards meeting by specified dates (Frieden 1998).[1] This unprecedented action attracted a range of criticism from countries, many of whom were pro-liberalisation, notably that the USA was contravening the WTO principles of Most Favoured Nation (MFN) and national treatment (Frieden 1998, p. 967). However, the US position on the matter was that the extent of its commitments in the WTO ABT, in particular (but not solely) regarding its agreement to liberalise international resale services, meant that its market was ripe for exploitation by those economies which did not make similar liberalising commitments. The FCC noted the two undesirable likely outcomes of one–way bypass and price squeeze to justify what it viewed as corrective action through the imposition of benchmarks on foreign carriers (Cowhey 1998, p. 902).[2]

The EU, too, unsurprisingly, turned its attention to international accounting rate issues. Since the emergence of policy activity in telecommunications at the EU level in the mid to late 1980s, the European Commission was made aware increasingly by large international corporate business users of the need for reform (interview, International Telecommunications Users Group, 1991). In its 1987 green paper, it noted that it was necessary to take action to ensure that the efficiency of the system increased (European Commission, 1987, p. 271). In the early 1990s, a more urgent tone was apparent on the matter. The situation reached a crucial stage in 1990, when the ITU's International Telegraph and Telephone Consultative Committee (ITTCC) met to examine the D–series of Recommendations related to the international call charging system (*Financial Times* 25.05.1990a). The Commission decided to challenge the ITU head–on on the matter by attending uninvited a meeting of the ITTCC's Study Group 3. In particular, it demanded that transparency be injected into the whole process and threatened, if necessary, to require PTTs to provide it with accounting information. However, this assault on the traditional PTT—national government axis was not popular, even among EU Member States, where the French delegation described the Commission's Action as 'inopportune and questionable' (*Financial Times*, 25.05.1990b). Further weight was added to the argument at the time when it was claimed that users worldwide were being overcharged by as much as between $10 billion and $20 billion per year for international calls (*Financial Times*, 29.01.1991).

As the 1990s proceeded, the liberalisation of the EU telecommunications sector (see Chapter 3) brought with it a change of attitude to the global telecommunications market and with it the system of international call charging. European operators now viewed international competition as an opportunity more than a threat and embraced the chance to lever open foreign markets. However, European companies were keen to ensure that reform, 'internally' in Europe and globally, occurred at a pace with which they were comfortable and would be able to take commercial advantage of.

The same goal was also, however, at the core of US moves to see reform of the system from which it had removed itself by the beginning of the 1990s. It expressed impatience at policy intransigence and foot-dragging reform wherever it was witnessed and thus, when the FCC embarked on its policy of bilateral call charging benchmarks, the EU did not escape scrutiny and action, even though its Member States had by this stage agreed to the full liberalisation of their telecommunications markets. This engendered some complaint from the EU, but also from Japan, though as Cowhey astutely points out, they were both aware that 'the United States will have to pay the political price for pushing a reform from which they benefit even if they temporize diplomatically' (Cowhey 1998, p. 911). The ITU itself began a process of reform of its international accounting rate system, though likewise, this has been criticised for being too slow and transitory, a facade of reform disguising deep seated reluctance to abandon the traditional system (ibid., p.910). In the meantime, such has been the recent rapid transformation in the international telecommunications voice traffic markets that the ITU has acknowledged the break up of the old system to a point where a substantial and growing element is catered for outside its remit (Tarjanne 1999, p. 54). In 1996, it established an Informal Expert Group to consider international accounting rate issues, resulting in the production of a number of guiding principles to frame future ITU work in the area, which fell very much in line with the new pro-liberalisation paradigm (Frieden 1998, p. 972–3).[3]

However, undertaking the kind of sea change required in the ITU to embrace the new telecommunications environment was never going to occur easily or quickly. As an organisation with a long history and firmly embedded institutions, norms and practices, the resulting path dependency would be difficult to overcome. Indeed, even if the fundamental shifts in thinking, which pervaded the 1990s, on how the telecommunications sector was to operate represented a critical moment in the history of the ITU in which fundamental change could occur, it is as yet uncertain whether enough policy learning has occurred for a transfer of neo-liberal policy practice to have fully taken place. An important event was the ITU's 1992 plenipotentiary conference at which it resolved to try and remodel itself to keep pace with the new emergent philosophy on telecommunications. Aside from some 'cosmetic' organisational change, it was agreed that the ITU would strive to become a more open organisation, encouraging a more eclectic range of private sector members and embracing new regulators, implying that these interests would be given greater weight than hitherto in the ITU's decision–making processes.

However, this reform process has been described as top–down in nature and doubts have been expressed over the extent to which complete transfer of what are relatively new ideas on the regulation of telecommunications has been embraced by its 'grassroots' members. The problem for those wishing to transfer policy ideas to the ITU is its essential eclecticism: with 189 members currently, many of whom are developing and less developed countries, there is much unwillingness to reform international call charging since it has provided historically an important source of much-needed revenue, which dwarfs the issue of free market cost – price proximity. Nonetheless, as the once pre-eminent international organisation for telecommunications regulation, it has become acutely aware of the need to maintain its technical excellence but also to expand into areas characteristic of a globally competitive sector, such as law, policy and trade.

THE WORLD TRADE ORGANIZATION AND TELECOMMUNICATIONS

The pressures outlined above for reform of international call charging can be viewed as part of a significant structural shift in the global regulation of telecommunications. As the 1990s progressed, the liberalising telecommunications sector became the subject of calls to project competition into the *inter*–national scenario. To do this would require two major items to be added to the global telecommunications policy–making agenda: international foreign direct investment and direct competition on international telecommunications routes. The promotion of the idea of international competition in telecommunications logically pointed to the increased significance of trade issues and trade regulation. Nonetheless, as Drake and

Nicolaidis (1992) point out, the acceptance of such a change of approach required nothing short of an attitudinal transformation among states, not least because of the significant risks and adjustment costs which it entailed. An important role in the international trade policy community was played by an epistemic community of experts, dominated in the first instance by Anglo–Americans. Here, at a generic level, the 'very act of defining services transactions as "trade" established normative presumptions that "free trade" was the yardstick for good policy against which regulations, redefined as non–tariff barriers (NTBs), should be measured and justified only exceptionally' (p. 40). This was soon to have significant impact in the sector–specific context of telecommunications.

An early proponent of this approach was the USA, which aside from its opposition to the old order of the ITU, also argued for international economic issues in telecommunications, such as international call charging, to be dealt with within generic global trade fora, notably the General Agreement in Trade and Tariffs. As shown in this volume, throughout the 1990s, ideas of globalist expansionism began to be more broadly accepted by most EU member countries, the EU too becoming, eventually, an advocate of developing a new global regulatory framework to cater for trade and investment in the telecommunications sector. As a consequence, the EU and the US developed something of a policy axis promoting the logic of global liberalisation, competition, trade and investment. To ensure the transfer of these policy ideas beyond North America and Western Europe to the remainder of the industrialised world and beyond required that both the ideology and the practices of neo-liberalism be 'learned'. The creation of the World Trade Organization on January 1st 1995 presented an important new institutional context within which efforts to effect this transfer might be partially undertaken.

Negotiations on the possible liberalisation of telecommunications trade began in the period of the Uruguay Round (1986–94) under the auspices of the General Agreement on Tariffs and Trade. A key issue for those wishing to make progress on the telecommunications issue was that the vast majority of revenue in the telecommunications sector is generated from services, not goods. Trade in the manufacturing component of telecommunications was, in comparison to the task of telecommunications service trade liberalisation, a relatively straightforward process. In any event, a qualitative change in the nature of structural arrangements for trade liberalisation was necessary if any negotiations on telecommunications services were to proceed. This change was partly assisted by the fact that the character of the global economy had been undergoing a profound change over a number of years. In its most industrialised (and most politically powerful) parts, the service economy was growing, accounting for an increasing proportion of wealth creation in the process. As such, there was a political push from the world's industrialised states for the establishment of a global trade in services regime. This duly occurred with the completion of the Uruguay Round and the signing of the General Agreement on Trade in Services (GATS), annexed to the GATT, on January 1, 1995 (WTO 1995). The World Trade Organisation was to be the institutional context within which GATS and other agreements would be administered and any future trade negotiations undertaken.

The current and potential value of the telecommunications sector was instrumental in negotiations which were undertaken with a view to securing the GATS. It was also the case that throughout the Uruguay Round (1986–94) efforts were made to put in place an agreement on telecommunications services trade liberalisation, though the acceptance of the commensurate opening of markets which this would precipitate was difficult to secure. In its efforts to create transference and acceptance of its neo-liberal policy agenda, the USA proposed that long distance voice telephonic services be liberalised, but later withdrew this proposal since it soon became clear that the vast majority of potential signatories (including the EU) were not at that stage ready to embrace such a radical liberalisation proposal (Fredebul–Krein and Freytag 1997, p. 483).

The creation of the GATS held general and specific relevance for the telecommunications sector. In broad terms, GATS specifies a series of General Obligations and Disciplines (GODs) and negotiated Specific Commitments on market access, national treatment and additional commitments. It also contains a series of annexes, one of which relates to telecommunications, indicating how the GATS GODs relate to key issues within the sector in question. Finally, GATS contains a series of National Schedules in which member governments state their Specific Commitments to market opening in the sector in question (Drake and Noam 1997, p. 801). As a consequence of the Uruguay Round of negotiations on telecommunications, a categorisation of 15 types of telecommunications service were identified. A total of 48 countries submitted national schedules of commitments liberalising trade in respect of services in various of the categories.

The limited nature of what was achieved is clear since whilst most of the parties to the Agreement made commitments on the liberalisation of what were broadly Value Added Services categories, only 19 members made very modest commitments on basic telecommunications services related to the provision of voice (and facsimile) telephony (Drake and Noam 1997, p. 802). Aside from the commitments made to liberalise VANS at the conclusion of the Uruguay Round, WTO Members also agreed an important Telecommunications Annex which might be regarded as a move to further embed the general process of global trade in services liberalisation. According to Luff (2004, p. 43), in legal terms this did not require specific liberalisation of telecommunications networks and services but was, rather, a measure designed to complement liberalisation commitments made by members in their GATS Schedules of Commitments. Consequently, 'to the extent international trade in a service [that is, any service] is authorised in a domestic market, the Annex on Telecommunications requires the competent national government to grant access to its public networks and services [in this case those of telecommunications] to whoever supplies it'.

The Annex on Telecommunications aside, the Agreement concluded as a consequence of the Uruguay Round, whilst undoubtedly significant, was viewed as merely the first staging post in the global liberalisation process and was for some rather modest and even stand–still in nature, since largely it did not go beyond the level of liberalisation which existed in the markets of its 57 signatories at the time (Cameron 2004). The next immediate goal to be pursued had two dimensions: to broaden the number of countries agreeing to open up markets to international trade and, second, to deepen the level of commitment to liberalisation by tackling basic telecommunications, once considered the 'sacred cow' of national protectionist telecommunications policy.

In the vanguard of the liberalisers, unsurprisingly, were the EU and the USA. The aim was to promote aggressively the transfer of ideas on telecommunications policy liberalisation, so avidly pursued in their jurisdictions, to the global forum of the WTO and in this they were soon to be successful. The ability of the EU to set and influence the agenda at the WTO is clear from the fact that the European Commission pressed hard and was ultimately successful in ensuring that audiovisual services were not subject to trade negotiations, in line with Europe's domestic, largely protectionist, policies on broadcasting, much to the chagrin of the USA. The French, in particular, pressed hard to ensure that, on grounds of cultural exemption, the audiovisual sector remained off the negotiating table (Doyle 2002a, p. 100). More precisely, whilst WTO members agreed that audiovisual services do come under the remit of GATS, they were permitted to exempt themselves from making commitments in relation to market access and national treatment in respect of audiovisual services and could exempt promotional measures relating to film and television programmes from the most–favoured nation treatment obligation. A general reticence to make commitments liberalising audiovisual services was evident in the low number of WTO members choosing this option – only 13 at the end of the Uruguay Round rising to 19 as a consequence of subsequent accessions (Nihoul 2004).

Nonetheless, the quid pro quo for this was an agreement to apply the principle of progressive liberalisation to the area, thus obligating a reconsideration of the issues at some unspecified future juncture (Beat Graber, 2004, pp. 165–6). However, with an eye firmly on the sort of trends in ICT convergence discussed in Chapter 6, Mueller (2004, p. 311) contends that:

> whether and how classical trade barriers in audio–visual services can be reconciled with the WTO agreement in basic telecommunications services is a reasonably interesting question in the short term. In the longer term it is a distraction. In a converged world the distribution of audio–visual services will take many new forms, producing new services and massive changes in market structures that will ultimately consume more regulatory attention than anything else. Most of these new forms of audiovisual distribution will not be subject to traditional trade protection or regulation.

A key element of the negotiations which ensued from 1995 onwards was the attempt to include in any agreement both networked service provision and resale of capacity, meaning that market access commitments were pursued regarding the commercial presence and cross–border modes of service provision and which underpinned the policy idea that trade and foreign direct investment in telecommunications were essential to secure a globally liberalised environment. In terms of market access, member governments were pressed to submit schedules of commitments giving at least partial, but preferably full, market access across the board of telecommunications services (Tuthill 1997, p. 786).[4]

Young (2002, pp. 67–75) provides a detailed picture of the key issues during the period of negotiation leading to the signing of the ABT. Here, the pivotal role of the European Commission as a conduit for Member State preferences but also as a partial shaper of the negotiations at critical points provide highly significant. The two issues which distinguished more liberal and less liberal EU Member States were national ownership restrictions on telecommunications companies and transitional periods to implement the agreements made in 1993 and 1994 to liberalise voice telephony services and infrastructures across the EU. With regard to the former, there was some willingness to be flexible in order to ensure similar access to foreign telecommunications markets.

In February 1996, the US government, in a bid to stimulate the EU, Japan and Canada to follow suit, put forward an improvement on its initial offer to include local telephony services and clarifying restrictions on foreign ownership of companies with common carrier radio licences. As Young (2002, p. 72) illustrates, this move precipitated an internal conflict among EU Member States and the Commission. Some of the former, such as the UK, Holland, Germany, Finland and Sweden did not have to make any concessions in order to match the US offer, whilst others, notably France, Spain and Portugal and Italy, were urged by the Commission to relinquish foreign ownership restrictions and speed up liberalisation. The French, in particular, were concerned that ambiguity in draft agreement documentation would lay Europe open to a flood of American online content (*European Voice* 30.01.1997). As a compromise, the EU merely confirmed the initial offer made but indicated a willingness to negotiate further concessions provided there was reciprocal willingness in evidence among other states. Whilst some further progress was made in the shape of new or improved offers from 28 governments, and despite claims that a deadline of 30 April 1996 to secure an agreement would be final (*European Voice*, 25.04.1996), the US government did not consider this enough and refused to press ahead with an agreement much to the consternation of the EU (*European Voice*, 02.05.1996).

However, talks re-commenced and, in February 1997, the ABT was eventually concluded. As Young points out, the European Commission played a key role in creating an improvement in the EU's offer through exercising its competition policy powers. The desire of telecommunications companies to form intra-European and global strategic alliances allowed the Commission, which held power to reject or ratify them, to force the Spanish government to remove foreign ownership restrictions on telecommunications companies and to accept a much reduced (11 months only) transition period to implement the 1998 telecommunications framework agreement in order for regulatory approval to be given to Telefonica to join the Unisource telecommunications service provider alliance. The Commission, through negotiation, also persuaded the Belgian government to declare that its public ownership restrictions would not act as a barrier to market entry, as well as to persuade the French government to reduce its ownership restriction in the area of radio communications infrastructures, a move choreographed with a similar pro-liberalisation move by the USA (see Young 2002, p. 74). Throughout the negotiations leading to the signing of the ABT, the drive by the EU and the US was powerful and, ultimately, it prevailed.

Here, 69 member states (now more than 80 at the time of writing) submitted schedules of commitments which applied significant liberalisation to their telecommunications sectors.[5] Yet the ABT was equally significant in respect of what became known as the Reference Paper – so called since its measures are integrated in GATS through reference to them in WTO members' ABT Schedules of Commitments (Luff 2004). The Paper, included as part of these Schedules by the majority of signatories (57 governments), contains a set of regulatory principles to be pursued in order to create and cement liberalisation in their telecommunications sectors. In this way, the Reference Paper consolidated, reinforced and, to a certain extent, served to operationalise the ABT and was an important political and practical commitment won by liberalisers. The Reference Paper's principles promised to ensure that the ideological transition of telecommunications from national protectionism to neo-liberal competition was transferred globally. The document focused on the key areas of anti-competitive behaviour, interconnection, licensing and regulatory independence as the conditions to be addressed *internally* by signatories to ensure the efficacy of the ABT which dealt with *inter*–national telecommunications trading and investment relationships. By contrast, and as what might be regarded as something of a concession, the Paper affirms the importance of securing universal telecommunications service, though its ideological underpinnings are designed to be neo-liberal in nature since it should be created and delivered in a competitively neutral way (Blouin 2000, p. 138).

In the ABT, a number of specific areas of liberalisation were addressed in the Schedules of Commitments put forward by the signatories. Whilst each state's commitment was not identical in its liberalising thrust, overall the Agreement represented a unique development in the history of international telecommunications policy coordination. Regarding voice telephony, 61 governments opened their market to competitive supply. There were commitments to introduce competition in the local voice telephonic market by 55 governments; by 52 governments in respect of long–distance voice telephony and by 56 governments in the area of international voice telephony. The potential for competition was spurred by 42 governments permitting resale of public voice services. A series of commitments were also made in areas such as liberalisation of data transmission (by 63 governments); competitive supply of leased circuit capacity (55 governments); cellular mobile services (60 governments) and satellite infrastructure and services (50 governments) (Drake and Noam 1997, p. 803). In terms of market access for international telecommunications services and infrastructures, it has been calculated that 29 governments, initially, and 23 more by 2006, made the commitment to liberalise in the 1997 Agreement. In terms of the establishment of commercial presence to provide telecommunications services through foreign direct investment, 27 governments initially and another 21 (mostly developing) states by 2004 made liberalising commitments, though there were notable exceptions taken here by countries such as France, Italy, Japan, Australia and Spain (Drake and Noam 1997, p. 804)[6].

From an EU perspective, the ABT and the Reference Paper were significantly in line with the nature and speed of telecommunications policy change in the vast majority of Member States and this was undoubtedly the most important factor for the EU being able to present a concerted negotiating position at the WTO. As noted in Chapter 3, the changing corporate strategies of a number of Europe's strongest PTOs at the beginning of the 1990s, in terms of their desire to enter new international markets and to develop strategic alliances, gave the European Commission, with its strong competition policy powers, a significant policy lever with which to push for the complete liberalisation of the EU's national voice telephonic markets. These changing corporate outlooks were influential, too, in encouraging the development of trade negotiations at the global level within the WTO.

In fact, the EU has subsequently used the GATS agreement as a lever to ensure that a decision by US competition authorities, which would have prevented Deutsche Telekom from acquiring the US company VoiceStream in 2000, was overturned, thus assisting the German operator's global corporate ambitions. An important issue for the EU and its Member States at the beginning of the negotiations concerned the competence of the EU to represent its Member States at the WTO. As Young (2002, p. 63) points out, at the start of the Uruguay Round, the 'doctrine of implied powers' was not applicable to telecommunications and, subsequent to this, the ability to deal with issues related to the establishment of commercial presence across the EU's markets was outside the EU's sphere of jurisdiction. However, these issues were resolved primarily because members states became convinced of the greater bargaining utility to be derived from presenting a united bargaining front in global trade negotiations and, second, because telecommunications negotiations were conducted within a broader battery of negotiations on trade where, overall, the EU did have jurisdiction. Nonetheless, it was decreed that any agreement reached would have to be ratified by all EU Member States for it to be adopted.

Throughout the Uruguay Round, the EU made offers relating only to the liberalisation of VANS, very much in line with the pace of domestic liberalisation within its Member States as a consequence of the 1990 Services Directive. However, as Chapter 3 has noted, the period around the conclusion of the Uruguay Round (1993–94) was highly significant for EU Member States since over this short period they made a commitment to liberalise voice telephonic services and infrastructures albeit with a 1 January, 1998, deadline. These moves signalled the possibility of moving the liberalisation agenda further forward at the global level, something strongly advocated by the USA and it was thus significant that, at the Uruguay Round's conclusion in 1994, governments agreed a 'Decision on Basic Telecommunications', the springboard for the series of voluntary negotiations which led eventually after the WTO's inception, to the ABT.

Indeed, the Reference Paper itself is striking in its similarities to the internal EU telecommunications policy agenda where out and out neo-liberalism dominates though the social policy goal of universal service is upheld and pursued. As international trade in services issues began to be debated more vigorously at the global level at the beginning of the 1990s, Drake and Nicolaidis (1992, p. 41) noted at this juncture that 'the balance of influence has shifted in recent years away from the largely American partisans of comprehensive liberalisation and towards analysts favoring a more European–style managed liberalism'. This would appear to have been reflected some years later in the substance of the ABT. At the very least, it is illustrative of the extent to which the EU was able to secure, at least in principle, the transference of its policy preferences into the global arena, though the fact that these were largely in line with those of the US should also not be forgotten since, for example, the latter has arguably more extensive universal service policy provision in place domestically.

The extent to which sufficient policy learning can take place to ensure not just policy transfer of ideas but also day–to–day regulatory practices is a more complex and thus problematic issue. In this regard, the ABT and the Reference Paper have been criticised for lacking enough specificity to deliver their general goals. Fredebul–Krein and Freytag (1999) argue that the Paper's provisions on anti-competitive behaviour leave scope, in particular, for governments to discriminate against foreign suppliers of telecommunications services. Regarding interconnection, there is no detailed treatment of the potentially thorny issue of interconnect price setting or network unbundling. Similarly, there is a lack of detail on the conditions for securing a telecommunications licence in a foreign territory, leaving open the possibility for discrimination. Equally, the Paper does not explicitly state that where full or partial state ownership of a telecommunications operator remains, the ministry of state responsible for that company must be structurally separate from the regulatory authority which the Paper requires to be established. In the EU itself, for example, conditions can be attached to the granting of general authorisations and licences in a series of areas (Fredebul–Krein and Freytag 1999, p. 637).[7]

The ABT and Reference Paper were produced in the shadow of continuing disagreement among WTO members regarding the international accounting rate system referred to above since even though international service revenue was just 10 per cent of the sectoral total, it was a business with huge profit margins (Cameron 2004). According to Cowhey (2004, pp. 51–64), the introduction of international simple resale as a consequence of the ABT was another important catalyst for the dissolution of the traditional regime, since it created opportunities for alternative international telecommunications service providers to initiate and terminate, on their own, international traffic and thus to bypass the accounting rate system. However, it also created the possibility that the markets of countries offering international simple resale could be exploited on the basis of Most Favoured Nation and national treatment obligations in GATS by other WTO members which had not made a similar agreement. Thus, the EU and the USA agreed tacitly that the former would not oppose the latter's unilateral imposition of individual international benchmark tariff reduction schemes for various countries to force a reduction in international settlement rates. The scheme was eventually modified to exempt those countries, most of which were from the OECD, which had significantly reduced international call charging rates as a result of increased competition between international carriers, both incumbent and new entrant alike.

THE NATURE OF THE WORLD TRADE ORGANIZATION

The conclusion of the Uruguay Round and, with it, the establishment of the WTO were two of the most important landmarks in the history of post–war international trade. The WTO was designed to provide a new legal basis and organisational context for international trade regulation across economic sectors and was heralded as a significant departure from the past and an opportunity to create a strong organisational base for the development, negotiation and deployment of international trade agreements. Nonetheless, whilst the WTO was a new organisation, its essential operational principles and norms drew on the institutional history of efforts at regulating international trade which were nurtured in GATT signed in 1947, most notably, Most Favoured Nation and national treatment; reciprocity; and dispute settlement (Wilkinson 2000). However, the WTO was unparalleled in the history of international trade regulation in that its breadth of coverage included not just the regulation of trade in goods (under GATT) but also agreements in agriculture and textiles and clothing, as well as a number of what were termed Plurilateral Agreements. Moreover, the launch of the WTO marked the first time an international trade organisation was given the remit of regulating trade related areas. This occurred through the Agreement in Trade Related Aspects of Intellectual Property and the Agreement on Trade Related Investment Measures which were considered to be essential to efficient production and thus, indirectly, trade (Wilkinson 2000, p. 57). Finally and very importantly, the conclusion of the Uruguay Round heralded the signing of the GATS which was central to the pursuit of telecommunications liberalisation.

The GATS relates to the service sector as a whole and distinguishes four modes according to which a service may be supplied: cross–territorially; in the territory of a country by servicing any consumer from another member country; by the service provider of one country through the establishment of commercial presence in the territory of another country; by one country's service provider through the presence of natural persons in the territory of another country (GATS Article 1, paragraph 2). GATS also contains a set of General Obligations which signatories must adhere to regarding MFN[8], transparency, national regulatory practices to ensure monopolies do not abuse their position; and restrictive business practices. Luff (2004, p. 49) argues that even in the case of services which a typical member makes no specific commitments on, the MFN obligation requires non–discriminatory treatment of all other members' service suppliers. The Agreement also makes provision for specific commitments on market access and national treatment which members must commit to in national schedules that they present in particular sectoral cases (Fredebul–Krein and Freytag 1997, p. 485).

Several features of the nature of the WTO provide an illustration of why it has become the most important focal point for the global liberalisation of telecommunications and why, as a consequence, more traditional organisations, such as the ITU, have become sidelined. These illustrate, too, why in the light of its gradual but steady development of a change of approach to the governance of telecommunications, the WTO has become such an important global policy focal point for the EU and its Member States. The WTO's core aim is to remove any barriers to the liberalisation of goods and services where they are deemed to exist. As such, the telecommunications sector as it was structured, and as it functioned historically, presented an ideal case for the WTO to turn its attention to in the eyes of those seeking globally liberalised markets. The WTO, very quickly, has become a powerful organisation at the centre of global trade regulation. Part of its goals are to develop mutually supportive relationships with other international organisations with complementary aims, such as the International Monetary Fund, the World Bank, the World Intellectual Property Organisation and others. Through this, a system of loose, nested governance within which policy ideas can be learned and transferred where appropriate is pursued. Furthermore, the WTO requires all the world's regional trade associations, including the EU, to register with it and conform to its rules (Simpson and Wilkinson 2002, p. 44).

The WTO also plays an important surveillance role, ensuring that signatories to Agreements, such as the ABT, comply with its requirements or alternatively, do not put in place any measures which might denude the nature and impact of liberalisation. A consequence of this is that there are in place the conditions within which policy learning can and, to a certain extent, must, take place. This is clearly illustrated in the case of telecommunications where according to Drake and Noam (1997, p. 807) 'the real significance of the...deal does not rest on how deeply countries have liberalised....What may matter more for the governance of the global information economy is that the deal signals the beginning of an evolutionary process of mutual adjustment that will unfold according to a clearly defined set of principles, baselines and mechanisms'. The ABT contains provision for information sharing procedures and dialogue, thereby creating the possibility for convergent regulatory thinking.

Finally, the WTO is notably different from its predecessors due to the establishment in its architectural principles and practices of dispute settlement. This system endows the WTO with the enforcement teeth necessary to ensure that Agreements, such as the ABT, are complied with. Should any party argue to the WTO that another member is contravening its commitments, then an examination of the complaint is triggered which, if proven valid, could result ultimately in the imposition of sanctions against the miscreant member. It is perhaps an indication of how significantly the neo-liberal model of telecommunications regulation has pervaded the industrialised world that, since the signing of the ABT only one dispute has been heard at the WTO in telecommunications, where the USA successfully challenged Mexico regarding the interconnection arrangements between the Mexican incumbent Telmex and US telecommunications operators (*Telecom Markets*, 22.03.2004).

ELECTRONIC COMMERCE, THE EU AND THE WTO

The WTO Agreement on Basic Telecommunications and associated Reference Paper provided a framework for the global liberalisation of telecommunications services between its signatories. However, the Agreement did not cover a potentially very important, and growing, element of all commercial activity conducted over electronic communications networks, namely what the EU has come to term broadly as Information Society services, epitomised more widely in electronic commerce. As Chapter 6 has illustrated, providing international, in this case European, regulatory solutions to issues which relate to the carriage of communications content has, to date, proved too demanding a policy hurdle for the EU and its Member States to negotiate. Similarly, as noted earlier in this chapter, in the context of GATT, it became clear in the mid–1990s that it would be impossible to conclude any liberalisation agreement on audiovisual products or services, an important part of communications content.

To what extent then, does electronic commerce differ from 'traditional' telecommunications and audiovisual services and to what extent has the WTO been able to secure the basis for a global trade agreement here? E-commerce refers to transactions which occur across electronic communications networks between businesses, private consumers and the public sector where, at a minimum, the good or service in question is ordered electronically, but, depending on its nature, might be paid for and/or delivered either electronically or 'physically'. In its earliest days, e-commerce was almost exclusively conducted between businesses (known as B2B) and was facilitated through the leasing of dedicated line capacity from fixed link telecommunications providers. Electronic Data Interchange (EDI) was one of the most notable early applications of business to business e-commerce activity, spawning, at the international level, several efforts to create a common regulatory approach, such as the 1987 Uniform Rules of Conduct for Interchange of Trade Data by Teletransmission (UNCID) concluded by the International Chamber of Commerce, in which the European Commission played a role.[9] The EU itself adopted the European model EDI Agreement (1994) and launched a promotional project, the Trade Electronic Data Interchange System programme (TEDIS). The United Nations Conference on International Trade Law produced, in 1996, an important Model Law on Electronic Commerce which set out a framework containing a series of measures for states to implement to ensure common international treatment of e-commerce trade issues and provided a signpost for the EU in its regulatory approach to the issues thereafter.[10]

However, it was really the growth of the Internet which broadened the possibilities for expansion of electronic commercial activity. As the Internet became more user–friendly due to a series of technical innovations, it became possible to allow computer owners from around the world to communicate with each other in a speedy, increasingly sophisticated and affordable manner. Unlike the rather more limited commercial environment of leased line based business–to–business e-commerce, the Internet, through the increasingly user–friendly World Wide Web, can offer searching, marketing, transaction and payment facilities for all goods and services as well as delivery for new so–called electronic goods (e.g. music, software) and services (e.g. insurance, financial).

Whilst the Internet initially evolved separately from telecommunications, in order to reach a global set of users it was necessary to utilise telecommunications infrastructures, particularly at the local level. The increasing value of the Internet to business interests, both potential vendors of goods and services across its space and those who provide access and infrastructural services related to its functioning, led to a consideration of how its governance might evolve at the international level. The high profile and ultimately short–lived 'dot–com' boom of the late 1990s, located primarily in the US, fuelled further the already heady expectations of Internet growth. The Internet is somewhat unique, in that, whilst originating in the USA, it did not develop within the strong state communications policy traditions associated with telecommunications and broadcasting which as this volume has illustrated, proved difficult to change, particularly in Europe. As a communications network with fundamentally global credentials, strong arguments were propounded to develop an appropriate regulatory apparatus for it at the global level, not least for its commercial aspects.

In this respect, Simpson and Wilkinson (2003a) have discerned a range of features of a loose, nascent, global system for e-commerce regulation. Most important among these is the ardent pursuit of global e-commerce liberalisation, underpinned by an ideological promulgation of open, international, competition. Here, the telecommunications liberalisation agenda has provided important foundational support in international fora for the pursuit of this goal. Also significant has been the attempt to ensure that systems of international property rights protection are extended from the non–electronic marketplace into its electronic equivalent (see May 2002), evident in deliberations taking place between parties in the World Intellectual Property Organization (WIPO). Third, the emergence of e-commerce has been associated with calls for the creation, where possible, of systems of self–regulation in which 'market players determine and monitor the implementation of standards of commercial behaviour as well as settle disagreements between each other without recourse to either external regulatory intervention or the legal system' (Simpson and Wilkinson 2003b, p. 12). The most notable embodiment of this kind of approach to Internet regulation is the ICANN, created in 1999 to manage the Internet's domain name and Internet Protocol address system (Klein 2002). As illustrated below, liberalisation, self–regulation and electronic property rights protection have become three central aspects of the WTO's examination of e-commerce issues.

As noted in Chapter 6, though relatively late in realising the importance of the Internet, the EU began to construct a series of policy initiatives related to its development and use. Nonetheless, though the epitome of ICT convergence in many respects, it was decided to exclude the Internet and, more specifically, content services (known broadly as Information Society services, including e-commerce) from its proposed common communications regulatory framework, the upshot of the convergence debate of the late 1990s. The evolutionary nature of the Internet and commercial activity being undertaken across it, combined with the inherently global nature of this activity, cautioned against any early, and thus a possibly too–restrictive and generally inappropriate, regulatory treatment. Nonetheless, as noted above, the roots of the EU's (essentially closed user group) e-commerce policy predated the Internet, though the emergence of the Internet did focus sharply the minds of policy makers within the EU on these issues (interview, European Commission, 2004).

In 1997, a promotional initiative on e-commerce was launched (European Commission 1997c) which advocated coordinative action in areas such as intellectual property rights, privacy and taxation, as well as the pursuit of a globally liberalised market for telecommunications infrastructures and services, thereby illustrating the importance of the perceived link between electronic commerce and telecommunications policy. The EU attempted to set up the basis of a regulatory framework for e-commerce, in 2000, through the passage of a Directive on E-Commerce (European Parliament and Council 2000b) which laid out a set of criteria for the common treatment of Information Society service provision throughout the EU. The aim of the directive is to stipulate the basic legal parameters for the creation of a single EU market in e-commerce with a focus on, *inter alia*, issues such as: information requirements; commercial communications; electronic contracting; liability of Internet intermediaries; codes of conduct and out–of–court dispute settlement procedures. Due to its transposition date of 17 January 2002, the Directive has been operational for only a very short period of time and it is difficult to judge its impact at the time of writing, complicated by the fact that, by December 2003, there were still three EU Member States (France, Holland and Portugal) which had not fully transposed its provisions into their national laws. It is also the case that despite the heady predictions of growth of the late 1990s, e-commerce still only accounts for approximately 1–2 per cent of total retail sales across the EU, though it has been predicted that as many as 54 per cent of European Internet users will make online purchases by 2006 (European Commission 2003d, p. 5). The EU also developed a significant policy position on the taxation of e-commerce in the late 1990s, when it was decided to introduce indirect taxation at the point of consumption for services delivered to, and consumed within, the EU's jurisdiction (European Commission 2000c).

The EU's motivation here was twofold. First, it was considered necessary to eradicate a competitive disadvantage which EU firms were deemed to be encumbered with in that, until this juncture, they were obligated to charge Value Added Tax (VAT) on services at the point of production, thereby being placed at a potential disadvantage vis-à-vis competitor firms in jurisdictions outside the EU whose governments did not impose this requirement. In the new regime, 'European companies would no longer have to charge any VAT on services which they exported from the EU to another jurisdiction. Whether (and how much) VAT was levied on these services would be up to the government of the consumer of the particular service in question' (Halpin and Simpson 2002, p. 289). Second, this decision sent an important signal to the international communications policy–making community of the EU's intent to ensure that e-commerce was utilised for revenue generating purposes by the public sector in Europe. This position stood in stark contrast to that of the US government which was strongly in favour of refraining from taxation of electronic commerce, at the very least until it became a well–established part of commercial activity domestically and internationally.

Given these characteristic features, it was of little surprise when, in 1998, the WTO launched a Work Programme which aimed to deal with e-commerce trade issues from the perspectives of its four main areas of responsibility: trade in goods, trade in services, intellectual property and development (WTO 1998). Since 2001, it has also considered a series of what have been described as cross–cutting issues within its General Council (WTO 2001). As an organisation whose remit is to promote and extend global trade liberalisation to as many sectors of the economy as possible, the WTO is faced with the somewhat unusual circumstances of addressing a new area of trade in which there are few regulations in existence at either the national or international level. Thus, evidence to date suggests that the most powerful state players within the WTO, principally the USA and the EU, have viewed its task as ensuring that the electronic trading environment remains as internationally open and competitive as possible with the number of new rules on e-commerce kept to a minimum (Simpson 2004b). It has been argued that the Telecommunications Annex, agreed at the conclusion of the Uruguay Round, covers Internet data services, due to its reference to freedom of choice of protocol and that the subsequent ABT is both technologically neutral in approach and specifically includes market access agreements for packet switched services (Cowhey 2004, p. 69). Moreover, the development of new Internet based services, most notably Internet telephony, has created new challenges for traditional telecommunications service providers since, *inter alia*, it presents another means of bypassing the international accounting rate regime (Frieden 2004).

To create and preserve a liberally ordered global e-commerce sector does not require states to undertake the journey of governance change which has characterised the last 20 years of the telecommunications sector. Thus, the movement from state ownership to the 'regulatory state' context of detailed sector specific regulation has not been mirrored in e-commerce. Arguably, a key goal of the EU's ECRF, namely to replace ex-ante sector specific regulation with general competition and consumer law in telecommunications, is similar to the preferences of the EU and the USA in the current debate on e-commerce regulation. In this way, the ideas and practices of global economic liberalisation are impacting on these two important parts of the communications sector, though in rather different contexts, respectively.

Nonetheless, despite the deliberations undertaken to date, it was not possible for members to agree sufficiently to be able to proceed to formal trade negotiations at the September 2003 WTO ministerial meeting in Cancun, Mexico. In fact, it was declared that more work was necessary on a range of issues such as: the classification of electronically transmitted content as goods or services (or both); the fiscal aspects of e-commerce; development issues related to e-commerce; jurisdictional and applicable law issues. This suggests that there is considerable uncertainty among states, particularly from developing regions, about the likely significance of e-commerce for them in the future and consequently a reluctance to make commitments which they might later learn are not in their interests (Simpson and Wilkinson 2003b).

Unsurprisingly, the main contributors to the debates have been those countries at the leading edge of e-commerce developments. In this regard, the EU has been prominent in putting across its policy model and appears to have achieved considerable success in ensuring its ideas have been prominent in the limited agreement achieved among WTO members to date. This is in no small part due to the fact that, in the main, it has shared a similar view to the USA on how e-commerce trade regulation should be shaped within the WTO, though as the divergent approach to the indirect taxation issue has shown, there have also been differences between the two. The recent conclusion of bilateral trade agreements between the USA and, respectively, Chile, Singapore, Australia and Central American states, each of which contain a chapter on e-commerce affirming free trade in digital products (Bernier 2004), may be indicative of the currently favoured US strategy in this area. It is important to note, too, that the structure of the EU's contrasting commitments to telecommunications and broadcasting at the WTO has the potential to become open to scrutiny due to the emergence of new hybrid Internet commerce services, notably the distribution of audio and video content through the Internet (Larouche 2004) and may create pressure in the future to modify current exemptions taken in the audiovisual sector, in particular.

Overall indications are that e-commerce issues are likely to be dealt with within a broadly neo-liberal framework underpinned, where possible, by self–regulation with rigorous and extensive protection of property rights, dealt with through existing and well–established WTO agreements, notably the GATS, the GATT and the Trade Related Aspects of Intellectual Property Agreement, a situation strongly supported by the EU and one from which it has most to gain should e-commerce expand further.

CONCLUSIONS

This chapter has focused on the development of global trade regulation in the electronic communications sector and the position of the EU in this complex milieu of change. As shown in Chapter 2, the changing nature of production in the latter part of the twentieth century, most notably its internationalisation, energised those interests which had called for a dismantling of the traditional telecommunications regulatory system. Expanding internationalisation of economic activities required communications tools and facilities commensurate with the desire of multinational firms to expand their global reach and new technological possibilities in telecommunications offered the requisite tools to facilitate international productive activities. However, aside from the national and regional level political and regulatory obstacles to change, as we have shown in this chapter, the traditional global arrangements for telecommunications regulation were considered to be, equally, in need of reform by those promoting the neo-liberal political–economic agenda.

To gain acceptance of a radically different regulatory model for international telecommunications was, as we have shown, a challenging task for its proponents. What occurred was a gradual, but steady, growth in the view that telecommunications should be reconstituted as a globally competitive sector, intra– and *inter*–nationally, and that this was best achieved by the creation of a regulatory regime at the global level to cater for the promotion of international trade and investment issues. The launch of the World Trade Organization in 1995 provided the appropriate institutional context for this to occur, though it is also the case that the significant pressure for such regulatory re–focusing of telecommunications played at least some part in the argument for creation of the WTO in the first place, evidenced by the fact that telecommunications liberalisation was one of the first tasks addressed. Thus, the kind of dialectical, mutually reinforcing, relationship between globalisation and telecommunications regulation referred to in Chapter 1 is evident in the connection between the telecommunications sector and the WTO.

The WTO (and its predecessor organisation, the GATT) also created a forum in which those advocating global telecommunications liberalisation could attempt to promulgate its logic and ensure transfer and acceptance of a new policy context in telecommunications regulation. Drahos and Joseph (1995, p. 627) argue that in respect of the uptake and diffusion of the National Information Infrastructure initiative, popularised in European Union political rhetoric and practice as the Information Society, 'a process of copying or imitation rather than...the exercise of power by interest groups' occurred. This idea is interesting and may account for some of the mechanics of the new emerging global system for telecommunications regulation which we have charted in this chapter. Nonetheless, a detailed explanation for the important events witnessed must incorporate more than a passive imitation process.

As we have shown, once created, the WTO, because of its 'command and control' functions exercised ultimately, though not solely, in its Dispute Settlement Mechanism, provided a forum in which further policy 'learning' could take place between signatories. It is also the case that as more countries 'buy in' to the liberalisation agenda, the greater is the 'shut out' pressure on those who do not wish to proceed with liberalisation at all, or would rather do so more slowly than they are being asked to. Pressure to adopt new policy ideas in telecommunications is also felt from the fact that aid is often associated with an acceptance of a liberalised, competitive paradigm as a starting point. Nonetheless, as we have shown, the process of change in international telecommunications has neither been completely smooth, nor as a consequence, complete. This has been reflected in the tension between the ITU, the bastion of traditional international telecommunications regulation and the WTO – the former has experienced a reduction in its institutional authority and has also been buffeted by those advocating reform of the international telecommunications system most aggressively, notably the USA. It has been argued that that there are signs that both organisations are settling into something of a partnership, where the ITU will deal with technical matters, leaving the WTO to deal with economic regulation (Larouche 2004), which is arguably more politically high profile, though the ITU's recent attempt to set the agenda in the global debate on Internet governance and the Information Society might suggest otherwise.

Those countries (mostly developing nations) wishing to proceed more slowly with reform have attempted to set a more gradual pace of change within the ITU as is witnessed by its allegedly ponderous reform of the international call charging system, increasingly outside its power nonetheless. At present, the growing internationalised, liberal telecommunications system does not encompass all economies of the world, though it is clearly the case that 'most of the world's international telecoms traffic, however, will flow within one or more of the Single Market Groups [created by the ABT], enabling the Single Market environment to shape the way such traffic is carried' (Tyler and Bednarczyk 1998, p. 799). The vital inclusion in the WTO's policy 'armoury' of the Dispute Settlement Mechanism has endowed the ABT with 'implementation teeth' absent from previous international regulatory agreements, such as those of the ITU. Whilst the latter's consensus derived treaties bound their members according to the conventions of international law (MacLean 1995, p. 177), in practice the loose intergovernmentalism of the ITU meant that settlement of any disputes occurred bilaterally, if at all.

In terms of the more content–rich elements of electronic communications services, the WTO has played a more limited role. In fact, to date, it has not been possible to create any sort of an agreement on audiovisual services where the national–centric gravitational pull of broadcasting has proven resistant to any efforts at global trade liberalisation. By contrast, e-commerce trade appears to be something of a tailor–made scenario for extending the WTO's governance remit, though whilst considerable deliberation has occurred, both the complexity of, and uncertainty surrounding, e-commerce has largely prevented a trade agreement from being signed, though there is strong evidence of the ideas and practices of neo-liberal international communications capitalism having been well established in this nascent policy area also. Many of the new convergent ICT services referred to in Chapter 6, which straddle the traditional vertical demarcations between telecommunications and broadcasting, for example, may create considerable debate in the future at the WTO in terms of whether they fall under existing agreements in telecommunications or, by contrast, are covered by exemptions taken by WTO members in audiovisual services. The lack of clear definitions of terms included in the WTO Classification List for communications services may have laid fertile ground for this to develop in (Nihoul 2004), though any perceived encroachment into the area of broadcasting is likely to be firmly resisted by the EU, its clear movements towards a more convergent approach to communications regulation notwithstanding (see Chapters 5 and 6).

The position of the EU in this evolving global communications policy context is highly significant. As is well known, it was not the initial proponent of liberalisation of telecommunications and even at the beginning of the 1990s many of its Member States' ex–PTTs were reluctant to see competition introduced into their national markets, let alone any disruption of their stable and secure commercial revenues streams easily garnered from international call charging. However, as the opportunities of competitive telecommunications environments became clear and as they learned to adapt to the new realities of the sector, the promulgation of a model at the global level which they had, for most, only recently accepted 'internally' within the EU, seemed increasingly logical. Thus, through their 'principal agent', the European Commission, they soon campaigned within global institutions for the adoption of liberalisation of telecommunications. In fact, since the conclusion of the ABT, the EU has pressed hard to ensure not only its implementation, but also its extension, in the process coming into conflict with influential WTO members such as Japan (*European Voice*, 01.03.2001). As we have shown, the ABT largely mirrors the EU policy model and is evidence of the success of the EU in securing, in outline at least, the transfer of its approach to telecommunications to the global level. Rather differently, the power of the EU as a global political actor in the communications sector was also clearly illustrated by its success in securing a cultural exemption for audiovisual products and services in the Uruguay Round negotiations.

By contrast, the implementation of the ABT has brought the EU into conflict with the USA. Here, the latter, spurred on by its telecommunications industry lobby groups and buoyed by its victory against Mexico in a WTO–adjudicated interconnection trade dispute (see above), has complained against what it alleges is unfair economic practice in the area of fixed–to–mobile international termination rates (*Telecom Markets*, 22.03.2004). These rates have been estimated to be at least three times higher than might be justified by the cost of provision, plus a reasonable profit margin to a telecommunications service provider (*CommunicationsWeek International*,

27.01.2003) and the issue, though remaining unresolved at the time of writing, is likely to precipitate a decline in rates factored by European operators into the fixed–to–mobile settlement process. The USA has also drawn on WTO trade agreements as a tool in its attempt to thwart what it considered to be EU efforts at imposing the technical standards for its Universal Mobile Telecommunications System (UMTS) which could work to the exclusion of alternative systems and, thus, service providers (*European Voice*, 08.10.1998; 07.01.1999).

The limited, though still significant, policy activity of the EU in the area of e-commerce has given it sufficient experience to be a policy leader in the deliberations which have taken place at WTO level thus far, where with the USA and other leading edge industrial states, it has propounded a minimalist, liberal regulatory model for the consideration of e-commerce trade issues underpinned by preference for the extension and enforcement of a strongly protective property rights regime to the electronic realm. Outside the confines of the WTO, the EU has also shown itself willing to stamp its own individual policy mark on the treatment of e-commerce, in the process challenging USA policy preferences, as evidenced by its landmark initiative on indirect taxation, as well bilateral negotiations on data privacy which produced the safe harbour compromise agreement with the US (see Farrell 2003). However, whilst undoubtedly successful in both the telecommunications and audiovisual policy contexts for very different reasons, it is as yet not possible to determine the extent to which the EU's policy preferences will be manifest in the trade regime for e-commerce which emerges from the WTO, though it is highly likely to be, for the most part, to the EU's satisfaction.

NOTES

1. Based on four levels of economic development standardised by the World Bank and the ITU: see Frieden (1998).
2. One-way bypass occurs where a foreign company could take advantage of leased line liberalisation in the USA to terminate calls there more cheaply that the settlement rate agreed between the two countries. Price squeezing occurs where a foreign company (which due to liberalisation is permitted to set up in the USA) is able to subsidise its affiliate there due to excess profit made from the above cost settlement rate on its transactions. This subsidisation may take the form of pricing below cost in order to squeeze out any competition on the route: see Cowhey (1998).
3. They comprise support for liberalisation; initiatives to compensate for lack of market forces; provision of accounting rate data; development of new cost principles; support for transitional arrangements for less developed countries in a global competitive marketplace.
4. These refer to market issues such as the number of suppliers permitted; total value of transactions; total quantity of output; number of employees permitted; any requirements for a specific type of legal entity e.g a joint venture; foreign equity ownership: see Tuthill (1997).

5. Only 55 schedules were submitted initially since the European Commission is the representative negotiator for EU Member States in the WTO.
6. There were other more limited commitments made by other countries in both market access and FDI areas.
7. Such as allocation of numbers, environmental planning, universal service obligations, permanence of the network or service in question.
8. However, Member States may refrain from MFN implementation if they sign the so-called negative list at the point of accession to the Organisation or thereafter by obtaining a special waiver from the ETO Ministerial Conference.
9. Other parties were the United Nations Conference on International Trade Law (UNCITRAL), the United Nations Conference on Trade and Development (UNCTAD), the United Nations Economic Commission for Europe (ECE), the Organisation for Economic Co-operation and Development (OECD), the International Organisation for Standardisation (ISO), the World Customs Organisation (WCO), the Organisation for Data Exchange by Tele-transmission in Europe (ODETTE) and the European Insurance Committee (EIC).
10. Issues dealt with in the Model Law relate principally to the formation and validation of electronic contracts.

8. Conclusions – globalisation, convergence and European telecommunications regulation

This volume has charted the unprecedented transformation in the ownership and governance of telecommunications across the EU in approximately the last 25 years. The accompanying changes which have occurred as a consequence of this, are of importance in two broad respects. First, they have called into question traditional assumptions about the structure, functions and role of telecommunications in the economies and societies of the European Union. Second, what has occurred in telecommunications provides an important example of the effects and their consequences of structural change, most outstandingly in this case, economic globalisation, on sectors of the European economy. This chapter has two main themes, reflective and forward looking respectively. It commences by drawing together the key themes of the volume and considering in summary how these have emerged in the evidence presented on the evolution of telecommunications regulation in previous chapters. The chapter then moves to a consideration of some of the key issues which are likely to influence the debate on the further evolution of the Electronic Communications Regulatory Framework. Here, consideration is given, in particular, to the relationship between the EU and national levels in an increasingly complex regulatory scenario, the prospects for further convergence in communications regulation in Europe and, finally, the place of public service provision in the communications sector which is increasingly likely to be dominated by sector–specific and more general regulatory measures with overwhelmingly economic goals.

GLOBALISATION AND REGULATORY CHANGE IN TELECOMMUNICATIONS

In Chapter 1, the conceptual framework for this volume's description and analysis of change in the governance of telecommunications across Europe was outlined. Centrally, the nature and direction of regulatory change in the sector, what we have described as our dependent variable, has been explained through the positing of a framework containing a set of important independent and intervening variables. Throughout the period of time covered in this volume, the multidirectional influence of these often interlinked and overlapping factors: technological change, globalisation, international regulatory competition in the context of the developing regulatory state, economic interests, and ideas has been in strong evidence. The well–known key broad additions to the technological 'portfolio' of telecommunications, most notably digitisation and digital compression, as well as fibre optical and microwave transmission, produced a context within which convergent business and governance strategies in telecommunications (and later the electronic communications sector as a whole) could be considered and pursued. These technologies underpinned the creation of a new and much more expansive range of services, many eagerly provided by companies from outside traditional telecommunications industrial circles. The broad common nature of technological change, too, made it possible to utilise new services for international communications purposes in sophisticated ways never before possible. The distance–defying potential of new telecommunications technology certainly laid a platform, at the very least, upon which converging expectations could be developed of what new services should constitute, the manner in which they should be delivered, and how much they should cost. By contrast, the pursuit of technological progress presented a series of new cost challenges to the manufacturing component of the telecommunications industry in which the pursuit of an international strategy – through direct sales expansion, international merger, full or partial acquisition, or even joint venture – became significant. Internationalisation of strategic responses to the cost challenges of technological change was yet another catalyst for more convergent patterns of activity to be developed in telecommunications, traditionally a nationally demarcated and ordered sector.

The internationalisation of telecommunications, part facilitated by technological change, has come to be recognised as a significant element of a recent broader phase of globalisation of the world economy. In fact, this volume has demonstrated that, in the first instance, it was trends and pressures associated with globalising economic activity which provided a vital spur for telecommunications reform. Thereafter, however, it is possible to argue that a bi–directional and mutually reinforcing, though not necessarily equal, relationship has developed between the two, most visible in the World Trade Organisation's treatment of telecommunications dealt with in Chapter 7. The globalisation of telecommunications has at least three dimensions. First, many producers and service providers in telecommunications, traditionally nationally rooted and focused, have developed through time strong international commercial outlooks and strategies. Second, telecommunications users, most particularly businesses, began to consider the global availability of advanced, high speed, and affordable communications services, to be not just an advantage in their pursuit of international market share gain, but even essential to it. As this volume has described, in Europe this translated into a political strategy to achieve their demands, pursued at both the national and EU levels. Third, as telecommunications has developed many more traits of internationalism (as opposed to its historically *inter*–national structure) international trade and international foreign direct investment issues have become so significant that a re–evaluation of global rules governing telecommunications has occurred. As Chapter 7 has shown, this has caused a clear shift in global institutional regulatory power in telecommunications from the ITU to the WTO.

One of the most important consequences of the above traits is the emergence of Cerny's (1997) 'competition states' in telecommunications. Recognised as a general phenomenon of economic globalisation (Chapter 1), the telecommunications sector provides a classic example of the international bandwagon effects of changes in governance in economic sectors. The analysis of the EU in this volume shows how states decided to alter their governance strategies through the introduction of competition into a highly uncompetitive sector. Second, states have made a clear decision to relinquish public ownership of telecommunications service providers, at least partly and, in many cases, completely. Third, a series of independent regulatory authorities have been created to implement a new set of rules aimed primarily, though not exclusively, at creating an environment of managed competition in telecommunications.

Here, there is very clear evidence of the evolution of Majone's (1996) 'regulatory state' in which a combination of neo-liberal and, somewhat paradoxically, neo-mercantilist, policies have been employed domestically and internationally. Once established in telecommunications, having been adopted by a number of leading edge industrial states, these regulatory arrangements were soon emulated by others. It is also possible to argue that the EU, through the European Commission's 'regulatory state–like' behaviour, has emerged as a major proponent and exponent of this approach. This volume has also illustrated how, once established, liberalising re-regulation itself became a reinforcing agent for more intensive globalisation of telecommunications, in that it soon became de rigeur in the global telecommunications policy–making scenario and was accepted by many states, particularly those with developing economies, which initially eschewed it.

Suffusing and to some extent framing the globalisation and competitive re-regulation of telecommunications has been the power of ideas in the shape of neo-liberalism. This seismic shift in perspective on the governance of telecommunications has involved a rejection of state ownership and direct state management of telecommunications in favour of the structure and disciplines of the market. There is no doubt that a competitively ordered, internationally open and independently regulated telecommunications sector has been promulgated (initially by those with the greatest material interest in securing it) and broadly accepted by the majority of nation states as a desirable state of affairs. Globalisation is bolstered and sustained by its own ideological discourse and norms which have questioned the suitability of traditional 'interventionist state' functions and international economic order and presented a new alternative as imperative and, thus, inevitable. As Chapter 7 has noted, negotiations which led to the signing of the 1997 Agreement on Basic telecommunications in the WTO, the Agreement itself, and changes in the nature of the international bastion of the old telecommunications order, the ITU, provide evidence that liberalised re-regulation is now viewed as the general normative framework within which the future developmental parameters of telecommunications are negotiated and constructed.

REFRACTING AND FILTERING STRUCTURAL CHANGES IN TELECOMMUNICATIONS: THE EU, NATIONAL POLICY CONTEXTS AND THE LIMITS TO CONVERGENCE

The above series of interlinked factors which have underpinned the transformation of telecommunications might be expected to result in the restructuring of those markets, whose states have accepted and adopted the norms and practices of neo-liberal economic order, in a very similar, if not identical, manner. However, this volume has shown that a prediction of this kind would prove much too deterministic, since it ignores the crucial influence of national and EU institutional contexts. First, as noted in Chapter 1, the domestic politics context can play an important 'refractory' role shaping the effects of global structural trends in particular and, ultimately, producing patterns of diversity within a similarly framed regulatory context. Second, the analysis of telecommunications governance in Europe has a further layer of complexity in the shape of the European Union, the institutions of which (in particular the European Commission) have proved to be important agents of Europeanisation of telecommunications governance. Third, as illustrated in Chapters 3, 4, 5 and 6 of this volume, as the Europeanised version of competitive telecommunications re-regulation has developed over the course of the last 20 years, an important bi-directional, multi-component, governance relationship has developed between the EU and national Member State levels.

For national Member States, the EU provided an important institutional context which could be utilised as a part of their response to the structural changes and strategic challenges of telecommunications. However, as this volume notes, many of the initial governance changes in the leading edge economies of Europe took place either before, or in tandem with, the regulatory package which was developed at EU level. Thus, this volume has argued that liberalising re-regulation would have occurred across Europe in the absence of the EU, though it would undoubtedly have been a different process in terms of structure and timing. Thus, the EU institutional context has been an important intervening variable, assisting Member States in 'making sense' of globalising telecommunications. Their signing up to the 'EU route' was part of a plan to maximise economic welfare in their jurisdictions from challenges and opportunities arising in the electronic communications sector. As shown, they have been able in numerous ways to 'upload' their interests to the EU level and ensure that they have borne some weight in negotiated policy outcomes (e.g. France and its 'service public'). Consequently, a distinctly 'European' character to liberalised and re-regulated telecommunications has become very much apparent. This is most obviously embodied in the package of legislative measures that has been developed since the late 1980s. However, Chapter 7 has also indicated that the EU's policy model for telecommunications regulation – essentially neo-liberal but with certain significant public service elements – has been at least partially adopted at the global level in the WTO Agreement on Basic Telecommunications, which bears remarkable similarity, by no coincidence, to the central elements of the EU's 1998 telecommunications regulatory framework.

Also, as explained in detail in Chapters 4 and 5, whilst the EU regulatory framework has provided a context within which approaches to the governance of telecommunications have converged along a series of regulatory lines, the transposition and implementation of the agreed EU telecommunications regulatory package clearly illustrates persistent diversity in EU Member States' interpretation of, and response to, new telecommunications environments, that is, they have downloaded the package in different ways. Here, the classic imprint of political–institutional traditions is evident in transposition patterns for EU legislation. However, there are two significant caveats to this. First, a small number of Member States, notably the UK and Sweden, had already undertaken significant telecommunications liberalisation ahead of agreements of a similar kind made at the EU level. Second, on occasion, the political–institutional context was able to facilitate swift transposition of EU legislation in states which had expressed a reluctance to liberalise at the outset, notably France. However, it is in the implementation of telecommunications legislation that a diversity of approaches to the new regulatory paradigm is most strongly evident. Thus, whilst liberalising re-regulation have become the watchwords of telecommunications in Europe as elsewhere in world, their pronunciation among EU Member States currently differs (Humphreys 2002, Simpson forthcoming). This echoes the findings of both Schmidt (2002) and Weiss (1998; 2003) on the consequences of economic globalisation in Europe.

However, it is the nature of the relatively new relationship between the EU–institutional and Member State levels that is the most unique characteristic response of the Europeans to structural change in telecommunications. Developing a vital part of the liberalised telecommunications framework at EU level promised advantages but also incurred a number of political costs to states. As Chapter 3 has noted, those Member States which had already liberalised could promote this course of action to a wider European audience in the knowledge that they were first movers in a new regulatory paradigm. By contrast, Member States with ideological and practical reservations about an out and out liberalising approach could attempt to utilise the EU as a protective mechanism against the more extreme elements of regulatory competition, in the process working from the inside to secure compromises which would shape liberalising re-regulation in ways more suited to their traditional politico–economic approach to the communications sector. Third, once Member States had embarked upon a process of liberalisation, the EU level could be used to undertake policy learning about the mechanics of new regulatory governance, as well to disseminate what was considered best practice to other states in the hope that it would gain EU–wide acceptance.

Nonetheless, the development of telecommunications policy at the EU level also resulted in the significant loss of control and commensurate uncertainty which is part and parcel of the Europeanisation of any policy area, though this was perhaps more starkly experienced by Member States in telecommunications, given its highly specific state–centric history. Aside from the obvious potential loss of control due to joint decision making with other Member States, this volume has shown that the European Commission has emerged as an important new institutional actor in EU telecommunications policy. The Commission has variously occupied the role of policy entrepreneur, lobbying point for commercial and governmental interests, administrative facilitator and collaborator for its Member States, sponsor of cross–national policy learning and transfer, and, occasionally, coercive agent (Humphreys 2004; Simpson forthcoming). The Commission is, arguably, likely to continue to play the most important role at EU level in the future implementation of the ECRF, as well as representing European interests in the WTO global trade forum. The remainder of this chapter focuses on some key current and likely future issues which will arise and partly determine the functioning and development of the new governance framework.

CHALLENGES AND FUTURE PROSPECTS FOR THE EU'S ELECTRONIC COMMUNICATIONS REGULATORY FRAMEWORK

As Chapters 5 and 6 have shown, the period preceding the proposal of the electronic communications regulatory framework involved an important debate on what should, and should not, be included therein, couched within a review of the convergence of the technologies and services of information and communications. This convergence was undoubtedly given impetus by the growth of the Internet through the 1990s and the short–lived 'dot–com' boom. Whilst the new framework excludes regulation of communications content relating most specifically to broadcasting, on the one hand, and Internet–based and Information Society services (electronic commerce), on the other, this does not mean that all of these important parts of the communications sector are outside the new framework. The fact that it does explicitly cover all communications infrastructures and services directly associated with the provision of infrastructures means that key elements of these sub—sectors of communications do form part of the new regulatory structure.

A number of factors will determine the extent to which both broadcasting and Internet *content services* might become a part of an expanded common electronic communications regulatory framework in the future. First, the Internet and broadcasting are sub-sectors of communications which are likely to witness continued growth in the short to medium term. In broadcasting, the take–up of digital TV, with all its associated multimedia and interactive applications, is proceeding apace. The Internet too, though well established in most parts of the EU, still has considerable capacity for growth (in terms of access) and development (in terms of new service offerings). Second, both digital television and the Internet are highly significant in that they are quintessential embodiments of convergence, since their technical platforms provide the potential to transmit and receive content services simultaneously combining voice, data, text and pictures. In terms of governing the conditions of *access* to these services and their precursors, there is already clear evidence of the EU staking out its regulatory territory. In 2002, for example, the Commission produced a working document for the Open Network Provision Committee considering the implications of the new common framework for broadcasting. This document noted that the new framework, principally through the Access and Universal Services directives, covered all of the following: authorisation of radio and broadcasting networks; the allocation and assignment of spectrum used for the provision of broadcasting transmission services; must–carry obligations on networks for radio and television broadcasts to the public; access to facilities such as conditional access systems, application programme interfaces and electronic programme guides; third–party access to broadcasting networks to distribute electronic communications services other than broadcast content; and interoperability between consumer digital television equipment (European Commission 2002c). The Commission has also released a communication, put together by Directorate–General Information Society, on interoperability of digital interactive television services, an issue covered by article 18 of the Framework Directive of the electronic communications regulatory package. Here the Commission, whilst finding no grounds to do so at present, has declared its willingness in the future to take action against Member States by mandating common standards, where it finds a lack of choice available to the consumer (European Commission 2004d).

In terms of the Internet, the transmission of video has been possible for sometime and is now common, though by no means ubiquitous, illustrating some degree of convergence with broadcasting. However, much more immediately relevant for the new EU framework and potentially crucial for traditional telecommunications providers, has been the emergence and growth of VoIP services. Here, the EU has already begun to address VoIP through considering access issues as part of the Electronic Communications Regulatory Framework. In a recent working document on the matter, the Commission produced a number of recommendations to Member States and their NRAs, in particular. These dealt with issues related to safeguarding the welfare of consumers in contexts where VoIP suppliers offer access to public telephone networks. Indicating the embryonic nature of regulatory thinking at present, the Commission also called for opinions on regulatory issues such as interconnection, interoperability, numbering and extra–territorial provision (that is outside the territory of a typical NRA's jurisdiction) related to VoIP services (European Commission 2004e). There are indications that major telecommunications incumbents, notably British Telecom, are in the process of re-modelling at least some of their strategies for future service provision around VoIP. Although impossible to determine with accuracy at the time of writing, developments in the service panorama of the Internet are likely to ensure that it will become a much more significant element of the EU's electronic communications regulatory framework in the future.

For both the Internet and broadcasting, the central significance of content in the service offerings of each ensured their exclusion, for the most part, from the framework to date. However, should convergent network and service contexts continue to develop, then the arguments for broadening the framework's remit to deal with content issues may gain ground. This would undoubtedly require wholesale and imaginative remodelling of the regulatory treatment of the public service dimension to communications and is some distance away, if it is indeed ever to be realised. However, there are signs that some Member States at least are moving in the direction of developing a common regulatory approach to communications. Most outstandingly, the UK and Italy have been the forerunners in creating convergent national regulators for all electronic communications. The UK's move in this direction was in some ways a surprise, given the lukewarm reception of the prospect in its government green paper of 1997 which quickly followed the Commission's own paper on the subject. However, the UK has shown itself to be in the vanguard of regulatory change in the communications sector over the course of the last 25 years – both in telecommunications and broadcasting – and such policy experimentalism does tally with past strategies. The UK was the neo-liberal forerunner of telecommunications reform in the EU in the early 1980s and, as this volume has indicated, the progress of its experiment was closely followed by other Member States, who were to some extent swayed by the practical benefits which began to be accrued from the changes wrought, ideological misgivings aside. Much the same may happen with the progress of its new convergent regulatory approach, launched at the end of 2003 with the mobilisation of a new regulator, the Office of Communications. It is too early to say at this stage whether Ofcom will prove something of a catalyst for similar regulatory changes across the EU.

Aside from whether completely convergent regulatory approaches are adopted at the national level by a greater number of EU Member States than at present, as Chapter 6 has noted, it is likely to require a quantum leap for the regulation of communications infrastructures and content to be dealt with comprehensively at the European level. Nevertheless, few if any at the beginning of the 1980s could have predicted the regulatory sea change which would occur over the following 20 years in European telecommunications. Moreover, there is strong circumstantial evidence to suggest that those in the European Commission, who have been championing a 'maximalist' convergence approach, have gained the upper hand in the Commission's internal politics, namely the recent transfer of the audiovisual and media units of DG Education and Culture (formerly DG X) to an expanded DG Information Society (formerly DG XIII), now called DG Information Society and Media.

THE EVOLVING RELATIONSHIP BETWEEN THE EU AND NATIONAL LEVEL IN COMMUNICATIONS REGULATION

For the foreseeable future, developments in the modalities of regulation of the telecommunications sector in the EU are most likely to concern the evolving relationship between the European Commission and National Regulatory Authorities. As Chapter 5 has illustrated, the parameters of this relationship have not yet been fully clarified and are likely to remain a key issue in the regulatory evolution of the new ECRF for some time to come. To date, there have been indications of an element of regulatory 'jostling for position' between the Commission and the national level. A key theme of this volume concerns how the agreed EU framework has been imbued with well–established national political–institutional traits in its transposition and implementation phases. Nonetheless, it is clear that more than 20 years of collective telecommunications policy making across the EU level have established a significant apparatus of governance at the EU level. Due to the gradual and constant evolution of a regulatory framework, the system has not yet reached a position of equilibrium in terms of the detailed balance of responsibility and authority between the European Commission and National Regulatory Authorities.

The decision by EU Member States to embark on a Europeanised re-regulatory liberalisation of their telecommunications sectors has, by necessity, required the construction of a complex system of regulation in which free market competition must be engineered and managed to a very considerable extent. The designation by the European Commission of as many as 24 markets within the telecommunications domain potentially requiring sector–specific ex-ante regulation reflects the degree to which the framing of the telecommunications sector within national and European general competition policy rules is still aspirational and, in a number of cases (due to the economics of the market in question) arguably, quite unrealistic.

Whilst major legislative and other decisions at EU level will continue to be taken by representatives of national government, the nature and dynamics of the day–to–day mechanics of regulation in this system deserve some scrutiny. Here, the relationship between the European Commission and national regulatory authorities will continue to be crucial. This volume has noted how EU level regulatory committees, such as those responsible for ONP and licensing, have proved to be an important context for epistemic policy learning among Member States and their regulators, particularly those new to a liberalise telecommunications environment striving to assimilate unfamiliar regulatory 'know–how'. However, the creation of the European Regulators Group by the European Commission in 2002 to 'advise and assist...with consolidating the internal market' (European Regulators Group 2004, p. 2) marked an important development.

First, it provides evidence of the European Commission's desire to gain an 'inside track' on regulatory issues as they arise. Not only does the Commission provide a secretariat for the Group, it is also represented in it. As argued in this volume, the ERG can be viewed as an attempt to usurp to some extent the influence of the Independent Regulators Group, established in 1997, and comprising a pan–European range of national regulatory authorities from within and outside the EU. This body, as its name suggests, was independent of direct government control and was, thus, outside the formal EU institutional framework. Importantly, the creation of the ERG has not resulted in the dissolution of the IRG, which has continued to carry out a number of studies on detailed aspects of regulating telecommunications markets. However, a close relationship between the two groups appears to be developing as evidenced by the joint approval of a recent IRG report on universal service designation (Independent Regulators Group 2003).

Second, the ERG provides more evidence that the Commission intends to play a proactive role in the shaping of regulatory thinking and dissemination of best practice in the new framework, complementing its veto rights stemming from Article 7 of the Framework directive. Third, it has been argued (*CommunicationsWeek International*, 04.03.2002) that the ERG may well represent the beginning of the creation of a European telecommunications regulator, an idea floated in the mid to late 1990s at EU level but which received little support from Member States (Bartle 1999). Even though the Group's decisions do not have any legal authority it is nonetheless the case that, de facto, they are likely to be very influential over the developmental course of the EU's telecommunications markets. Should the ERG evolve in the medium term into a European telecommunications regulatory authority of some kind, it is likely to operate in much more of an intergovernmental than a supranational fashion.

Equally important would be the determination of the exact terms of reference of its relationship with the European Commission and national Member States, a task demanding considerable endeavour. As has been the case throughout the development of EU telecommunications policy, much will hinge on the support that such a move would garner from telecommunications operators. The emergence of relatively new 'peak level' organisations, such as ETNO and ECTA, the former representing mainly incumbents and the latter representing mostly newer entrants to the telecommunications market, provides a clear indication of how the EU level has grown in significance for the telecommunications industry and has become normalised as a lobbying focus. This volume has highlighted evidence of support from both established and newer players for the regulatory intervention of the Commission, which might be viewed as something of an 'honest broker' in regulatory disputes. Indeed, guarded support has also been expressed for the mutation of the ERG into a European regulator (*CommunicationsWeek International*, 04.03.2002).

THE FUTURE OF PUBLIC SERVICE GOALS IN THE NEW ELECTRONIC COMMUNICATIONS REGULATORY FRAMEWORK

As noted in this volume, the development of telecommunications policy at EU level, whilst overwhelmingly neo–liberal in focus, has nonetheless been characterised by a tension between the traditional public service goals which played a significant part in justifying the historic organisation of the sector and new policy priorities centred on creating and managing competition in telecommunications markets. Highly noteworthy is the fact that at critical junctures in policy development, such as the 1987 single telecommunications market Green Paper, the negotiations on what materialised as the 1998 package and the current ECRF, public service provision, essentially embodied in universal service, has been provided for at the EU level. The approach taken in both the 1998 and 2002 directives covering universal service has been to specify a minimum standard of basic telecommunications service which Member States must make available to users at an acceptable level of quality. This involves voice telephony (either through fixed or mobile networks), *ability* to access the Internet (as opposed to actual access), as well as operator assistance, directory enquires and public payphone services. Should the financial burden of making these services available be judged as unfair on the telecommunications incumbent, then its net cost can be shared through the creation of a universal service fund, a facility set up at the time of writing only in France and Italy.

Characteristic of the general approach to liberalisation, states are permitted to mandate a more expansive range of services should they wish to do so, though the cost of this would have to be generated from the public purse rather than as a specific tax on its telecommunications sector operators (European Parliament and Council 1998; 2002b).

Whilst the Europeanisation of universal service as part of the EU telecommunications regulatory framework was something fought hard for by the more dirigiste Member States and is regarded as a counterweight to the out-and-out liberalising thrust of the rest of the framework, it is a loosely defined and rather modest measure on the whole. Given the state of the art of technological and service developments, a debate has arisen around the possibility of extending the basic minimum scope of universal service provision. Policy changes at EU level, most notably a prioritisation of the idea of the European Information Society, have turned thoughts towards, and presented visions of, a much more widespread and sophisticated social use of ICT services. Whilst the policy discourse which has developed may be regarded as optimistically naïve, it has been used, at the level of EU Heads of State, for example, as a political justification for programmes such as the eEurope programme, setting a series of targets which, if successfully attained, will achieve a much more limited version of the Information Society than often trumpeted by its advocates.

As noted in Chapter 6, the convergence of communications technologies and services, most notably between telecommunications and broadcasting, created a context within which the practices and values of these two parts of the communications sector have been compared closely. The emergence of the Internet too, has, in a high-profile way, pointed up the possibility of enriched, convergent, communications services delivered over, in considerable part, the traditional telecommunications infrastructure. As content has become an increasingly significant element of services delivered through the telecommunications network, it has been suggested that the debate on universal service should, at the very least, consider elements of public service provision traditionally associated with broadcasting. In particular, issues which have been traditionally important in the latter sector, such as access to, and diversity of, content, may now or in the near future be indispensably part of a revised universal service charter (Simpson 2004a; Michalis 2002). So far, arguably, the direction of convergence policy has been more a movement to a telecommunications regulatory approach, providing for *access* to basic services, than a genuinely balanced telecommunications/broadcasting one, catering for the *provision* of public service content for the new electronic communications services. Indeed, it is possible that public service broadcasters' existing Internet content provision may soon be limited by European competition policy due to complaints from commercial providers.

Nihoul (2004) argues that given the EU's resolve to move more closely towards technologically neutral regulatory contexts within which issues, most notably those of competition, are dealt with 'generically' across platforms, then the same sort of approach might be applied to communications public service issues. However, for a number of reasons, it is highly unlikely that, in the short to medium term, such a revised universal service package will be legislatively created at the EU.

First, the debate on ICT convergence has thus far been noteworthy for a diffusion of policy ideas on liberalisation and competition from telecommunications to broadcasting, as opposed to a diffusion of ideas on public policy content regulation in the opposite direction. In the UK, which has pioneered the creation of a convergence regulator for ICT (Ofcom), for example, it appears that the idea that economic regulation, and thus by definition that the market forces subject to this regulation, can be utilised to deliver public policy goals, has achieved primacy. Equally, the concept of, and delivery mechanisms for, public service broadcasting have come under significant scrutiny and face considerable opposition from opposing commercial and political interests.

Second, as Michalis (2002) has pointed out, any extension of basic universal service public provision in the communications sector is unlikely to have its origins at EU level, not least due to the difficulties faced so far in tackling and securing agreement on regulation of broadcasting content. It appears that change, if it occurs at all, will take place at the national level and that if such a 'convergent' expansion of basic universal service becomes commonplace throughout the EU, it might eventually be ensconced in EU level legislation. However, should an enhanced provision for universal service arise, the current very loose system employed in respect of universal service in telecommunications, leaving considerable discretion to the Member States, will almost certainly be maintained.

Third, at a much more practical level, the cost of extending the current basic provision of universal service is likely to prove prohibitive for the ten new Member States of the EU that joined in May 2004. A related consideration is that even in the most wealthy economies of the EU, mandating and subsidising new services through the public purse could result in the assistance of 'pioneer' users rather than those in the lowest income groups, in situations where more content–rich services are not the established norm. It would be equally difficult to justify (and would probably be politically impossible to implement due to the power of the communications industry) the imposition of a sector–specific tax on the telecommunications sector for such a provision.

Fourth, the by now well embedded, though arguably questionable, principle that in telecommunications market forces will always deliver both efficiency in the allocation of economic resources and social welfare maximisation, has clearly developed through a predominantly neo-liberal discourse and practice across Europe in the last 20 years, and this received wisdom is likely to endure. Fifth, and consequently, universal service provision in telecommunications, and perhaps increasingly throughout the communications sector, will continue to be a 'safety net' mechanism, employed where market forces have resulted in under–provision of services which have otherwise become commonplace (in geographically disadvantaged areas and to certain socio–economic groups of the population).

CONCLUSIONS

The remarkable transition in the character, structure and functioning of the telecommunications sector in Europe has produced convergence in two fundamental ways. First, deliberate strategic reorganisation of their policies on telecommunications by a number of 'first mover' nation states, principally the USA and the UK, has precipitated similar moves by other governments which, for the EU, has transformed the governance of the sector around the poles of liberalisation and re-regulation to create a structure of managed competition. The aim of states has been, broadly, to capitalise upon important structural changes, most outstandingly the recent phase of economic globalisation of the world economy. As a consequence, a dynamic, mutually reinforcing, dialectical relationship has developed between regulatory change in telecommunications and the complex process of globalisation itself. However, as this volume has shown, it is vital to understand that such policy convergence is producing similar, rather than identical, policy reform in telecommunications. The steady creation of an elaborate and detailed policy framework at EU level, where previously none had existed, represents a distinct European strategic response to the opportunities and challenges presented by technological and economic change occurring in telecommunications. Analysis of this framework – in terms of the various Member State interpretations of the liberalisation/re-regulation discourse during negotiation, transposition and implementation – has also revealed diversity in detail, within a commonly chosen approach.

Second, and in a much more limited way, there is evidence that, within the EU, convergence among different parts of the ICT sector, most notably between the historically separated telecommunications and broadcasting sectors, has occurred. A combination of new opportunities to develop convergent commercial service offerings based on technological progress and the largely unanticipated emergence of the Internet into mainstream communications in the mid–1990s, led policy makers to consider the possibilities for creating convergent governance arrangements at EU level. Whilst the degree to which this occurred has proved to be limited, the policy change enacted has been centred on further development of the existent body of telecommunications regulation in a more convergent direction, 'pulling in' elements of broadcasting and other communications infrastructures, and has resulted in its current presentation as the EU's Electronic Communications Regulatory Framework.

The caveats of the two constituents of this convergence aside, it is clear that the model of liberalising re-regulation has been accepted by EU Member States and is likely in the future to become further refined and, in the process, more deeply established. Nonetheless, for the EU and its Member States at least two main challenges lie ahead.

First, the current framework, though a product of some 20 or more years of political negotiation and agreement, is relatively new. The pursuit of the regulatory state, even when confined purely to its own geo–political boundaries, requires a major reconstitution of the basic parameters of governance and the mobilisation of a new institutional context whose practices must be reconciled with, or supersede, traditional, long established structures and modes of governance. To Europeanise successfully many of the ideas and practices of the regulatory state is even more challenging, and as noted above, requires the development of a substantial, trusted, governance and administrative apparatus at the supranational level. Moreover, this must be created alongside evolving national systems of regulation in a compatible, mutually supportive, fashion. The EU, through its Electronic Communications Regulatory Framework, has merely established the foundation for such a system to develop at this stage and many obstacles lie ahead in terms of securing its workable fine detail, not least regarding the specific relationship to be elaborated and embedded between the European (be it an EU or some other as yet unprescribed institutional context) and national levels. The EU must also ensure that the new framework is compatible with the current and future global system of communications market regulation at the WTO. Recent concern over possible inconsistency between the ECRF's and ABT's approach to ensuring cost orientation regarding interconnection rates between telecommunications suppliers with major market shares provides an early example of challenges which lie ahead as the detailed regulatory mechanics of liberalising global electronic communications come under scrutiny (*Telecom Markets*, 22.3.2004).

Second, and very much tied into the first challenge, the EU, as in all other policy areas, must aim to integrate fully the ten new member countries which acceded to it in May 2004. Whilst considerable work has been done on this already in ensuring, in particular, that new Member States are able to transpose the elements of the ECRF into their domestic legal systems, this says nothing of their institutional capacity to satisfactorily comply with the implementation of the detail of the new framework. It may well be that much policy energy is expended by the EU over the forthcoming years in this regard, delaying, in the process, further development of the communications governance model in the direction of both of the kinds of convergence written about in this volume. The technical, institutional and human resources demanded here may even require a fundamental re-think of the social dimension to EU communications policy, introducing a new redistributional and capacity building element, though any such change will undoubtedly be rooted firmly in the values and practices of neo-liberal telecommunications reform which has so fundamentally altered the shape of   European telecommunications.

References

Albert, Michel (1993), *Capitalism Against Capitalism*, London: Whurr Publishers.

Allen and Overy (1991), *Telecommunications and 1992*, London: Allen and Overy.

Andersen, Jeffrey (2003), 'Europeanization in context: concept and theory', in Kenneth Dyson and Klaus H. Goetz (eds), *Germany, Europe and the Politics of Constraint*, Oxford: Oxford University Press, pp. 37–53.

Armstrong, Kenneth and Simon Bulmer (1998), *The Governance of the Single European Market*, Manchester: Manchester University Press.

Bartle, Ian (1999), 'European Union policy making and globalization: A comparative study of the liberalization of telecommunications and electricity', PhD thesis, Liverpool University.

Bartle, Ian (2001), 'Is the European Union an "agenda setter's paradise"? The case of a possible European regulatory authority for telecommunications', *Currrent Politics and Economics of Europe*, **10** (4), 439–59.

Bartle, Ian (2002a), 'Competing perspectives on European Union telecommunications policy', in Peter Humphreys (ed.), Special Issue on Telecommunications in Europe, *Convergence: The Journal of Research into New Media Technologies*, **8** (2), 10-27.

Bartle, Ian (2002b), 'When institutions no longer matter: reform of telecommunications and electricity in Germany, France and Britain', *Journal of Public Policy*, **22** (1), 1–27.

Bartle, Ian, Markus M. Müller, Roland Sturm and Stephen Wilks (2002), *The Regulatory State: Britain and Germany Compared*, London: Anglo-German Foundation.

Bauer, Johannes (2002), 'Normative foundations of electronic communications policy in the European Union', in Jacint Jordana (ed.), *Governing Telecommunications and the New Information Society in Europe*, Cheltenham, UK and Northampton, MA, USA: Edward Elgar, pp. 110–133.

Beat Graber, Christoph (2004) 'Audiovisual policy: the stumbling block of trade liberalisation?', in David Luff and Damien Geradin, *The WTO and Global Convergence in Telecommunications and Audiovisual Services*, Cambridge: Cambridge University Press, pp. 165–214.

Bennett, Colin (1988), 'Different processes, one result: the convergence of data protection policy in Europe and the United States', *Governance*, **1** (4), 415–41.

Bennett, Colin (1991a), 'Review article: what is policy convergence and what causes it?', *British Journal of Political Science*, **21**, 215–33.

Bennett, Colin (1991b), 'How states utilize foreign evidence', *Journal of Public Policy*, **11** (1), 31–54.

Bernier, Ivan (2004) 'Content regulation in the audio-visual sector and the WTO', in David Luff and Damien Geradin (eds), *The WTO and Global Convergence in Telecommunications and Audiovisual Services*, Cambridge: Cambridge University Press, pp. 215–42.

Blouin, Chantal (2000), 'The WTO agreement on basic telecommunications: a reevaluation', *Telecommunications Policy*, 24, 135–42.

Börzel, Tanja A. (2002), 'Pace-setting, foot-dragging, and fence-sitting: member state responses to Europeanization', *Journal of Common Market Studies*, 40 (2), 193–214.

Börzel, Tanja A. and Thomas Risse (2000), 'When Europe hits home: Europeanization and domestic change', *European Integration Online Papers* (EioP), 4 (15), at http://eiop//or.at/eiop/texte/2000-015a.htm

Bulmer, Simon and Martin Burch (2001), 'The Europeanisation of central government: the UK and Germany in historical institutionalist perspective', in Gerald Schneider and Mark Aspinwall (eds), *The Rules of Integration: Institutionalist Approaches to the Study of Europe*, Manchester: Manchester University Press, pp. 73–96.

Bulmer, Simon, David Dolowitz, Peter Humphreys and Stephen Padgett (2003), 'Electricity and telecommunications: fit for the European Union' in Kenneth Dyson and Klaus Goetz (eds), *Germany, Europe and the Politics of Constraint*, Oxford: Oxford University Press, pp. 251–69.

Cameron, Kelly (2004) 'Telecommunications and audiovisual services in the context of the WTO: today and tomorrow", in David Luff and Damien Geradin (eds), *The WTO and Global Convergence in Telecommunications and Audiovisual Services*, Cambridge: Cambridge University Press, pp. 21–33.

Campbell, John L. and Leon N. Lindberg (1991), 'The evolution of governance regimes', in John L. Campbell, J. Rogers Hollingsworth and Leon N. Lindberg (eds), *Governance of the American Economy*, Cambridge: Cambridge University Press, pp. 319–55.

Cave, Martin (2000), 'Barriers to entry in European telecommunications markets', in Jacint Jordana (ed.), *Governing Telecommunications and the New Information Society in Europe*, Cheltenham, UK and Northampton, MA, USA: Edward Elgar, pp. 47–65.

Cawson, Alan, Kevin Morgan, Douglas Webber, Peter Holmes and A. Stevens (1990), *Hostile Brothers: Competition and Closure in the European Electronics Industry*, Oxford: Clarendon Press.

Cerny, Philip (1997), 'Paradoxes of the competition state: the dynamics of political globalisation', *Government and Opposition*, 32 (2), 251–74.

Christiansen, Thomas (1997), 'Tensions of European governance: politicized bureaucracy and multiple accountability in the European Commission', *Journal of European Public Policy*, 4 (1), 73–90.

Christensen, Thomas and Per Laegreid (2002), *The New Public Management: The Transformation of Ideas and Practice*, Aldershot: Ashgate.

Christou, George and Seamus Simpson (2004), 'Internet policy implementation and the interplay between global and regional levels – the Internet Corporation for Assigned Names and Numbers (ICANN) and the European Union (EU)', paper for European Consortium for Political Research Joint Sessions, Workshop 1: 'International Organisations and Policy Implementation', Uppsala, Sweden, April 13–18. http://www.essex.ac.uk/ecpr/events/jointsessions/paperarchive/uppsala/ws1/Simpson.pdf

Cini, Michele and Lee McGowan (1998), *Competition Policy in the European Union*, Basingstoke: Macmillan.

Coen David (1997) 'The evolution of the large firm as a political actor in the European Union', *Journal of European Public Policy*, 4 (1), 91–108.

Coen, David and Chris Doyle (2000), 'Liberalisation of the utilities and evolving European regulation', *Economic Outlook*, April 2000 issue, 18–26.

Coen, David and Adrienne Héritier (2000), 'Business perspectives on German and British regulation: telecoms, energy and rail', *Business Strategy Review*, **11** (4), 29–37.

Coen, David, Adrienne Héritier and Dominik Böllhof (2002), *Regulating the Utilities: the UK and Germany Compared*, London: Anglo-German Foundation for Industrial Society.

Cohen, Elie (1995), 'France: national champions in search of a mission', in Jack Hayward (ed.), *Industrial Enterprise and European Integration: From National to International Champions in Western Europe*, Oxford: Oxford University Press, pp. 23–47.

Collins, Richard (1994), *Broadcasting and Audio-visual Policy in the European Single Market*, London: John Libbey.

CommunicationsWeek International (04.03.2002), 'European regulators form new group'.

CommunicationsWeek International (06.05.2002), 'Competitive operators change tack from networks to services', p. 3.

CommunicationsWeek International (20.05.2002), 'Europe attacks regulatory logjam', p. 1.

CommunicationsWeek International (20.05.2002), 'ECTA calls for leased line price points: but the disparity in pricing leased lines is being hindered by the inability to track excess pricing, according to some observers', p. 14.

CommunicationsWeek International (03.06.2002), 'Mobile operators put pressure on for spectrum trading review', p. 3.

CommunicationsWeek International (15.07.2002), 'Divest from local loops, say competitive telcos', p. 4.

CommunicationsWeek International (09.09.2002), 'EU "stalls" mobile operators', p. 3.

CommunicationsWeek International (25.11.2002), 'Let's stop playing the 3G blame game: everyone makes excuses for the delays in mobile data services, but the real issue here is the inherent lack of demand for new technology', p. 10.

CommunicationsWeek International (16.12.2002), 'Big brass get heavy with the regulators: incumbent operators and vendors are claiming that light touch regulation is the key to growth of broadband in Europe', p. 12.

Communications Week International (27.01.2003), 'US targets high mobile rates in Europe'.

Cowhey, Peter (1998), 'FCC benchmarks and the reform of the international telecommunications market', *Telecommunications Policy*, **22** (1), 899–911.

Cowhey, Peter (2004), 'Accounting rates, cross-border services and the next round on basic telecommunications services' in David Luff and Damien Geradin (eds), *The WTO and Global Convergence in Telecommunications and Audiovisual Services*, Cambridge: Cambridge University Press, pp. 51–82.

Cram, Laura (1994), 'The European Commission as a multi-organisation: social policy and IT Policy in the EU', *Journal of European Public Policy*, **1** (2), 195–217.

Dan Nygen, Godefroy (1986), 'A European telecommunications policy - which instruments for which prospects?', unpublished paper, Brest: ENST.

Dandelot, Marc (1993), *Le Secteur des Télécommunications en France; Rapport au Ministre de L'Industrie, des Postes et Télécommunications et du Commerce Extérieur*, Paris: PTT Ministry.

Dolowitz, David (1997), 'British employment policy in the 1980s: learning from the American experience', *Governance,* **10** (1), 23–42.

Dolowitz, David and David Marsh (1996), 'Who learns what from whom: a review of the policy transfer literature', *Political Studies*, **44**, pp. 343–57.

Dolowitz, David and David Marsh (2000), 'Learning from abroad: the role of policy transfer in contemporary policy-making', *Governance*, **13** (1), 5–24.

Dolowitz, David R. Hulme, N. Nellis and F. O'Neal (2000), *Policy Transfer and British Social Policy: Learning from the USA?*, Buckingham: Open University Press.

Department of Trade and Industry (1990) 'Internal brief on EC telecommunications policy', London: DTI, 14 September.

Doyle, Gillian (2002a) *Understanding Media Economics,* London: Sage.

Doyle, Gillian (2002b) *Media Ownership,* London: Sage.

Drahos, Peter and Richard A. Joseph (1995), 'Telecommunications and investment in the great supranational regulatory game', *Telecommunications Policy*, **19** (8), 619–35.

Drake, William and Eli Noam (1997), 'The WTO deal on basic telecommunications - big bang or little whimper?', *Telecommunications Policy*, **21** (9/10), 799–818.

Drake, William and Kalypso Nicolaidis (1992) 'Ideas, interests and institutionalisation: "trade in services" and the Uruguay Round', *International Organization*, **46** (1), winter, 37-100.

DTI/DCMS (1998), *Regulating Communications: Approaching Convergence in the Information Age*, London: Department of Trade and Industry/Department of Culture, Media and Sport.

DTI/DCMS (1999), *Regulating Communications: The Way Ahead. Results of the Consultation on the Convergence Green Paper*, London: Department of Trade and Industry/Department of Culture, Media and Sport.

Dyson, Kenneth and Peter Humphreys (eds) (1986), *The Politics of the Communications Revolution in Western Europe*, London: Frank Cass.

Dyson, Kenneth and Peter Humphreys (1990), 'Introduction: politics, markets and communication policies', in Kenneth Dyson and Peter Humphreys (eds), *The Political Economy of Communications: International and European Dimensions*, London and New York: Routledge, pp. 1–32.

Eliassen, Kjell A. and Marit Sjøvaag (eds) (1999), *European Telecommunications Liberalisation*, London and New York: Routledge.

Esser, Josef (ed.) (1997), *Europäische Telekommunikation im Zeitalter der Deregulierung: Infrastruktur im Umbruch*, Münster: Verlag Westfälisches Dampfboot.

European Broadcasting Union (1998), 'EBU reply to the convergence green paper'. http://www.ispo.cec.be/convergencegp/ebucon.htm.

European Commission (1984), *Communication From the Commission to the Council on Telecommunications: Progress Report on the Thinking and Work Done in the Field and Initial Proposals for an Action Programme*, Luxembourg: Office of Official Publications of the EC, Com(84)277, 18.5.84.

European Commission (1985a), *Proposal for a Council Directive on Standardisation in the Field of Information Technology and Telecommunications and Proposal for a Council Directive Concerning the first Phase of the Establishment of the Mutual Recognition of Type Approval of Telecommunications Terminal Equipment*, Luxembourg: Office of Official Publications of the EC, Com(85)230, 25.6.85.

European Commission (1985b), *White Paper on Completion of the Single European Market*, CEC Luxembourg: Office of Official Publications of the EC, Com(85)658 final, 1985.

European Commission (1985c), *15th Competition Report*, CEC Luxembourg: Office of Official Publications of the EC.

European Commission (1986a), *Proposal for a Council on the Coordinated Introduction of the Integrated Services Digital Network (ISDN) in the European Community*, Luxembourg: Office of Official Publications of the EC, Com(86)205.

European Commission (1986b), *Communication from the Commission to the Council on European Telecommunications Policy*, Luxembourg: Office of Official Publications of the EC, Com(86)325,1986.

European Commission (1986c), *Proposal for a Council on the Coordinated Introduction of the Integrated Services Digital Network (ISDN) in the European Community*, Luxembourg: Office of Official Publications of the EC, Com(86)205.

European Commission (1987a), *Communication from the Commission - Green Paper on the Development of the Common Market for Telecommunications Services and Equipment*, Luxembourg: Office of Official Publications of the EC, Com(87)290, 30.6.87.

European Commission (1987b), *Communication from the Commission - Green Paper on the Development of the Common Market for Telecommunications Services and Equipment Summary Report*, Com(87)290. Luxembourg: Office of Official Publications of the EC, 30.6.87.

European Commission (1988a), *Communication from the Commission - Towards a Competitive Community-wide Telecommunications Market in 1992 - Implementing the Green Paper on the Development of the Common Market for Telecommunications Services and Equipment up to 1992*, Luxembourg: Office of Official Publications of the EC, Com(88)48, 09.02.1988 .

European Commission (1988b), *Commission Directive of 16th May 1988 on Competition in the Markets in Telecommunications Terminal Equipment*, Luxembourg: Office of Official Publications of the EC, 88/301/EEC, 27.5.88.

European Commission (1989a), *Directive on the Second Stage of Mutual Recognition of Type Approval for Telecommunications Terminal Equipment*, Luxembourg: Office of Official Publications of the EC.

European Commission (1989b), *Commission Directive on Competition in the Markets for Telecommunications Services*, Luxembourg: Office of Official Publications of the EC, Com(89)671.

European Commission (1989c), *Revised Proposal for a Council Directive on the Establishment of the Internal Market for Telecommunications Services Through the Implementation of Open Network Provision*, Luxembourg: Office of Official Publications of the EC, Com(89)325.

European Commission (1990a), *A European Market for Telecommunications - the Twelve Give Their Political Agreement to Liberalise Services*, Luxembourg: Office of Official Publications of the EC.

European Commission (1990b), *Directive of 28 June 1990 on Competition in the Markets for Telecommunications Services*, Luxembourg: Office of Official Publications of the EC, OJL192/10, 90/388/EEC, 24. 07.90.

European Commission (1992a), *Review of the Situation in the Telecommunications Sector*, SEC(92) 1048 final. 21.10.92.

European Commission (1992b), *Pluralism and Media Concentration in the Internal Market*, Brussels: Com(92)480, 23.12.02.

European Commission (1993), *Growth, Competitiveness and Employment: The Challenges and Way Forward into the Twenty First Century*, Brussels: European Commission, Com(93) 700 final.

European Commission (1994a), *Europe and the Global Information Society; Recommendations to the EC*, Brussels: European Commission. (The 'Bangemann Report').

European Commission (1994b) *Commission Directive of 13th October 1994 Amending Directive 88/301/EEC and Directive 90/388/EEC in Particular with Regard to Satellite Communications*, 94/46/EC, OJL268/15, 19.10.94

European Commission (1995) *Commission Directive of 18th October 1995 Amending Directive 90/388/EEC with Regard to the Abolition of the Restrictions on the Use of Cable Television Networks for the Provision of Already Liberalised Telecommunications Services*, 95/51/EC, OJL256/49, 26.10.95.

European Commission (1996a), *Commission Directive Amending the 1990 'Competition Directive' to Ensure Full Competition in Telecommunications Markets*, Brussels: European Commission, 96/19/EC.

European Commission (1996b) *Commission Directive of 16th January 1996 Amending Commission Directive 90/388/EEC with Regard to Mobile and Personal Communications*, 92/2/EC OJL20/59, 26.1.96.

European Commission (1997a) *Green Paper on the Convergence of the Telecommunications, Media and Information Technology Sectors, and the Implications for Regulation. Towards an Information Society Approach*, Brussels, Com(97)623, 3.12.98.

European Commission (1997b), *Green Paper on the Convergence of the Telecommunications, Media and Information Technology Sectors and the Implications for Regulation. Towards an Information Society Approach*, Brussels: European Commission, Com(97)623, 23.9.97.

European Commission (1997c) *A European Initiative in Electronic Commerce*, Brussels: Com(97)57.

European Commission (1997d), *Action Plan on the Safe Use of the Internet*, Brussels: Com (97) 582.

European Commission (1998a), *European Commission, Communication from the Commission to the Council, the European Parliament, the Economic and Social Committee and the Committee of the Regions; Third Report on the Implementation of the Telecommunications Regulatory Package*, Brussels: Com (1998) 80 final.

European Commission (1998b), 'Working Document of the Commission: Summary of the Results of the Public Consultation on the Green Paper on the Convergence of the Telecommunications, Media and Information Technology Sectors; Areas for Further Reflection, SEC(98)1284, www.ispo.cec.be/convergencegp/gpworkdoc.html.

European Commission (1999a), *Communication from the Commission to the European Parliament, the Council, the Economic and Social Committee and the Committee of the Regions. Fifth Report on the Implementation of the Telecommunications Regulatory Package,* Brussels: Com (1999), 537 final.

European Commission (1999b), *Towards a New Framework for Electronic Communications Infrastructure and Associated Services. The 1999 Communications Review*, Brussels: Com (1999) 539.

European Commission (1999c), *The European Union's Telecommunications Policy*, Brussels: Information Society Directorate-General.

European Commission (2000a), *Communication from the Commission to the Council, the European Parliament, the Economic and Social Committee and the Committee of the Regions; Sixth Report on the Implementation of the Telecommunications Regulatory Package*, Brussels: Com (2000) 814.

European Commission (2000b), *Commission Recommendation of 25 May 2000 on Unbundled Access to the Local Loop: Enabling the Competitive Provision of a Full Range of Electronic Communications Services including Broadband Multimedia and High-Speed Internet*, 2000/417/EC.

European Commission (2000c), 'Commission proposes value added tax on e-commerce', *E-Policy News*, Brussels: European Commission, June.

European Commission (2001a), *Seventh Report on the Implementation of the Telecommunications Regulatory Package*, Brussels: Com (2001) 706.

European Commission (2001b), *Communication from the Commission on the Application of State Aid Rules to Public Service Broadcasting*, Official Journal of the European Communities, 2001/C 320/04.

European Commission (2002a), *Eighth Report from the Commission on the Implementation of the Telecommunications Regulatory Package: European Telecoms Regulation and Markets 2002*, Brussels, COM (2002) 695 final.

European Commission (2002b), *Commission Guidelines on Market Analysis and the Assessment of Significant Market Power under the Community Regulatory Framework for Electronic Communications Networks and Services*, Luxembourg: OJ C 165, 11.7.2002, pp. 6–31.

European Commission (2002c), *Open Network Provision Committee Working Document: The 2003 Regulatory Framework for Electronic Communications – Implications for Broadcasting*, Brussels, June 14.

European Commission (2003a), *Commission Recommendation of 11 February 2003 on relevant product and service markets within the electronic communications sector susceptible to ex ante regulation in accordance with Directive 2002/21/EC of the European Parliament and of the Council on a common regulatory framework for electronic communication networks and services*, OJ L 114, 8.5.2003, pp. 45–49.

European Commission (2003b), *Commission Recommendation of 23 July 2003 on notifications, time limits and consultations provided for in Article 7 of Directive 2002/21/EC of the European Parliament and of the Council on a common regulatory framework for electronic communications networks and services*, OJ L 190, 30.7.2003, pp. 13–18.

European Commission (2003c), *Communication from the Commission to the Council, the European Parliament, the European Economic and Social Committee and the Committee of the Regions. European Electronic Communications Regulation and Markets 2003*, Brussels, 19.11.2003 Com (2003) 715 final.

European Commission (2003d), *Report from the Commission to the European Parliament, the Council and the European Economic and Social Committee: First Report on the Application of Directive 2000/31/EC of the European Parliament and of the Council of 8 June 2000 on Certain Legal Aspects of Information Society Services, in Particular Electronic Commerce, in the Internal Market (Directive on Electronic Commerce)*, Brussels: Com(2003)702 final, November 21.

European Commission (2004a), *Communication from the Commission to the Council, the European Parliament, the European Economic and Social Committee and the*

Committee of the Regions. European Electronic Communications Regulation and Markets 2004, Brussels, 2.12.2004 Com (2004) 759 final.

European Commission (2004b*), Commission Staff Working Paper. Annex to the European Electronic Communication Regulation and Markets 2004 (10th Report)*, Volume 1, Brussels 2.12.2004 (SEC (2004) 1535.

European Commission (2004c*), Commission Staff Working Paper. Annex to the European Electronic Communication Regulation and Markets 2004 (10th Report)*, Volume 2, Brussels 2.12.2004 (SEC (2004) 1535.

European Commission (2004d), *Communication from the Commission to the Council, the European Parliament, the Economic and Social Committee and the Committee of the Regions on Interoperability of Digital Interactive Television Services*, Brussels, Com(2004)541 final, SEC(2004)1028, July 30.

European Commission (2004e), *Commission Staff Working Document on the Treatment of Voice Over Internet Protocol (VoIP) under the EU Regulatory Framework – An Information and Consultation Document*, Brussels, June 14.

European Council of Ministers (1986), *Council Directive of 24th July 1986 on the Initial Stage of the Mutual Recognition of Type Approval for Telecommunications Terminal Equipment*, Luxembourg: Office of Official Publications of the EC, OJ L217/21, 86/361/EEC, 5.8.86.

European Council of Ministers (1988), *Council Resolution of 30 June 1988 on the Development of the Common Market for Telecommunications Services and Equipment up to 1992*, (88/C 257/01) OJ C 257/1, 4th October.

European Council of Ministers (1993) *Council Resolution of 22nd July 1993 on the Review of the Situation in the Telecommunications Sector and the Need for Further Development in that Market*, Luxembourg: 93/C213/01, 06.08.1993.

European Council of Ministers (1994), *Council Resolution of 22nd December 1994 on the Principles and Timetable for the Liberalisation of Telecommunications Infrastructures*, Luxembourg: Office of Official Publications of the EC, OJ No C 379, 31.12.94.

European Council of Ministers (1999), *Resolution of the Council and of the Representatives of the Governments of the Member States, Meeting within the Council of 25th January 1999 concerning Public Service Broadcasting*, Luxembourg: Office of Official Publications of the EC, OJ No C 30/01, 5.2.99.

European Court of Justice (1982), *Judgment on 'European Commission versus British Telecom'*, Luxembourg: Office of Official Publications of the EC, OJ L360/36, 10.12.82.

European Court of Justice (1988), *France versus the European Commission*, Luxembourg: Office of Official Publications of the EC, case 202/88,1988.

European Court of Justice (1991), *Judgment of the Court of 19th March 1991 on Case C-202/88: French Republic v. European Commission (Competition in the Markets in Telecommunications Terminal Equipment)*, 91/C96/04, OJ C 96/06, April 12.

European Court of Justice (1992*), Judgment of the Court of 17 November 1992 in Joined Cases C-271, C-281 and C-289/90: Kingdom of Spain and others v. European Commission (Competition in the Markets for Telecommunications Services)* 92/C 326/08, OJ C 326/8, December 11.

European Parliament and Council (1997a), *Directive of 30 June 1997 on Interconnection in Telecommunications with Regard to Ensuring Universal Service and Interoperablility through Application of Open Network Provision*, 97/33/EC, OJL199/32, 26.7.97.

European Parliament and Council (1997b), *Directive of 10 April 1997 on a Common Framework for General Authorisations and Individual Licences in the Field of Telecommunications Services*, 97/13/EC, OJL117/15, 7.5.97.

European Parliament and Council (1998), *Directive of 26 February 1998 on the Application of Open Network Provision to Voice Telephony and on Universal Service for Telecommunications in a Competitive Environment (replacing European Parliament and Council directive 95/62/EC)*, 98/10/EC OJL101/41, 1.4.98.

European Parliament and Council (2000a), *Regulation (EC) No 2887/2000 of the European Parliament and of the Council of 18 December 2000 on Unbundled Access to the Local Loop*, Official Journal of the European Communities, 30.12.2000, L 336/4–8.

European Parliament and Council (2000b) *Directive 2000/31/EC of the European Parliament and of the Council of 8th June 2000 on Certain Legal Aspects of Information Society Services, in Particular Electronic Commerce, in the Internal Market (Directive on Electronic Commerce)*, OJ L178/1, 17.7.2000.

European Parliament and Council (2002a), *Directive of the European Parliament and Council on a Common Regulatory Framework for Electronic Communications Networks and Services (Framework Directive)*. Brussels: 4 February, PE-CONS 3672/01.

European Parliament and Council (2002b), *Directive of the European Parliament and of the Council on Universal Service and User's Rights relating to Electronic Communication Networks and Services (Universal Services Directive)*. Brussels, 4 February, PE-CONS 3673/01.

European Parliament and Council (2002c), *Directive 2002/19/EC of the European Parliament and of the Council of 7th March 2002 on Access to and Interconnection of, Electronic Communications Networks and Associated Facilities (Access Directive)*, Brussels, OJL 108/7-20, April 24.

European Regulators Group (2004), *ERG Annual Report*, ERG Secretariat, January.

European Voice (25.04.1996), 'Hopes rise for WTO telecoms deal', **2** (17).

European Voice (02.05.1996) 'US scuppers deadline for WTO telecoms deal', **2** (18).

European Voice (30.01.1997), 'Prospects good for telecoms agreement', **3** (4).

European Voice (08.10.1998), 'Fresh trade row with US looms over mobile phones', **4** (36).

European Voice (05.11.1998), 'Van Miert's TV plans get scrambled', **4** (40).

European Voice (12.11.1998), 'Ministers to warn EU off public broadcasting', **4** (41).

European Voice (07.01.1999) 'US warning on mobile phone standards', **5** (1).

European Voice (14.10.1999), 'Liikanen aims to simplify EU telecoms rules', **5** (37).

European Voice (04.05.2000), '2 May: Telecoms Council', **6** (18).

European Voice (08.06.2000), 'Firms attack telecoms package', **6** (23).

European Voice (13.07.2000), 'Berlin attacks telecoms "unbundling" plan', **6** (28).

European Voice (14.09.2000), 'Market spots loopholes in telecoms plan', **6** (33).

European Voice (23.11.2000), 'Industry angered by French plan to change key plank of telecoms plan', **6** (43).

European Voice (01.02.2001), 'Telecoms at risk from "arbitrary" regulation', **7** (5).

European Voice (01.03.2001a), 'Local loop unbundling "massive flop", says industry giant', **7** (9).

European Voice (01.03.2001b), 'EU defends WTO threat against Tokyo over telecoms' , **7** (9).

European Voice (22.03.2001), 'Liikanen "not to blame" as phone regulation fails to ring the changes', 7 (12).

European Voice (05.07.2001), 'Watchdog warns bid to veto telecom rules will stifle industry development', 7 (27).

European Voice (05.07.2001), 'Belgacom chief urges regulators to show restraint', 7 (27).

European Voice (29.11.2001), 'National regulators fight Brussels' veto', 7 (44).

European Voice (06.12.2001), 'Telecoms industry hopeful of deal on veto', 7 (45).

Farrell, Henry (2003), 'Constructing the international foundations of e-commerce - the EU-US safe harbour agreement', *International Organisation*, **57** (1), 277–306.

Featherstone, Kevin and Claudio Radaelli (eds) (2003), *The Politics of Europeanization*, Oxford: Oxford University Press.

Financial Times (29.01.1991), 'Cartel called into account'.

Financial Times (21.06.2000), '"Unbundling" deadline in danger'.

Financial Times (02.02.2001), 'Telecoms operators in rules plea'.

Financial Times (06.04.2001), 'Crossed lines for EU telecoms: Commission wants shake-up but member states think sector is still too young for competition, reports Daniel Dombey'.

Fraser, Matthew (1996) 'Television', in Kassim Hussein and Anand Menon (eds), *The European Union and National Industrial Policy*, London: Routledge, pp. 204–25.

Fredebeul-Krein, Markus and Andreas Freytag (1997) 'Telecommunications and WTO discipline - an assessment of the WTO Agreement on Telecommunication Services', *Telecommunications Policy*, **21** (60), 477–91.

Fredebul-Krein, Markus and Andreas Freytag (1999), 'The case for a more binding WTO agreement on regulatory principles in telecommunications markets', *Telecommunications Policy*, **23**, 625–44.

Frieden, Rob (1998), 'Falling through the cracks – international accounting rate reform at the ITU and the WTO', *Telecommunications Policy*, **22** (11), 963–75.

Frieden, Rob (2004), 'Whither convergence: legal, regulatory and trade opportunism in telecommunications', in David Luff and Damien Geradin (eds), *The WTO and Global Convergence in Telecommunications and Audiovisual Services*, Cambridge: Cambridge University Press, pp. 323-56.

Grande, Edgar (1989), *Vom Monopol zum Wettbewerb: die neokonservative Reform der Telekommunikation in Großbritannien und der Bundesrepublik Deutschland*, Wiesbaden: Deutscher-Universitäts-Verlag.

Grande, Edgar (1994), 'The new role of the state in telecommunications: an international comparison', *West European Politics*, **17** (3), 138-58.

Grande, Edgar and Volker Schneider (1991a), 'Reformstrategien und staatliche Handlungskapazitäten: Eine vergleichende Analyse institutionellen Wandels in der Telekommunikation in Westeuropa', *MPIFG Discussion Paper*, no. 3, Cologne: Max-Planck-Institut für Gesellschaftsforschung.

Grande, Edgar and Volker Schneider (1991b), 'Reformstrategien und staatliche Handlungskapazitäten: Eine vergleichende Analyse institutionellen Wandels in der Telekommunikation in Westeuropa', *Politische Vierteljahresschrift*, **32** (3) (1991b), 452–78.

Green Cowles, Maria, James Caporaso and Thomas Risse (eds) (2001), *Transforming Europe: Europeanization and Domestic Change*, Ithaca and London: Cornell University Press.

Haas, Peter (1992), 'Introduction: epistemic communities and international policy coordination', *International Organization*, **46** (1), 1-35.

Hall, Peter A. (1986), *Governing the Economy*, Cambridge: Polity Press.

Hall, Peter A. and David Soskice (eds) (2001), *Varieties of Capitalism: the Institutional Foundations of Comparative Advantage*, Oxford: Oxford University Press.

Hall, Peter A. and Rosemary C.R. Taylor (1996), 'Political science and the three new institutionalisms', *Political Studies*, **44** (4), 936-57.

Halpin, Edward and Seamus Simpson (2002), 'Between self-regulation and intervention in the networked economy: the European Union and internet policy', *Journal of Information Science*, **28** (4), 285–96.

Hayward, Jack (1986), *The State and the Market: Economy: Industrial Patriotism and Economic Intervention in France*, Brighton: Harvester Wheatsheaf.

Héritier, Adrienne (1999), *Policy-Making and Diversity in Europe: Escape from Deadlock*, Cambridge: Cambridge University Press.

Hills, Jill (1986), *Deregulating Telecoms: Competition and Control in the United States, Japan, and Britain*, Westport, CT: Quorum.

Hills, Jill (1992), 'The politics of international telecommunications reform', in Harvey M. Sapolsky, Rhonda J. Crane, W. Russell Neuman and Eli M. Noam (eds), *The Telecommunications Revolution: Past, Present and Future*, London and New York: Routledge, pp. 120–39.

Hills, Jill and Maria Michalis (1997), 'Technological convergence: regulatory competition. The case of British digital television", *Policy Studies*, **18** (3/4), 219–37.

Hills, Jill and Maria Michalis (1999) 'Telecommunications and broadcasting convergence: How convergent can the EU regulatory regime be?', paper presented at the European Consortium for Political Research workshop 'Regulating communications in the multimedia age', Mannheim, 26-31 March.

Hulsink, Willem (1999), *Privatisation and Liberalisation in European Telecommunications: Comparing the Netherlands and France*, London and New York: Routledge.

Humphreys, Peter (1990), 'The political economy of telecommunications in France: a case sudy of "telematics"', in Kenneth Dyson and Peter Humphreys (eds), *The Political Economy of Communications: International and European Dimensions*, London and New York: Routledge, pp. 198–228.

Humphreys, Peter (1992), 'The politics of regulatory reform in German telecommunications', in Kenneth Dyson (ed.), *The Politics of German Regulation*, Aldershot: Dartmouth, pp. 105–36.

Humphreys, Peter (1994), *Media and Media Policy in Germany. The Press and Broadcasting since 1945*, Oxford and Providence, USA: Berg.

Humphreys, Peter (1996), *Mass Media and Media Policy in Western Europe*, Manchester: Manchester University Press.

Humphreys, Pcter (1999), 'Regulating for pluralism in the era of digital convergence', paper presented to the *ECPR Joint Research Sessions*, Mannheim, Workshop 24: 'Regulating Communications in the Multimedia Age', 26-31 March.

Humphreys, Peter (2002), 'Europeanisation, globalisation and policy transfer in the European Union', in Peter Humphreys (ed.), Special Issue on Telecommunications in Europe, *Convergence: The Journal of Research into New Media Technologies*, **8** (2), 52–79.

Humphreys, Peter (2004), 'Globalisation, regulatory competition and EU policy transfer in the telecoms and broadcasting sectors', in David Levi-Faur and Eran Vigoda-Gadot (eds.), *International Public Policy and Management: Policy Learning Beyond Regional, Cultural and Political Boundaries*, New York: Marcel Dekker, pp. 91–120.

Humphreys, Peter and Matthias Lang (1998), 'Digital television between economy and pluralism', in Jeanette Steemers (ed.), *Changing Channels: The Prospects of Television in a Digital World*, Luton: John Libbey Media, pp. 9-35.

Humphreys, Peter and Stephen Padgett (forthcoming), 'Globalisation, the European Union and domestic governance in telecoms and electricity'. *Governance,* **19**: 3, July 2006.

Humphreys, Peter and Seamus Simpson (1996), 'European telecommunications and globalization', in Philip Gummett (ed.), *Globalization and Public Policy*, Cheltenham, UK and Brookfield, USA: Edward Elgar, pp. 105–124.

Immergut, Ellen M. (1998), 'The theoretical core of the new institutionalism', *Politics and Society*, **26** (1), pp. 5-34.

Independent Regulators Group (2003), *Universal Service Designation – A Report on the Designation Mechanisms for Universal Service Providers in Different IRG Countries and Evaluation of the Impact of Divergences on the Internal Market*, IRG, October.

International Telecommunications Union (2003a), 'ITU overview – history', http://www.itu.int/aboutitu/overview/history.htm

International Telecommunications Union (2003b) 'ITU member states'.,http://www.itu.int/cgi-bin.../mm.list?_search=ITUstates&_languages.htm

International Telecommunications Union (2003c), 'Overview of ITU and its three Sectors – Standardisation Sector'. At: http://www.itu.int/aboutitu/overview/o-s.htm

INTUG (1989) 'INTUG VIEWS – telecommunications initiatives related to the Single Market in Europe – background, status and action steps', London: International Telecommunications Users Group, Issue No. 2.

Johnson, Chalmers (1982), *M.I.T.I. and the Japanese Miracle: The Growth of Industrial Policy,* 1925–1975, Stanford, CA: Stanford University Press.

Jordana, Jacint (ed) (2002), *Governing Telecommmunications and the New Information Society in Europe*, Cheltenham, UK and Northampton, MA, USA: Edward Elgar.

Jordana, Jacint and David Levi-Faur (eds.) (2004), *The Politics of Regulation: Institutions and Regulatory Reforms in the Age of Governance*, Cheltenham, UK and Northampton, MA, USA: Edward Elgar.

Jordana, Jacint and David Sancho (2002), 'Institutional constellations and regulatory policy', paper prepared for the Politics of Regulation workshop, Pompeu Fabre University, Barcelona, 29–30 November.

Jordana, Jacint, David Levi-Faur and David Vogel (2002), 'The internationalization of regulatory reforms: the interaction of policy learning and policy emulation in the diffusion of the reforms', draft chapter circulated to the Politics of Regulation workshop, Pompeu Fabre University, Barcelona, 29–30 November.

Jordana, Jacint, David Levi-Faur and Puig Imma (2003), 'The limits of Europeanization: telecommunications and electricity liberalisation in Spain and Portugal', paper presented at the 2nd *ECPR General Conference*, Marburg, Germany, 18–21 September.

Joseph, Richard (1993), 'Converging telecommunications technologies: challenges facing government and regulators in Australia and New Zealand', paper presented at the Pacific Telecommunications Council 15th Annual Conference, Honolulu, Hawaii, USA, 17–20 January.

Joseph, Richard (1997), 'Political myth, high technology and the information superhighway: an Australian perspective', *Telematics and Informatics*, **4** (4) 289-301.

Karlsson, Magnus (1998), *The Liberalisation of Telecommunications in Sweden*, Linköping, Sweden: Department of Technology and Social Change, Linköping University.

Kingdon, John W. (1984), *Agendas, Alternatives and Public Policies*, Boston, MA: Little Brown.

Klein, Hans (2002), 'ICANN and Internet governance: leveraging technical coordination to realise global public policy', *Information Society*, **18**, 193–207.

KPMG (1996), *Public Policy Issues Arising from Telecommunications and Audiovisual Convergence. Report for the European Commission*, London: KPMG.

Knill, Christoph (2001), *The Europeanization of National Administrations: Patterns of Institutional Change and Persistence*, Cambridge: Cambridge University Press.

Knill Christoph and Andrea Lenschow (1998), 'Coping with Europe: the impact of British and German administrations on the implementation of EU environmental policy', *Journal of European Public Policy*, **5** (4), 595-614.

Ladrech, Robert (1994), 'Europeanisation of domestic politics and institutions: the case of France', *Journal of Common Market Studies*, **34** (1), 69-88.

Larouche, Pierre (2004), 'Dealing with convergence at the international level', in David Luff and Damien Geradin (eds), *The WTO and Global Convergence in Telecommunications and Audiovisual Services*, Cambridge: Cambridge University Press, pp. 390–422.

Lehmke, Thomas and Karin Waringo (1997), 'Frankreich: Aufstieg und Niedergang des High Tech-Colbertismus', in Joseph Esser (ed.), *Europäische Telekommunikation im Zeitalter der Deregulierung: Infrastruktur im Umbruch*, Münster: Verlag Westfälisches Dampfboot, pp. 113–146.

Levi-Faur, David (1999), 'The governance of competition: the interplay of technology, economics, and politics in European Union electricity and telecom regimes', *Journal of Public Policy*, **19** (2), 175–207.

Levi-Faur, David (2002) 'On the "net impact" of Europeanization: the EU's telecoms and electricity regimes between the global and the national', *European Integration Online Papers*, 6, ECSA Austria. Available at: http://eiop.or.at.eiop/.

Levy, David (1997), 'Regulating digital broadcasting in Europe: the limits to policy convergence', *West European Politics*, **20** (4), 24–42.

Levy, David (1999), *Europe's Digital Revolution: Broadcasting Regulation, the EU and the Nation State*, London and New York: Routledge.

Lewin, David, David Rogerson, Peter Alexiadis and Miranda Cole, *Barriers to Competition in the Supply of Electronic Communications Networks and Services*, A final report for the European Commission, Ovum, November 2003.

Lijphart, Arend, Thomas C. Bruneau, P. Nikiforos Diamandouros and Richard Gunther (1988), 'A Mediterranean model of democracy? The southern European democracies in comparative perspective', *West European Politic*, **11** (1), 7-25.

Lindberg, Leon N., John L. Campbell, and J. Rogers Hollingsworth (1991), 'Economic governance and the analysis of structural change in the American economy', in John

L. Campbell, J. Rogers Hollingsworth and Leon N. Lindberg (eds), *Governance of the American Economy*, Cambridge: Cambridge University Press, pp. 3-34.

Lindblom, Charles (1977), *Politics and Markets*, New York: Basic Books.

Longuet, Gérard (1988), *Télécoms. La Conquête de Nouveaux Espaces*, Paris: Dunod.

Luff, David (2004), 'Current international trade rules relevant to telecommunications services', in David Luff and Damien Geradin (eds), *The WTO and Global Convergence in Telecommunications and Audiovisual Services*, Cambridge: Cambridge University Press, pp. 34–50.

Lüthje, Boy (1997), 'Bundesrepublik Deutschland: Von der "Fernmeldeeinheitstechnik" zum universellen Netzwettbewerb' in Josef Esser (ed.), *Europäische Telekommunikation im Zeitalter der Deregulierung: Infrastruktur im Umbruch*, Münster: Verlag Westfälisches Dampfboot, pp. 147–81.

MacLean, Donald J. (1995), 'A new departure for the ITU – an inside view of the Kyoto plenipotentiary conference', *Telecommunications Policy*, **19** (3), 177–90.

MacLean Donald J. (1999), 'Open doors and open questions: interpreting the results of the 1998 ITU Minneapolis plenipotentary conference', *Telecommunications Policy*, **23**, 147-58.

Majone, Giandomenico (1994), 'The rise of the regulatory state in Europe', *West European Politics*, **17** (3), 77–101.

Majone, Giandomenico (1996), *Regulating Europe*, London and New York: Routledge.

Majone, Giandomenico (1997), 'From the positive to the regulatory state: causes and consequences of changes in the mode of governance', *Journal of Public Policy*, **17** (2), 139-67.

Majone, Giandomenico (2000), 'The credibility crisis of community regulation', *Journal of Common Market Studies*, **38** (2), 273–302.

Marsden, Christopher T. (2000) (ed.), *Regulating the Global Information Society*, London and New York: Routledge.

May, Christopher (2002), 'The political economy of proximity: intellectual property and the global division of information labour', *New Political Economy*, **7** (3), 317–42.

McKenzie, Richard B. and Dwight R. Lee (1991), *Quicksilver Capital: How the Rapid Movement of Wealth Has Changed the World*, New York: Free Press.

Mény, Yves, Pierre Muller and Jean-Louis Quermonne (eds) (1996), *Adjusting to Europe. The Impact of the European Union on National Institutions and Policies*, London and New York: Routledge.

Michalis, Maria (1999) 'European Union broadcasting and telecoms: towards a convergent regulatory regime?', *European Journal of Communication*, **14** (2), pp. 141-71.

Michalis, Maria (2002), 'The debate over universal service in the European Union – plus ça change, plus c'est la même chose', *Convergence*, **8** (2), 80–98.

Michalis, Maria (2004), 'Institutional arrangements of regional regulatory regimes: telecommunications regulation in Europe and limits to policy convergence', in Erik Bohlin, Stanford L. Levin, Nakil Sung and Chang-Ho Yoon (eds), *Global Economy and Digital Society*, Amsterdam: Elsevier, pp. 285–300.

Mishra, Ramesh (1999), *Globalization and the Welfare State*, Cheltenham, UK and Northampton, MA, USA: Edward Elgar.

Monopolkommission (1981), *Die Rolle der Deutschen Bundespost im Fernmeldewesen. Sondergutachten der Monopolkommission*, **9**, Baden-Baden: Nomos Verlag.

Moran, Michael (1991), *The Politics of the Financial Services Revolution: The USA, UK and Japan*, New York: St. Martins Press.

Moran, Michael (2002), 'Understanding the regulatory state', *British Journal of Political Science*, **32**, 391–413.

Moran, Michael (2003), *The British Regulatory State: High Modernism and Hyper-Innovation*, Oxford: Oxford University Press.

Morgan, Kevin and Douglas Webber (1986), 'Divergent paths: political strategies for telecommunications in Britain, France and West Germany', in Kenneth Dyson and Peter Humphreys (eds), *The Politics of the Communications Revolution in Western Europe*, London: Frank Cass, pp. 56–79.

Mueller, Milton (2004), 'Convergence: a reality check', in David Luff and Damien Geradin (eds), *The WTO and Global Convergence in Telecommunications and Audiovisual Services*, Cambridge: Cambridge University Press, pp. 311-22.

Murphy, Craig N. (1994), *International Organisation and Industrial Change – Global Governance Since 1885*, Cambridge: Polity Press.

Natalicchi, Giorgio (2001), *Wiring Europe: Reshaping the European Telecommunications Regime*, Lanham, Boulder, CO, New York, and Oxford: Rowman and Littlefield.

Nihoul, Paul (2004), 'Audiovisual and telecommunications services: a review of definitions under WTO law', in David Luff and Damien Geradin (eds), *The WTO and Global Convergence in Telecommunications and Audiovisual Services*, Cambridge: Cambridge University Press, pp. 357-89.

North, Douglass (1990), *Institutions, Institutional Change and Economic Performance*, Cambridge: Cambridge University Press.

OECD (1997), *Global Information Infrastructure-Global Information Society (GII-GIS) - Policy Recommendations for Action*, Paris, OECD.

Ohmae, Kenichi (1991), *The Borderless World. Power and Strategy in the Interlinked Economy*, London: Fontana.

Pauwels, Caroline (1998), 'Integrating economies, integrating policies: the importance of anttrust and competition policies within the global audiovisual order.', *Communications and Strategies*, **30**, 103-132.

Peltzman, Sam (1976), 'Towards a more general theory of regulation', *Journal of Law and Economics* **19**, 211-40.

Peterson, John and Margaret Sharp (1998), *Technology Policy in the European Union*, London: Macmillan.

Pitt, Douglas (1989), *Government and Industry Relations: Key Issues in the U.S. Telecommunications Industry*, London: Economic and Social Research Council.

Pitt, Douglas and Kevin Morgan (1992), 'Viewing divestment from afar', in Harvey M. Sapolsky, Rhonda J. Crane, W. Russell Neuman and Eli M. Noam (eds), *The Telecommunications Revolution: Past, Present and Future*, London and New York: Routledge, pp. 45-64.

Radaelli, Claudio (2000a), 'Policy transfer in the European Union: institutional isomorphism as a source of legitimacy', *Governance*, **13** (1), 25-43.

Radaelli, Claudio (2000b), 'Whither Europeanization? Concept stretching and substantive change', *European Integration Online Papers* (EioP), 4 (8), at http://eiop/or.at/eiop/texte/2000-008a.htm

Rhodes, Martin and Bastiaan van Apeldoorn (1997), 'Capitalism versus capitalism in Western Europe' in Martin Rhodes, Paul Heywood and Vincent Wright (eds.), *Developments in West European Politics*, Basingstoke: Macmillan, pp. 171-89.

Risse, Thomas, Maria Green Cowles, and James Caporaso (2001), 'Europeanization and domestic change: introduction', in Green Cowles, Maria, James Caporaso and Thomas Risse (eds) (2001), *Transforming Europe: Europeanization and Domestic Change*, Ithica and London: Cornell University Press, pp. 1-20.

Robinson, Kenneth (1992), 'The significance of Telecom 2000', in Harvey M. Sapolsky, Rhonda J. Crane, W. Russell Neuman and Eli M. Noam (eds), *Telecommunications Revolution: Past, Present and Future*, London and New York; Routledge, pp. 28-38.

Roy, Simon (2000), *Overview of Telecommunications Regulatory Regimes in the EU-15*, ESRC project internal report, May 2000.

Roy, Simon (2002), 'Telecommunications policy in the European Union', in Peter Humphreys (ed.), Special Issue on Telecommunications in Europe, *Convergence: the Journal of Research into New Media Technologies*, 8 (2), 100-13.

Sally, Razeen (1993), 'Alcatel's relations with the French state: the political economy of a multinational enterprise', *Communication and Strategies*, 9, Montpellier: IDATE.

Sancho, David (2002), 'European national platforms for the development of the Information Society', in Jacint Jordana (ed.), *Governing Telecommunications and the New Information Society in Europe*, Cheltenham, UK and Northampton, MA, USA: Edward Elgar, pp. 202-27.

Sandholtz, Wayne (1993), 'Institutions and collective action. The new telecommunications in western Europe', *World Politics*, 45 (2), 242-70.

Sandholtz, Wayne (1998), 'The emergence of a supranational telecommunications regime', in Wayne Sandholtz and Alexander Stone Sweet (eds), *European Integration and Supranational Governance*, Oxford: Oxford University Press, pp.134-63.

Sandholtz Wayne and John Zysman (1989), '1992: Recasting the European bargain', *World Politics*, 42 (1), 95-128.

Schiller, Dan (1999), *Digital Capitalism – Networking the Global Market System*, Cambridge, MA and London: the MIT Press.

Schmidt, Susanne K. (1996), 'Sterile debates and dubious generalisations: European integration theory tested by telecommunications and electricity', *Journal of Public Policy*, 16 (3), 233-71.

Schmidt, Susanne K. (1997), 'Behind the Council agenda: the Commission's impact on decisions', *MPIfG Discussion Paper 97/4*, Cologne: Max-Planck-Institut für Gesellschaftsforschung.

Schmidt, Susanne K. (1998a), *Liberalisierung in Europa: die Rolle der Europäische Kommission*, Frankfurt/New York: Campus Verlag.

Schmidt, Susanne K. (1998b), 'Commission activism: subsuming telecommunications and electricity under European competition law', *Journal of European Public Policy*, 5 (1), 169-84.

Schmidt, Vivien A. (1996a), *From State to Market? The Transformation of French Business and Government*, Cambridge: Cambridge University Press.

Schmidt, Vivien A. (1996b), 'The decline of traditional state dirigisme in France: the transformation of political economic policies and policymaking processes', *Governance: An International Journal of Policy and Administration*, 9 (4), 375-405.

Schmidt, Vivien A. (1999), 'Convergent pressures, divergent responses: France, Great Britain and Germany between globalization and Europeanization', in D.A. Smith, D.J. Solinger and S.C. Topik (eds) *States and Sovereignty in the Global Economy*, London and New York: Routledge, pp. 172-192.

Schmidt, Vivien A. (2002), *The Futures of European Capitalism*, Oxford: Oxford University Press.

Schneider, Volker (2002), 'The institutional transformation of telecommunications between Europeanization and globalization', in Jacint Jordana (ed.), *Governing Telecommunications and the New Information Society in Europe*, Cheltenham, UK and Northampton MA, US: Edward Elgar, pp. 27-46.

Schneider, Volker and Raymund Werle (1990), 'International regime or corporate actor? The European Community in telecommunications Policy', in Kenneth Dyson and Peter Humphreys (eds), *The Political Economy of Communications. International and European Dimensions*, London and New York: Routledge, pp. 77-106.

Schneider, Volker, Godefroy Dang-Nguyen and Raymund Werle (1994), 'Corporate actor networks in European policy-making: harmonizing telecommunications policy', *Journal of Common Market Studies*, **32** (4), 473-98.

Schneider, Volker and Thierry Vedel (1999), 'From high to low politics in Franco-German relations: the case of telecommunications', in Douglas Webber (ed.), *The Franco-German Relationship in the European Union*, London and New York: Routledge, pp. 75-92.

Seidman, Harold and Robert Gilmour (1986), *Politics, Position and Power. From the Positive to the Regulatory State*, Oxford: Oxford University Press.

Simpson, Seamus (1992), 'Restructuring European telecommunications: the efficacy of European Community (EC) strategies', CNAA doctoral thesis, Manchester Polytechnic (now Manchester Metropolitan University).

Simpson, Seamus (2004a), 'Universal service issues in converging communications environments: the case of the UK', *Telecommunications Policy*, **28**, 233-48.

Simpson, Seamus (2004b) 'Explaining the commercialisation of the Internet: a neo-Gramscian contribution'. *Information, Communications and Society*, 7 (1), 50-69.

Simpson, Seamus (forthcoming), 'Explaining market liberalisation and the emergence of a European Union regulatory framework in telecommunications: structural change and the interplay between national and European levels', in Mine Bek and Deirdre Kevin (eds) *Communications Policies of the EU and Turkey*, Ankara: University of Ankara Press.

Simpson, Seamus and Rorden Wilkinson (2002), 'Regulatory change and telecommunications governance: a neo-Gramscian analysis', in Peter Humphreys (ed.), Special Issue on Telecommunications in Europe, *Convergence: The Journal of Research into New Media Technologies*, **8** (2), 30-51.

Simpson, Seamus and Rorden Wilkinson (2003a), 'Governing e-Commerce: prospects and problems', paper presented to the 31st Telecommunications Policy Research Conference, 'Communication, Information and Internet Policy', National Center for Technology and Law, George Mason University School of Law, Arlington, Virginia, USA, 19-21 September. Available at: http://www.tprc.org.

Simpson, Seamus and Rorden Wilkinson (2003b), 'First-mover preferences, structural power and path dependency: the World Trade Organization and e-Commerce' paper presented to the International Research Foundation for Development, World Forum on the Information Society, Geneva, Switzerland, 8-10 December.

Steinfeld, Charles (1994), 'An introduction to European telecommunications', in Charles Steinfeld, Johannes M. Bauer and Laurence Caby (eds), *Telecommunications in Transition: Policies, Services and Technologies in the European Community*, London: Sage, pp. 3-17.

Steinfeld, Charles, Johannes M. Bauer and Laurence Caby (eds) (1994), *Telecommunications in Transition: Policies, Services and Technologies in the European Community*, London: Sage.

Stevers, Esther (1990), 'Telecommunications regulation in the European Community - the European Commission as regulatory actor', San Domenico: European University Institute , EUI Working Paper, No 89/421.

Stigler, George (1971), 'The theory of economic regulation', *Bell Journal of Economics and Management Science*, **2**, 3-21.

Strange, Susan (1994), *States and Markets*, London: Pinter, 2nd edn.

Strange, Susan (1996), *The Retreat of the State: The Diffusion of Power in the World Economy*, Cambridge: Cambridge University Press.

Swank, Duane (2002), *Global Capital, Political Institutions, and Policy Change in Developed Welfare States*, Cambridge: Cambridge University Press.

Tarjanne, Pekka (1999), 'Preparing for the next revolution in telecommunications: implementing the WTO agreement', *Telecommunications Policy*, **23**, 51-63.

Telecom Markets (27.02.1997), 'Oftel backs away from planned fund to finance universal service', **310**, 1, 12.

Telecom Markets (13.03.1997), 'UK opposes EC's equal-access approach to telecoms competition', **1**, 12-14.

Telecom Markets (03.07.97), 'EU ministers back equal access as UK goes for compromise solution', **318**, 1, 11-12.

Telecom Markets (04..12.1997a), 'New German regulator hit by resignation crisis', **328**, p. 3.

Telecom Markets (04..12.1997b), 'Cruickshank admits mistakes in UK regulation, but points to benefits', **328**, p. 13.

Telecom Markets (04..12.1997c), 'Cruickshank slams Germany's progress on liberalisation', **328**, p. 14.

Telecom Markets (12.03.1998), 'Belgium licenses new competitors including BT', **334**, 5-6.

Telecom Markets (30.07.1998), 'Oftel blamed for UK delay in introducing carrier pre-selection', **343**, 2-4.

Telecom Markets (28.01.1999), 'Deutsche Telekom cable spin-off may be anti-competitive, says EC', **354**, 4-5.

Telecom Markets (25.03.1999), 'EC set for major inquiry into Europe's telecoms industry', **358**, 1-10.

Telecom Markets (06.05.99), 'UK government attacks barriers to entry in EU telecoms markets', **360**, 1, 7-8.

Telecom Markets (03.06.1999), 'Dutch newcomers lament high cost of number portability', **362**, 1-4.

Telecom Markets (17.06.1999), 'German regulator says it got the price right for local-loop access', **363**, 7.

Telecom Markets (01.07.1999), 'Entrants say France Telecom fails to provide proper price information', **364**, 2-4.

Telecom Markets (07.10.1999), 'EC report says leased line prices are far too high', **370**, 1, 9-10.

Telecom Markets (21.10.1999), 'EC set to unveil new regulatory framework for telecom sector', **371**, 1, 9-10.

Telecom Markets (11.02.2000), 'European Commission grants CPS laggards grace period', **378**, 1-2.

Telecom Markets (28.07.2000), 'EU's regulation ovrrides member states' unbundling law', **388**, 1-2.

Telecom Markets (27.10.2000), 'Final EU regulation wording favours incumbents', **393**, 5.

Telecom Markets (19.12.2000), 'Commission equivocal on Euro-regulators' progress', **397**, 5-7.

Telecom Markets (16.01.2001), 'LLU prices of concern across Europe', **398**, 3-4.

Telecom Markets (27.03.2001), 'EU to streamline competition rules', **403**, 7.

Telecom Markets (10.04.2001), 'EU Council votes against some Commission proposals', **404**, 7

Telecom Markets (22/05/2001), 'Two acts in competition to define telecoms fair play', **406**, 1-3.

Telecom Markets (03.07.2001), 'Independent regulators voice concerns over future Europe-wide regulation', **409**, 1.

Telecom Markets (31.07.2001), 'European regulators make flat-rate internet progress', **411**, 4-6.

Telecom Markets (23.10.2001), 'NRA/Commission at loggerheads over telecoms law', **416**, 1-2.

Telecom Markets (18.12.2001), 'EU telecoms framework nears adoption', **424**, 5.

Telecom Markets (07.05.2002), 'European bodies remain split ahead of vote on Data Protection Directive', **428**, 3-4.

Telecom Markets (02.07.2002), 'European Commission finally publishes draft relevant markets list', **432**, 6-7.

Telecom Markets (16.07.2002), 'IRG to continue, despite ERG launch', **433**, 6-8.

Telecom Markets (10.09.2002), 'NRAs consider outside firms for telecoms-package analysis', **436**, 1.

Telecom Markets (24.09.2002), 'Regulators move to modernise operators' cost-accounting practices', **437**, 3-4.

Telecom Markets (25/02/2003), 'NRAs get green light for market reviews', **447**, 1-3.

Telecom Markets (25.03.2003), 'Oftel submits market definitions to Brussels veto process', **449**, 1-2.

Telecom Markets (08.04.2003), 'Member states likely to add other markets in EU reviews', **450**, 7.

Telecom Markets (20/05/2003), 'Commission looks for areas where further regulation should be considered', **452**, 4-6.

Telecom Markets (03.06.2003), 'German draft telecoms law at odds with European framework', **453**, 1-4.

Telecom Markets (15.07.2003), 'Consensus on remedies tops Euro regulators' agenda', **456**, 4-6.

Telecom Markets (04.11.2003), 'European Parliament and Commission step up pressure on member states to pass new laws', **463**, 4-5.

Telecom Markets (16.12.2003), 'Carriers concerned over possibility of more EU telecoms regulation', **466**, 4-5.

Telecom Markets (22.03.2004), 'US-Mexico interconnection dispute resolved – Europe next?', **472**, 1-2.

Thatcher, Mark (1999), *The Politics of Telecommunications: National Institutions, Convergence, and Change*, Oxford: Oxford University Press.

Thatcher, Mark (2001a), 'The Commission and national governments as partners: EC regulatory expansion in telecommunications 1979-2000', *Journal of European Public Policy*, **8** (4), 558-84.

Thatcher, Mark (2001b), 'Delegation to independent regulatory agencies in western Europe', ECPR Working Paper, Joint Sessions, University of Grenoble, 6-11 April.

Thatcher, Mark (2002a), (ed.) 'Analysing regulatory reform in Europe', a special issue of the *Journal of European Public Policy*, 9 (6).

Thatcher, Mark (2002b), 'Regulation after delegation: independent regulatory agencies in Europe', *Journal of European Public Policy*, 9 (6), 954-72.

Thatcher, Mark (2002c), 'The relationship between national and European regulation of telecommunications', in Jacint Jordana (ed.), *Governing Telecommunications and the New Information Society in Europe*, Cheltenham, UK and Northampton, MA, USA: Edward Elgar, pp. 66-85.

Thatcher, Mark (2004a), 'Varieties of capitalism in an internationalized world: domestic institutional change in European telecommunications', *Comparative Political Studies*, 37 (7), pp. 1-30.

Thatcher, Mark (2004b), 'Winners and losers in Europeanisation: reforming the national regulation of telecommunications', *West European Politics*, 27 (2), 284-309.

Tongue, Carol (1998), 'Submission on the Commission's green paper on convergence of the telecommunications, media and information technology sectors and the implications for regulation'. http://www.poptel.org.uk/carole-tongue/index2.html.

Treaty of Amsterdam Amending the Treaty on European Union, the Treaties Establishing the European Communities and Certain Related Acts (1997), *Protocol on the System of Public Broadcasting in the Member States*, http://europa.eu.int/comm/dg10/avpolicy /key_doc/amsprot_en.html.

Tunstall, Jeremy (1986), *Communications Deregulation: The Unleashing of America's Communications Industry*, Oxford: Basil Blackwell.

Tuthill, Lee (1997), 'The GATS and new rules for regulators', *Telecommunications Policy*, 21 (9/10), 783-98.

Tyler, Michael and Susan Bednarczyk (1998), 'International economic relationships in telecommunications – a painful transformation', *Telecommunications Policy*, 22 (10), 797-816.

Ungerer, Herbert with Nicholas Costello (1990), *Telecommunications in Europe: Free Choice for the User in Europe's 1992 Market: The Challenge for the European Communities*, Brussels: Office of Official Publications of the European Communities.

US Department of Commerce (1998) *Management of Internet Names and Addresses* (Green Paper), 63 Fed. Reg., 31,741.

Vogel, David (1995), *Trading Up. Consumer and Environmental Regulation in a Global Economy*, Cambridge, MA: Harvard University Press.

Vogel, Steven (1996), *Freer Markets, More Rules: Regulatory Reform in Advanced Industrial Countries*, Ithaca, US, and London: Cornell University Press.

Vogel, Steven (1997), 'International games with national rules: how regulation shapes competition in "global markets" ', *Journal of Public Policy*, 17 (2), 169-93.

Waesche, Niko M. (2001), 'Global opportunity and national political economy: the development of Internet ventures in Germany', PhD thesis, London School of Economics and Political Science.

Waesche, Niko M. (2003), *Internet Entrepreneurship in Europe: Venture Failure and the Timing of Telecommunications Reform*, Cheltenham, UK and Northampton, MA, USA: Edward Elgar.

Wallace, Helen (2000), 'Europeanisation and globalisation: complementary or contradictory trends?', *New Political Economy*, 5 (3), 369-82.

Ward, David (2002), *The European Union Democratic Deficit and the Public Sphere: An Evaluation of EU Media Policy*, Amsterdam: IOS Press.

Webber, Douglas and Peter Holmes (1985), 'Europe and technological innovation', ESRC Newsletter 55.

Weiss, Linda (ed.) (1998), *States in the Global Economy: Bringing Domestic Institutions Back In*, Cambridge: Cambridge University Press.

Weiss, Linda (2003), *The Myth of the Powerless State: Governing the Economy and a Global Era*, Cambridge: Cambridge University Press.

Werle, Raymund (1999), 'Liberalisation of telecommunications in Germany', in Kjell A. Eliassen and Marit Sjøvaag (eds), *European Telecommunications Liberalisation*, London and New York: Routledge, pp. 110-27.

Werle, Raymond (2002), 'Internet @ Europe: Overcoming Institutional Fragmentation and Policy Failure', in Jordana, Jacinct, (2002) *Governing Telecommunications and the New Information Society in Europe*, Cheltenham, UK and Northampton, MA, USA: Edward Elgar.

Wessels, Wolfgang (1998), 'Comitology: fusion in action. Politico-administrative trends in the EU system', *Journal of European Public Policy*, 5 (2), 209-34.

Wilkinson, Rorden (2000), *Multilateralism and the World Trade Organisation*, London: Routledge.

Wilks, Stephen (1996), 'Regulatory compliance and capitalist diversity in Europe', *Journal of European Public Policy*, 3 (4), 536-59.

Woolcock, Stephen, Michael Hodges and Kristin Schreiber (1992) *Britain, Germany and 1992: The Limits of Deregulation*, London: Royal Institute of International Affairs.

WTO (1994) *The General Agreement on Trade in Services (GATS)*.

WTO (1998) *Work Programme on Electronic Commerce*, 25 September. WT/L/274 (98-3738)

WTO (2001) 'Dedicated discussion on electronic commerce under the auspices of the General Council on 15 June 2001'. (01-3355), WT/GC/W/436, July 6.

Young, Alisdair R (2002), *Extending European Cooperation: The European Union and the 'New' International Trade Agenda*, Manchester: Manchester University Press.

Zysman, John (1983), *Governments, Markets and Growth: Financial Systems and the Politics of Industrial Change*, Ithaca, NY: Cornell University Press.

Index